The Learned Practice of Religion in the Modern University

Scientific Studies of Religion: Inquiry and Explanation

Series editors: Luther H. Martin, Donald Wiebe, William W. McCorkle Jr.,
D. Jason Slone, and Radek Kundt

Scientific Studies of Religion: Inquiry and Explanation publishes cutting-edge research in the new and growing field of scientific studies in religion. Its aim is to publish empirical, experimental, historical, and ethnographic research on religious thought, behavior, and institutional structures. The series works with a broad notion of scientific that includes innovative work on understanding religion(s), both past and present. With an emphasis on the cognitive science of religion, the series includes complementary approaches to the study of religion, such as psychology and computer modelling of religious data. Titles seek to provide explanatory accounts for the religious behaviors under review, both past and present.

The Learned Practice of Religion in the Modern University

Donald Wiebe

BLOOMSBURY ACADEMIC

LONDON • NEW YORK • OXFORD • NEW DELHI • SYDNEY

Bloomsbury Publishing Plc
50 Bedford Square, London, WC1B 3DP, UK
1385 Broadway, New York, NY 10018, USA
29 Earlsfort Terrace, Dublin 2, Ireland

BLOOMSBURY, BLOOMSBURY ACADEMIC and the Diana logo are trademarks
of Bloomsbury Publishing Plc

First published in 2020
This paperback edition published in 2021

Bloomsbury Publishing Plc does not have any control over, or responsibility for, any
third-party websites referred to or in this book. All internet addresses given in this
book were correct at the time of going to press. The author and publisher regret any
inconvenience caused if addresses have changed or sites have ceased to exist, but
can accept no responsibility for any such changes.

A catalogue record for this book is available from the British Library.

Library of Congress Cataloging-in-Publication Data
Names: Wiebe, Donald, 1943- author.
Title: The learned practice of religion in the modern university / Donald Wiebe.
Description: London; New York: Bloomsbury Academic, 2019. |
Series: Scientific studies of religion: inquiry and explanation |
Includes bibliographical references and index.
Identifiers: LCCN 2019021176 (print) | LCCN 2019980997 (ebook) |
ISBN 9781350103436 (hardback) | ISBN 9781350103450 (epub) |
ISBN 9781350103443 (pdf)
Subjects: LCSH: Religion–Study and teaching (Higher) | Theology–Study and
teaching (Higher) | Religious education.
Classification: LCC BL41 .W469 2019 (print) | LCC BL41 (ebook) |
DDC 200.71/1–dc23
LC record available at https://lccn.loc.gov/2019021176
LC ebook record available at https://lccn.loc.gov/2019980997

ISBN: HB: 978-1-3501-0343-6
PB: 978-1-3502-5795-5
ePDF: 978-1-3501-0344-3
eBook: 978-1-3501-0345-0

Series: Scientific Studies of Religion: Inquiry and Explanation

Typeset by Deanta Global Publishing Services, Chennai, India

To find out more about our authors and books visit www.bloomsbury.com
and sign up for our newsletters.

In Memory of
Gary Lease (1940–2008)
University of California, Santa Cruz

A champion of the scientific study of religion

Contents

Acknowledgments

The fifteen chapters published in this volume were written over the past two decades. Ten appeared in earlier publications (Chapters 1–3; 5–7, 9, 10, 13, and 14). Four chapters are published here for the first time (Chapters 8, 11, 12, and 15). Chapter 4 was first delivered as a plenary address to the European Association for the Study of Religion but portions of it appeared in print as two separate articles: one in *Religio* and the other in *Einheit der Wirklichkeiten*. Aside from minor corrections, references updated and reformatted, and slight amendments to titles in order to bring out their common focus in this book, these papers appear as first published.

I am most grateful to the editors and publishers listed below for permission to include in this volume the chapters listed below.

"Religious Studies." In John R. Hinnells (Ed.), *The Routledge Companion to the Study of Religion*. London: Routledge (Taylor and Francis), 2005: 98–124.

"Secular Theology Is Still Theology, Not the Study of Religion." *Bulletin of the Council of Societies for the Study of Religion* 37/3 (2008): 77–81

"The Scientific Study of Religion and Its Cultured Despisers." In Willi Braun and Russell T. McCutcehon (Eds.), *Introducing Religion: Essays in Honor of Jonathan Z. Smith*. London: Equinox, 2008: 467–79.

"Religious Biases in Funding Religious Studies Research." *Religio* 17/2 (2009): 302–18.

"An Encroaching Spirituality: What Hope Remains for a Science of Religion." In Eva-Maria Glasbrenner and Christian Hackbarth-Johnson (Eds.), *Einheit der Wirklicheiten: Festschrift anlässlich des 60. Gebürtstags von Michael von Brück.* (München: Manya Verlag, 2009): 302–18.

"The Learned Practice of Religion: A Review of the History of Religious Studies in Canada and Its Portent for the Future." *Studies in Religion/Sciences Religieuses*, 35/3–4 (2006): 475–501.

"Harold Coward: Fifty Years of Religious Studies in Canada: A Personal Retrospective." *Religion*, 46/2 (2016): 291–95.

"Religion Thin and Thick: On the Development of 'Religious Studies' in the American University." Reviews in *Religion and Theology*, 8/2 (2001): 126–32.

"American Influence on the Shape of Things to Come: Religious Studies in the Twenty-First Century." *Journal of the Korean Association for the History of Religions*, 20 (2000): 1–24.

"Religious Studies in North America During the Cold War." In Luther H. Martin, Dalibor Papusek, and Iva Dolezalova (Eds.), *The Academic Study of Religion During the Cold War* (New York: Peter Lang Press, 2001): 267–88.

"Modernism." In Willi Braun and Russell T. McCutcheon (Eds.), *Guide to the Study of Religion* (London: Cassell): 351–64.

"An Old Methodenstreit Made New Again: Rejecting a 'Science-Lite' Study of Religion." In A. K. Petersen, I. S. Gilhus, L. H. Martin, J. S. Jensen, and J. Sorensen (Eds.), *Evolution, Cognition, and the History Of Religion: A New Synthesis*, Festschrift in Honour of Armin W. Geertz, (Leiden: Brill, 2019) 130–40.

I also wish to acknowledge and thank colleagues and friends who have read and criticized earlier drafts of one or more of these chapters: Marsha Hewitt, Abrahim (Ivan) Khan, Russell McCutcheon, Rosalind Hackett, Martha Cunningham, Gary Lease, Tom Lawson, and Luther Martin. Luther has read most of these chapters, often more than once, providing critically important feedback on my views of the long struggle to see the scientific study of religions gain some headway in our colleges and universities. I also wish to thank Dr. Jonathan Lofft (a post-doctoral fellow in the Faculty of Divinity in Trinity College) for putting these chapters into final form for publication. I am also deeply indebted to my copy editor, Nandini Satish, for her knowledge and efficiency in dealing with this ms, and to Leeladevi Ulaganathan, Project Manager, for this title, for her patience in getting me through the final stages of this project. Finally, I wish to thank Lucy Carroll, Bloomsbury's assistant editor for religious studies, for the encouragement, advice, and practical support she provided me in bringing this project to completion.

Abbreviations

AAR	American Academy of Religion
ASSR	American Society for the Study of Religion
AATS	American Association of Theological Schools
ACLS	American Council of Learned Societies
AHA	American Historical Association
CCSR	Canadian Corporation for Studies of Religion
CJT	Canadian Journal of Theology
CSR	Cognitive Science of Religion
CSSR	Canadian Society for the Study of Religion
IACSR	International Association for the Cognitive Science of Religion
IAHR	International Association for the History of Religions
IASR	Institute for the Advanced Study of Religion (Toronto)
IASSR	International Association for the Scientific Society for the Study of Religion
NAASR	North American Association for the Study of Religion
NABI	National Association for Biblical Studies
SBL	Society of Biblical Literature
SR	Studies in Religion/Sciences Religieuses
SSSR	Society for the Scientific Study of Religion

Introduction

I was the seventh of nine children born to a Canadian Mennonite family and was nurtured and educated in a small but vibrant religious community. In my late teens I began to be intellectually interested in my religious experience, becoming a bit of an enigma to my cohort and, with increasingly persistent questioning, a pain to my elders. Eventually I considered becoming a minister or missionary and was informed that, to be given serious consideration for such a profession, I would have to get some post-secondary education and training. I enrolled in two baccalaureate degree programs at the Mennonite Brethren Bible College and College of Arts in Winnipeg, Manitoba—one in theology and the other in arts. The B.Th. program included a field education component involving door-to-door visits and led to an internship in rural ministry that involved loading up a sound system on the back of a 1950s half-ton pickup truck and preaching on Main Street on Saturday nights in the small rural town of Winnipegosis, Manitoba. The BA program, on the other hand, introduced me to a wider range of subjects including philosophy which was later to become the primary focus of my intellectual interests.

It was concern over the epistemic credibility of my religious beliefs that ultimately influenced my career. My "secular" courses and my extracurricular reading and research, especially with respect to the natural and social sciences, presented a challenge to the religious worldview in which I had grown up. Upon completion of these programs I accepted an invitation to teach at the Winkler Bible Institute in southern Manitoba. My newfound philosophical interests, however, ultimately led to being fired for heresy from the institute, which I "interpreted" as an opportunity to enter a graduate program in philosophy in the "secular" educational context. The peculiar nature of the modern research university since that time has been the common denominator in all of my "academic" work, although my focus has not always been on the question of the nature of the study of religions and religion in that context.

My MA work at the University of Guelph in Canada and my work as part of the doctoral program at the University of Lancaster in England were focused on creating what might be called a "compatibility system" in which religious knowledge claims would not be considered beyond the boundaries of epistemic legitimation. My MA thesis at Guelph sought to answer the question "Can Theology Survive the Impact of Science?" (1970). I published a summary of my affirmative answer to this question in an essay entitled "Comprehensively Critical Rationalism and Commitment" (1974). I then enrolled in a doctoral program at McMaster University. Having run into trouble with Professor George Grant at McMaster for my lack of interest in religious questions,

I transferred, at the recommendation of one of my mentors at Guelph, to the University of Lancaster to study with Ninian Smart, a phenomenologist and philosopher of religion. In my doctoral thesis under Smart's supervision I continued my MA work on building a "science-religion" compatibility system but with attention now to a broader set of epistemic questions than those raised in the MA thesis. I completed the doctoral thesis in 1974 under the rather grandiose title of *Science, Religion, and Rationality: Questions of Method in Science and Theology* (1974). Despite spending several years of research and writing some 1,150 pages in support of claims by theologians to scientific legitimacy, I could not come to a clear conclusion. All I could muster in my defense of this expenditure of energy was the following:

> A precise conclusion or set of conclusions can hardly be expected in bringing a project like this to a close. In an enterprise of this sort, the work undertaken is not so much completed as temporarily suspended, for the dissolution of long-standing myths is never likely to be the result of one quick, direct assault, but rather the product of a steady erosion, over a long period of time, of the uncritical foundations upon which they rest. And the assumption of an inherent conflict between science and religion which has been under scrutiny in the preceding pages is just such a long-standing myth. (694)

What I failed to notice in these works, however, is the fact that I had tackled the question of the relationship of religious thought to scientific thought without being aware that I was using the concepts of "theology" and "religion" (i.e., religious thought) interchangeably—as if they were mere synonyms. A change in the course of my involvement in the Religious Studies Department at Lancaster, however, would eventually lead to my questioning this assumption as being a necessary step in search of an appropriate methodology for the study of religious phenomena.

Even though my original objective of building a science-religion (theology) compatibility system was not achieved, I nevertheless proceeded with this project given that "our modern Western-European/Anglo-American-civilization," as I phrased it later in my *The Irony of Theology and the Nature of Religious Thought* (1991), is essentially both religious and scientific. That historical fact alone, I felt, demanded that we find "a way of reconciling the meaningful and vital aspects of our religious tradition with the spirit and findings of modern science" (1974: ii). And my intention was to provide a persuasive apology for religious belief that I thought could be achieved simply by way of independent and comparative analyses of the structure of argument in support of the knowledge claims of both the scientific and religious communities (1974: ii). Unlike the argument in my master's work, however, I was now aware that the complexity of the epistemic, methodological, and other issues involved in the compatibility question would require some form of what was known in philosophy of religion circles as a cumulative argument in support of religion (1974: iii).

Before the start of my final year at Lancaster, Professor Smart asked whether I would be interested in teaching the course on "Theories of Religion" for the department. There were good pragmatic reasons for accepting the invitation but the results of actually taking up the task were of far greater importance. Teaching the course provided me with an entirely new, non-religious, focus suited to my interests in epistemology and research in the philosophy of science. Although I did not immediately give up my interests in constructing a "reasonable compatibility system," teaching the theory course brought me into the orbit of historians, phenomenologists, and comparativists in the study of religions and religion. I now changed the focus of my attention from the "philosophy of religion" to what the "philosophy of science" might be able to contribute to the study of religion. I began by critically examining what the roles of such concepts as belief, truth, explanation, and theory, among others, played in religious studies. I submitted my first paper in this vein—"Explanation and the Scientific Study of Religion"—to the Lancaster journal *Religion* in 1974 (published in 1975). Research for teaching the course and writing that early article became an enticement for analyzing the field as a whole, which began with preparation for a paper I delivered at the thirteenth congress of the International Association for the History of Religions (IAHR) held in Lancaster in 1975. That paper—entitled "Is a Science of Religion Possible?"—was my first attempt at assessing the central methodological problems faced by students of religion. I delivered the paper with a good deal of trepidation knowing that two new friends I had made at the congress—professors E. Thomas Lawson and Luther H. Martin—had informed me that I couldn't possibly treat such a topic responsibly and that they would put me to the test in the question period. I can no longer remember the questions—if any—that were raised, but the friendship with Lawson and Martin, and the common interests we had in understanding the nature of the field of "religious studies," was an important impetus in my eventual transformation from "religious apologist" to "naturalistic student of religion."

After completion of my doctoral program at Lancaster I was invited to take up a position as assistant professor at Canadian Nazarene College (CNC) in Winnipeg, a religious institution in the Wesleyan holiness tradition. While an undergraduate, I had taught courses in Koiné Greek for their ministerial students and I was now asked to return to teach philosophy of religion and to head up their "Division of Liberal Arts." The appointment was serendipitous in that the IAHR had accepted the invitation to hold its fourteenth international congress in Winnipeg under the supervision of the Religious Studies Department of the University of Manitoba and the Canadian Society for the Study of Religion (CSSR). I had agreed to oversee "local arrangements" for this event. However, not all members of the Religious Studies Department had been in favor of hosting the congress and, under considerable pressure, the chair of the department relinquished oversight of the process in 1978, leaving the CSSR responsible for finding someone from outside the department who could convince the president of the university to remain the host institution for this event. A short time before the development of the internal squabbles in the Religious Studies Department at Manitoba, I had been fired for heresy again, this time by CNC, which made me available to take up this task, and the CSSR moved quickly to ask me to become the executive director for the congress.

Given my new circumstances, I focused less attention on religious matters and more on trying to understand the character of the "religious studies" enterprise with which I was now engaged. I was particularly interested in elaborating a methodology for the study of religion generally: clearly, a far too ambitious project for a neophyte in the field. However, having analyzed the import of the notion of truth in the study of religion in a paper for the CSSR just before taking up my post at CNC, I was determined to provide at least the outlines of such a methodology. That "study" was published in my first book, *Truth and Religion: Towards an Alternative Paradigm for the Study of Religion* (1981). Despite the title, I was not engaged here in a philosophical exercise to determine the truth or falsity of religion. I was concerned, rather, to point out that one needed to recognize that assuming religion to be true would result in a radically different type of explanation of it from those based on leaving the truth question unanswered. Nevertheless, my earlier theological concerns did migrate into my attempt to understand what would constitute a genuine "science of religion." However, by the mid-1980s, especially in my article "The Failure of Nerve in the Academic Study of Religion" (1984), I no longer doubted that a science of religion would have to be entirely naturalistic, leaving the "truth question" about religion out of the picture and adopting a methodological atheism. In this article (and subsequently others) I wished to clarify for myself why I had simply assumed in my early academic work that theology was a religious mode of thought. *The Irony of Theology and the Nature of Religious Thought* (1991) was dedicated to that task. It was based, in part, on my paper on Lévy-Bruhl and the "pre-logical mentality" that I had read at the fifteenth international congress of the IAHR in Australia in 1985 which ultimately convinced me that one could not simply assume "theology" and "religion" (religious thought) to be synonymous terms. Although my erstwhile friends from Lancaster days (Lawson and Martin) had mercilessly mocked my adoption of what was then considered an outdated view of the archaic human mind—and warned me that if I published these views I would ruin my academic career even before it had a chance to emerge—I nevertheless presented the paper (published it in 1987) and incorporated its argument in the *Irony* volume.

It was clear to me now that analysis of religious thought and theology involved distinct cognitive capacities and intellectual operations. Theology is, clearly, a second-order mode of thinking with the objective of providing a rational justification and systematic elaboration of a religious community's explicit and implicit thought and belief. I set out, therefore, to account for the nature of that first-order thinking that gave rise to religions and religious belief and I attempted to show it to be mythopoetic in the Lévy-Bruhlian sense rather than scientific in the sense of being dedicated to gaining knowledge of the world and its contents for its own sake. Although theology is a second-order mode of thinking, it is unlike the sciences in that its objective is not to gain knowledge for the sake of knowledge alone but rather to provide religious belief, and the religious mode of thought generally, with scientific credibility. Therefore, I concluded that insofar as theology is engaged in an apologetic defense of religion it is an incoherent hybrid mode of thought constrained both by mythic and by rational criteria, making it, like mythopoetic and religious thought, an object of scientific interest in need of explanation.

Having settled my concern with the nature of religious thought, and with its peculiar relationship with theology in the *Irony* volume, I took up in earnest the question of whether—in "religious studies" departments in our modern research universities today—there is a clear line of demarcation between religious belief and the practice of religion on the one hand, and the study of religion as a scientific enterprise on the other. To answer that question with cogency, I began to consider the history and fundamental objectives of the modern research university. I also set out to provide a history of the study of religion (i.e., of "religious studies" departments)—along with an analysis and assessment showing that they, for the most part, appear to function religiously in the context of the modern university. That is why I have given serious attention to the creation and support of a science of religion concerned only with obtaining "public knowledge" about "public religion" (i.e., religious thought and behavior) expressible in propositional claims that can be subjected to empirical confirmation. I am aware that the arguments supporting the replacement of most forms of "religious studies" found in our modern research universities today with a genuine "science of religion" has been in the past, and will be in the future, vigorously opposed. That opposition, however, is predicated on the assumption—direct or indirect—of the truth of religion which, I argue in these chapters, shows religious studies departments in our modern research universities to amount to something more like "classroom religions" than scientific enterprises.

The most fundamental reality that "grounds" the argument in the chapters in this volume, and the rest of my work since the publication of *The Irony of Theology*, is the conviction that the modern university, although emerging from, is not simply a continuation of the medieval and early modern Christian university. It cannot be denied, nor should it be surprising, that the makers of the modern university carried much "Christian" baggage along with them in restructuring the earlier institution. Nevertheless, the modern university, as Thorstein Veblen puts it, is unlike its predecessors because it took "no responsibility for its students' fortunes in the moral, religious, pecuniary, domestic, or hygienic respect" (1908: 21). Rather, it created a specialized institution "to fit men for a life of science and scholarship" (20). The modern university, that is, has been purpose-designed simply to obtain empirically and theoretically testable knowledge about the world and its contents, whether natural and social/cultural, including religions and "religion." Arguments in support of this view of the study of religion in the modern university will be found throughout this volume.

*   *   *

Interest in a scientific study of religion emerged in late nineteenth-century European and North American colleges and universities as a new kind of academic enterprise distinct from the devotional, catechetical, and theological scholarship that characterized the study of religion in the medieval and early modern European universities. Since the mid-twentieth century "religious studies" has been the most common designation for these "new" non-theological departments of religion. However, the academic work carried out under that rubric has remained an essentially "faith-imbued" form of scholarship. Although emancipated from direct ecclesiastical control and, to some extent, from confessional sectarian theologizing, "religious studies" research and scholarship in the new departments failed to break free from fideistic biases. "Religious studies" departments generally reject the simple scientific aim of gaining objective knowledge—empirical, explanatory, and theoretical—about religious thought and behavior, believing that it is possible to blend the epistemic objectives of scholarly research with a quest for humanistic—moral and spiritual—truths. But in blending those disparate objectives "religious studies" has become a crypto-religious and crypto-theological enterprise.

I have repeatedly argued that given the crypto-religious and crypto-theological character of most "academic" study of religions and religion departments in college and university classrooms today, this enterprise amounts to a new "failure of nerve" by twentieth- and twenty-first-century scholars in this field, preventing them from following through on the nineteenth-century ideal of an objective scientific study of religious thought and behavior. Although it is unlikely that the chapters published in this volume will convince all who read them that such a massive failure of nerve actually describes the field today, I hope they will at least provide them with evidence of *a long struggle for the development of a science of religion* more appropriate to the modern research university—in other words, for the creation of a scientific endeavor no longer pervaded by religious and moral agendas or a blurring of the boundary between the search for "knowledge about religions and religion" for its own sake and "religious education for the betterment of individuals and society." I argue that these chapters will show that, up until now, the so-called new discipline of "religious studies" in the modern university essentially amounts to what we might think of as the "learned practice of religion."

The majority of the chapters collected here are responses to invitations to contribute to "guides" or "companions" to the study of religion (Chapters 1 and 13), contributions to Festschrifts (Chapters 3 and 14), presentations to general university audiences (Chapters 12 and 15), and plenary addresses to national or regional associations for the study of religion (Chapters 4 and 9). The remaining chapters include formal articles read at academic conferences (Chapters 5 and 10), critical responses to books on themes related to this volume (Chapters 6, 7, and 11), a response to a symposium on the place of "secular theology" in the modern university (Chapter 2), and a chapter specifically written for this volume on the religious import of recent AAR presidential addresses (Chapter 8). Chapters 5, 6, 7, and the Conclusion have not previously been published.

Although the style of argumentation and presentation differs across these genres, each essay, article, or review provides a picture of the current academic study of religion in the modern research university as "conspicuously" unscientific. They also provide a critique of today's majority view of the field because of its un-argued (or poorly argued) disenchantment with science (Part One: Chapters 1–6), its unjustified rejection of the modern epistemic tradition that otherwise characterizes the research carried out in the natural and social sciences in our modern universities (Part Two: Chapters 7–11), and its simple assertion that the search for a culture-transcending objective knowledge of the natural and social worlds is chimerical (Part Three: Chapter 12–14). In the concluding essay I argue that both a scientific study (or studies) of religions and religion need not remain conspicuously unscientific in comparison with the other sciences and that, in light of the purpose-designed character of the modern research university, the humanities are conspicuously inappropriate conversation partners for those in departments for the study of religions.

Donald Wiebe
Trinity College
University of Toronto

Part One

Disenchantment with Science in the Academic Study of Religion

1

Including Religion in "Religious Studies"

Including the notion of "religious studies" as one discipline among many for description and analysis in *The Routledge Companion to the Study of Religion* suggests that there is broad agreement among those who study religion in the modern Western university as to the meaning of the term. Unfortunately, this is not the case. There is a vast literature committed to providing an understanding of the nature and value of the enterprise, but, as I shall show, there is little agreement to be found among those who have put their hand to the task. Not only is the term "religious studies" ambiguous with respect to the enterprise it designates but the very idea of "a discipline" is itself vigorously contested; and it is quite obvious that whether or not religious studies can justifiably be called a discipline depends wholly upon the understanding of "discipline" which is operative. As one scholar has put it, the term is used with more passion than precision (Benson 1987: 91). There is, moreover, considerable debate about the nature of the modern university within which "religious studies" as "a field of study" exists, so that to equate "religious studies" with "the academic study of religion" provides little—if any— clarification as to the nature or structure of this venture beyond information about its institutional location. Indeed, depending upon the assumptions one makes about the raison d'être of the modern university, there is no guarantee that "religious studies" as "the academic study of religion" can even be clearly differentiated from the scholarly study of religion carried on in other institutions, including religious institutions. It is no surprise, therefore, that some who have attempted to set out the meaning of the term "religious studies" have remarked that perhaps the clearest thing that can be said about it is that it "appears to be the designation of choice for the academic study of religion in the college and university setting" (Olson 1990a: 549). There is, perhaps, equal agreement that this designation for the study of religion, "legitimated" by virtue of inclusion in the curriculum of the university, came into use only after the Second World War, primarily since the 1960s. Providing a singular, overarching definition of "religious studies" as it is carried out in the modern university, therefore, is hardly possible; at the very least, such an exercise is unlikely to be either persuasive or helpful. To understand "religious studies" is to understand the diverse and nuanced way in which the term is used. And in a sense, one must follow the principle that to understand a concept it is important to be familiar with its history. This is not to say that no generalization is possible, but it does require that a thorough knowledge of the debate over the use of the term is essential before proposing one use of the concept over another. Much of this essay, therefore, will consist of a critical examination of the diverse ways in which the notion is understood in the reflective methodological literature in the field. Given the proliferation of relevant publications, however, this review cannot hope to be comprehensive. Accordingly, I restrict my analyses to Anglo-American (including Canadian) treatments of the subject, beginning with the attempts to provide a definitive statement on the notion in representative encyclopedias and encyclopedic dictionaries. Despite the diversity of views that will emerge in this analysis of the literature about the study of religion as it is currently carried out in colleges and universities, I shall attempt in the conclusion to draw out some warrantable generalizations about "religious studies" that may assist those coming new to the field.

Encyclopedic treatment of the notion of religious studies

Encyclopedic treatments of "religious studies" consider the term to refer to a new kind of study of religious phenomena—an exercise free from narrow ecclesiastical interference and more general religious influence. Religious studies, that is, is often taken to be other than a religious quest or undertaking and, unlike earlier scholarly studies within the framework of the academy (colleges and universities), seems to work on the assumption of religion's status as a purely social phenomenon. There is agreement not only that there existed a scholarly study of religion in the university prior to the emergence of religious studies departments in the modern university but also that it was religious or theological in character. ("Theology" is often used in the literature to refer not only to a particular discipline but also, more generally, to denote any kind of confessional or religious orientation.) Indeed, not only was it religious, it was parochial, exclusivist, and therefore sectarian and ideological. As I show here, however, the encyclopedia portraits are not internally coherent in their accounts of this enterprise and therefore leave much to be desired with respect to defining the term.

Those who consult the new *Encyclopedia of Religion* (Eliade 1987) for enlightenment on the notion of "religious studies" (Vol. XII: 334) will find the cross-reference "Study of Religion, article on Religious Studies as an Academic Discipline" (Vol. XIV)—an entry that consists of essays by Seymour Cain ("History of Study"), Eric J. Sharpe ("Methodological Issues"), and Thomas Benson ("Religious Studies as an Academic Discipline"), the last of which purports to trace "the development of religious studies as part of the liberal arts curriculum of secular and sectarian institutions of higher learning during the latter half of the twentieth century" (64). According to Benson, religious studies is a scholarly or academic undertaking aimed at "fostering critical understanding of religious traditions and values" (89) as opposed to a religious exercise designed to nurture faith. It is therefore a new enterprise, distinct from an earlier style of "faith-based" study of religion in the university that is usually referred to as "theology."

Harold Remus, in the *Encyclopedia of the American Religious Experience* (1988, Vol. III), claims that the development of new academic disciplines, such as sociology, anthropology, and psychology, applied to the study of religion at the end of the nineteenth century "led eventually to the development of an academic field designated *religion* or *religious studies* that was dedicated in principle to the academic study of religion" (1658). There is a clear line of demarcation, he insists, between this new discipline and its forerunner (the religiously committed study of religion). Religious studies, he warns, must not be confused with religious education which, like theology, is confessional in nature. "Religious studies," he writes, "does not seek to inculcate religious doctrines or specific religious values, to strengthen or win commitment to a religious tradition or institution, or to provide instruction preparatory to professional training for the ministry or rabbinate" (1653). For Remus, therefore, religious studies cannot involve instruction *in* religion but can nevertheless teach *about* religion (1657).

Alan Olson presents a similar picture of "religious studies" in the *Encyclopedia of Religious Education* (1990a), insisting that such studies are "to be distinguished from theological studies programs at the some two hundred and fifty seminaries and divinity schools in the United States and Canada" (549). For more than a century, he claims, religious studies has been trying to differentiate itself from religious and theological enterprises as a study that excludes personal belief. In his view, "religious studies is meant to identify an objective, scientific, non-biased study of religion as distinct from 'theological' and/or 'confessional' study for the purpose of increasing the faith, understanding, and institutional commitment of individual degree candidates in a particular religion" (549–50). Thus, according to Olson, whereas the academic study of religion in the United States had been primarily in the care of religiously founded institutions until well into the twentieth century—and, therefore, had been essentially religious in character—by the 1950s it became more scientific and "emerged as an important interdisciplinary, polymethodological, and cross-cultural area of academic inquiry" (551).

The entry by Ninian Smart on "Religious Studies in Higher Education" in John Hinnells's *The New Penguin Dictionary of Religions* (1995) echoes Olson's description. After acknowledging the existence of long-standing traditional approaches to the study of religion in institutions of higher learning, Smart maintains that "Religious Studies as a new multidisciplinary subject incorporating history of religions, cross-cultural topics, social-scientific approaches and ethical and philosophical reflections . . . came to prominence chiefly in the 1960s and early 1970s" (420). The significance of the new "discipline," it is suggested, is that the academic study of religions in the modern university made possible a variety of scholarly approaches different from those sanctioned up to then by the traditional theological framework. Smart argues that this shift of approach clearly broadened the scope of studies in religion.

Despite the advent of a new and clearly defined scholarly approach to religious studies, that new study does not consistently reflect the neutral status of an objective science. Benson points to this, for example, arguing that even though admitting religious studies results from secularizing forces in society, what lies behind the emergence of this new field is not primarily a scientific impulse. Religious studies programs, he notes, have usually been created in response to student and community interests, so that, even though such studies of religion are not as overtly religious as they once were, they are nevertheless concerned with more than scientific knowledge, for they are often touted as an important element in the "liberal education" dedicated to the cultivation of the self. As he puts it, religious studies is "generally influenced by pluralistic assumptions and [has] tended toward global perspectives on the nature and history of religion" (1986: 89). As a consequence, religious studies, even while bringing a broader curriculum to the religion department and considerably undermining the traditional seminary model, has unfortunately held the door open to "a crazy quilt of courses encompassing many disciplines, eras, regions, languages, and methods of inquiry" (91)—including traditional seminary-type offerings of Christian history, theology, biblical studies, religious ethics, religious thought, and religious education. The survival of religious studies in the United States, he suggests, is therefore tied not to the social sciences but rather to the fate of the humanities which are, like theology in the past, directed not only toward providing knowledge about the human estate but also to the search for meaning, the inculcation of values, and the formation of the character of students. Recognizing this, Benson points to the vestigial religious overtones to "religious studies" in the university context, noting that in the publicly funded university, the study of religion occasionally raises apprehension "concerning church–state relations and the constitutional status of state-funded religious studies" (89). Objections to such studies in the public university context, he suggests, have eased in the light of court decisions that have distinguished teaching about religion (even with the overtones described) from religious indoctrination, implying that only self-ascribed sectarian religious education need be excluded from the field. In Benson's estimation, therefore, religious studies seems to connote a broadly liberal religious education directed toward the formation of character and the betterment of society rather than scientific study aimed at knowledge and explanation of religious phenomena. He admits that in the 1960s there was deep interest in gaining disciplinary status for religious studies, but not on the grounds of its being a science. Rather, such status was sought on the basis of scholarly interest in a common subject matter: "The nature and diverse manifestations of religious experience" (91). But this, he declares, is not sufficient to warrant its recognition as a discipline, because it clearly does not have a method peculiar to itself. "Religious studies are, perhaps, best understood," he therefore concludes, "as a community of disciplines gathered around the complex phenomenon of religious belief and practice" (92).

Although Remus argued for a line of demarcation between instruction *in* religion and teaching *about* religion, he also noted that such teaching *about* religion is of particular importance to liberal education (1988: 1658). And in so doing, he seems to suggest that religious studies is more than merely a scientific undertaking, despite his insistence that it is not the task of liberal education to make the university a religious place (1658). He claims, for example, that it is not only the emergence of the social sciences that provided an impetus to the development of this new field, but that a "decline in institutional religions has also been a factor in enrolment in religious studies courses" (1658), suggesting thereby that the new enterprise has become in some sense an ersatz religion. Courses available in the new departments, that is, provide students with "opportunities to pursue some of the basic human issues—such as freedom, justice, love, evil, death—that universities were often bypassing in favor of technical and analytical study" (1659). Thus, although not intending to indoctrinate, the new religious studies department nevertheless constitutes an element in the student's search for meaning in life; it is not simply concerned with obtaining empirical and theoretical knowledge about religion.

Olson's demarcation of religious studies from a religio-theological study of religion is at least as ambiguous. For Olson, however, the reasons no such clear demarcation is possible are connected to the nature of science rather than to the nature of either religion or religious studies. A proper understanding of "science," Olson insists, will be seen to exclude all possibility of providing a fully naturalistic explanation for religion. "Religious studies," he writes, "has greatly contributed to the growing awareness that *true science* does not have to do with the development of a monolithic discipline, but with the collective efforts of a community of scholars illuminating one or more facets of the truth" (1990a: 551, emphasis added). In an article on the university in the same encyclopedia (1990b), Olson's notion of religious studies is further clarified in his claim that the discipline is an important element in the humanities because it provides sustained attention to religious values, making knowledge alone an insufficient goal of the enterprise. Consequently, for Olson—although he does not spell it out in great detail—a scientific study of religion that seeks to study religion wholly objectively is little more than an ideology of secular humanism.

The essay by Smart in Hinnells's *The New Penguin Dictionary of Religions* also acknowledges that the so-called new religious studies is not altogether new; in fact, it offers programs that often parallel those offered in divinity schools and departments of theology. It is acknowledged, moreover, that, at least in part, religious studies is fueled by "a growth in questing and questioning" rather than by the ideal of obtaining objective knowledge about religion (1995: 420–21). Thus, even though involving the sciences in the study of religion, the new religious studies is not unambiguously scientific in intent or in practice. Not only is it determined by a religious or theological agenda, it is also shaped, Smart argues, by other ideological agendas. Since its emergence in the 1960s, it has been profoundly affected by newer, non-objectivist approaches to the understanding of human phenomena such as feminism and postmodernist theorizing (421). Smart then concludes by pointing out how important religious studies is to the humanities—and by implication—to the humanist (and "liberal education") agenda: "Religious Studies is in one sense a branch of social science but has also begun to play a vital role in the humanities, both because of its cross-cultural commitments and because of its serious consideration of diversity of human world-views" (421).

In light of this analysis of the encyclopedists' efforts to provide an account of "religious studies"—of the academic study of religion in the university context—scholars will have to acknowledge, as does Adrian Cunningham (1990), that "perhaps 'religious' [in the phrase 'religious studies'] may still carry hints of its earlier usage to describe adherents, and of the ambiguities of 'religious education'" (30). Michael Pye (1991) makes the same point more forcefully, arguing that "the adjective 'religious' can easily suggest, and sometimes may be intended to suggest, that these 'studies' are supposed to be religious in orientation and not simply studies *of* religion" (41). The term is often used, he maintains, to designate those subjects and activities which in the past have constituted theological enterprises and must therefore be taken as "camouflage for theology" (42).

The lack of clarity and precision in the encyclopedia definitions of "religious studies" is not surprising for it reflects current practices in the enterprise as it is observed in college and university departments. A critical review of the self-reflective literature on "religious studies" as it is carried on in Canada, Great Britain, the United States, and elsewhere in the world will, I suggest, lend credence to Cunningham's and Pye's assessment that the field fails to live up to the implicit ideal of it as a scientific rather than a religious undertaking found in the encyclopedic accounts.

"Religious studies" in Canada

The character of the academic study of religion is thoroughly analyzed in the ambitious state-of-the-art reviews of religious studies in Canadian universities directed by Harold Coward. Six volumes of the study appeared between 1983 and 2001, covering the provinces of Alberta (Neufeldt 1983), Quebec (Rousseau and Despland 1988), Ontario (Remus et al. 1992), Manitoba and Saskatchewan (Badertscher et al. 1993), British Columbia (Fraser 1995), and New Brunswick, Prince Edward Island, Nova Scotia, and Newfoundland (Bowlby 2001).

Although entitled *The Study of Religion in Canada/Sciences Religieuses au Canada*, the projected study is described in the editor's introduction to each volume as "a State-of-the-Art Review of *religious studies* in Canada" (emphasis added), which seems to identify "religious studies" in university departments very broadly with any and every type of study of religion carried on in institutions of higher learning. The ambiguity of the project description, in fact, provides Brian Fraser all the encouragement needed for dealing not only with the academic study of religion in the university setting but also with the religious and theological study of religion in other post-secondary educational institutions from bible schools to seminaries. Indeed, Fraser entitles his state-of-the-art review not "Religious Studies in British Columbia" but *The Study of Religion in British Columbia* (1995), and makes it very clear early on in the volume that he believes the ambiguity of the project title leaves room for argument to the effect that the kinds of study carried on in these very different institutions are not only complementary but in some fundamental sense the same. "In the other volumes in the Canadian Corporation for the Study of Religion (CCSR) series on the study of religion in Canada," he writes, "the focus has been on religious studies in the secular university, with minimal attention being paid to various approaches of theological studies" (viii). As there is only one department of religious studies in universities in British Columbia (UBC), and because Fraser works, as he puts it, from a "vocational base in theological studies," he chose "to focus on the broader subject indicated by the original designation of the series as a whole, i.e., the study of religion" (viii–ix). A comprehensive review of the state-of-the-art in that province, he insists therefore, "requires that appropriate attention be paid to both religious studies and theological studies" (ix). This, in his view, moreover, is not mandated simply by the fact that two radically different kinds of study of religion exist in institutions of higher education. It exists also because they have complementary interests, so that a proper study of "religious studies" requires that this fact be recognized. According to Fraser, for example, both types of study of religion exact an element of commitment aside from that found in religious institutions, for, while religious institutions of higher learning are committed to enhancing "participation in and contribution to religious traditions and communities that govern the institutions in which the study takes place" (viii), the so-called neutral and non-advocative study of religion in the university is also directed toward results "that intend to elucidate the questions of human existence that religions have always tried to confront" (viii). Religious studies, therefore, even though having "nothing whatsoever to do with the professional training of ministers" (20), seems to be a kind of non-sectarian civil religion or general theology fit for "a public and pluralistic institution" (viii) because it engages fundamental questions of meaning in human existence. His views in this regard are clearly exhibited in his praise for the work of the Centre for Studies in Religion and Society at the University of Victoria, which, he claims, emerged in part as "the result of the need for an expanded view of studies in religion" (109) wherein the "interdisciplinary nature of its commitment brings together the various voices of the scholarly worlds, while not ignoring the community at large, [to address] major challenges of global concern" (109). And it is in light of this kind of project that Fraser expresses the hope for an integration of the various approaches "to the study of religion and the religions themselves[,] and for the development of a [university-based] doctoral program in *religious/theological studies*" (109, emphasis added).

Had Fraser consulted the first volume in this series, he would not have needed to provide justificatory argument for his study of religious and theological programs of study in British Columbia's religious institutions. For in Ronald W. Neufeldt's (1983) account of "religious studies" in Alberta, he acknowledges that some scholars "expressed some opposition to the inclusion of theological colleges and bible colleges and institutions" (xi) but nevertheless in his study proceeded to support such an expanded notion of the field—as has every subsequent study. Neufeldt's justification for proceeding in this fashion is both practical and theoretical, and it is particularly symptomatic of the confusion that plagues the notion of religious studies as a new kind of academic undertaking. Among the practical reasons for including religious institutions in his account of religious studies in Alberta, Neufeldt cites the fact that "particular courses in theological colleges are recognized by universities either as religious studies courses or as arts options" (xi), pointing to the practice that "students from Bible colleges are sometimes given block credit for courses taken in a Bible college, or are exempted from taking introductory courses in religious studies in the universities" (xi). Although such practices suggest a profound confusion of the natures of the new study of religion, on the one hand, and theological studies, on the other, Neufeldt supports the practice on theoretical grounds, none of which is persuasive. He insists, for example, that "the confessional stance of a particular institution should not automatically be taken to mean that the programs and research in such institutions have no academic integrity at all," as if that fact provides grounds for the integration of the two approaches to the study of religion in the university context. He suggests that the courses in the theological schools for which transfer credit is given are all at the descriptive level and therefore not likely to differ greatly from the descriptive courses provided in university departments. Should this prove otherwise, however, Neufeldt is ready with further methodological argument. "In effect," he writes, "the argument made here is for a humanities model for religious studies rather than [for] a model in which the predominant note is critical analysis and theory" (xii). And such a model, he claims (on the authority of Smart's analysis of religious studies in his *The Science of Religion and the Sociology of Knowledge* (1973)), shows religious studies to be open to aims beyond those of science: beyond merely seeking a theoretical account of religion. Neufeldt acknowledges that religious studies in Alberta is dominated by "textual and theological/philosophical studies" (76), and while believing this needs correction through cooperation with cognate disciplines, nevertheless insists that the effort "to hire scholars who are trained in other approaches to the study of religion" must not eclipse those trained in the theological traditions (77). For Neufeldt, evidently, religious studies is not clearly distinguishable from a study of religion that is a religious undertaking.

Les Sciences Religieuses au Québec depuis 1972 (1988), by Louis Rousseau and Michel Despland, traces the declining influence of the Roman Catholic Church on religious studies since 1960, but they point out that a claim to neutrality for religious studies cannot be made. Although they argue that the major societies and associations related to the field of religious studies show a marked move toward "pluridisciplinarity," they nevertheless maintain that theology and Christian studies still dominate departmental programs and scholarly research interests. Indeed, they argue that the situation in Quebec institutions is still extremely unfavorable to freedom of teaching and research, disputing the claim that religious studies programs in the secular universities have eliminated theological approaches to the subject. According to Rousseau and Despland, therefore, the field of religious studies in Quebec integrates the approaches associated with theology and the sciences of religion; thus there is no indication of a decisive move from theology to the social-scientific study of religion.

Religious Studies in Ontario: A State-of-the-Art Review (1992) by Harold Remus, William James, and Daniel Fraikin also fails to provide a clear analysis of the theology/religious studies problem. The authors, drawing on Charles Anderson's study in the early 1970s, suggest that universities drew a clear distinction between religious and secular study (58), but they erred in extending their history of the field to programs operating in Bible colleges, which, by definition, take a faith-based, rather than a scientific, approach to their curriculum and therefore were presenting not religious studies as much as theology. They reason, in part, that contemporary theology is discontinuous from its "traditional" predecessor, therefore "mak[ing] it possible for Ontario religious studies departments to offer such courses today" (33). That claim, however, is predicated on the assumption that religious studies is not reducible simply to the scientific study of religion. Consequently, the authors maintain that students of religion must get on with the study of religion and stop the "by now, sterile wrangling over the 'theology-and-religious studies'" issue (33). Religion, they note, "is studied in a number of academic fields other than theology and in ways that are helpful to religious studies scholars . . . [and that that] too, is 'the state-of-the-art,' in religious studies in general and in Ontario religious studies in particular" (34). Religious studies as a new hybrid discipline, it appears therefore, is also appropriately carried on in the context of the modern university.

The response of one theological reviewer of the Ontario study is particularly perceptive with respect to this religiously significant understanding of religious studies. Jean-Marc Laporte, the director of the Toronto School of Theology, expresses gratitude for the authors' understanding of religious studies because it sees religious studies and theology as allies engaging "the world and its problems" (1993: 249). The essential task of each, is identical—but that is largely because the fundamental task of religious studies has been assimilated to that of theology. This is lauded by Laporte, who writes: "While the authors prize the academic objectivity of religious studies, they are far from advocating bloodless sterility. Professors of religious studies ought to respond to existential concerns and be free to disclose their own personal convictions in appropriate, non-proselytizing ways" (249). And this is not surprising for, as Laporte points out, the authors claim both that "the matrix out of which religious studies emerged as a distinct reality is a theological one" and that "the pioneers of this discipline in Ontario universities by and large did not make a clean break from their origins" (249).

The story of the rise of religious studies departments in the universities of Manitoba and Saskatchewan (Badertscher et al. 1993) reveals the same picture of religious origination and influence on the academic study of religion found in the other state-of-the-art studies, with the exception of the department at the University of Regina in Saskatchewan. As in Manitoba, claims Roland Miller, "university education . . . grew out of a close association with an original perspective that viewed arts and theology as colleagues in the educational enterprise" (101). Theology consequently dominated the notion of religious studies, but only at the University of Saskatchewan (Saskatoon). The development of the department at the University of Regina, at first simply an extension of the department at the University of Saskatchewan, was radically different, even though it found itself involved with legally and financially autonomous, but academically integrated (federated), religious colleges. Nevertheless, its programs, Miller argues, "grew out of a genuine recognition of the importance of the subject material and out of concern for a secular approach to its academic study" (83). The University of Regina, he continues, "was interested in pursuing the direction that might be summed up by the phrase 'science of religion,' although those words do not appear in any of the materials" (83).

In *Religious Studies in Atlantic Canada*, Paul W. R. Bowlby works with a definition of the field that excludes schools preparing people for professional work in religious institutions but includes religious colleges and universities that have accepted public funding and have to some degree, therefore, been secularized. Nevertheless, he is well aware that most of the departments of religion included in his study have evolved from departments of theology and that they have followed a conventional pattern of curriculum development, with particular emphasis on biblical and Christian studies. He maintains that these institutional structures have seen significant development (such as the introduction of comparative, social-scientific, and gender-critical approaches to the study of religion) yet also admits that the influence of Christianity on the field in this region of the country has hindered the advancement of "religious studies" as a scientific discipline.

In all of the programs described in the Canadian studies, only that of the University of Regina is (in theory at least) purely epistemic in orientation. And its view about the nature of the discipline clearly places it in a minority. There were some early indications that religious studies would be identified primarily with a non-religious, scientific approach to understanding religion (Anderson 1972), but, as the state-of-the-art studies make clear, such views did not have a significant impact on the development of the field in Canada. Charles Davis's essay on "The Reconvergence of Theology and Religious Studies" (1974–5) better captures the aims and desires of those involved in Canadian university departments of religion, as is clearly evident in the majority of the contributions to the more recent volume of essays, *Religious Studies: Issues, Prospects and Proposals* (1991), edited by Klaus Klostermaier and Larry Hurtado. While recognizing something new in contemporary religious studies, the editors nevertheless pointedly invited participants to the conference "to consider the study of religion at public universities *as a continuation of the intellectual examination of religion which goes back over the ages*" (ix, emphasis added). This is also clearly evident in the character of the research activities of the majority of those who contribute to the Canadian journal *Studies in Religion/Sciences Religieuses*, whose pages are for the most part filled with religious and theological research rather than with scientific studies of religion (Riley 1984). Indeed, as I have shown elsewhere, religious studies in Canada, for the most part, has been more concerned with a "learned practice of religion" rather than with seeking a scientific explanation of it (Wiebe 2006a).

"Religious studies" in Great Britain

Although there are no other state-of-the-art reviews of the field of religious studies as extensive as that undertaken by the Canadians, the festschrift for Geoffrey Parrinder, edited by Ursula King and entitled *Turning Points in Religious Studies* (1990), provides a comparable one-volume review of the emergence, development, and current state of religious studies in Great Britain. This volume is of particular interest because it unequivocally presents itself as providing an account of religious studies as a new discipline, clearly distinguishable from the theological approaches to the study of religion that had until recently characterized university scholarship. As the fly-leaf notice about the volume puts it: "Religious Studies was first introduced as *a new discipline* in various universities and colleges around the world in the 1960s. This discipline brought about a *reorientation of the study of religion*, created new perspectives, and influenced all sectors of education" (emphasis added). The clarity of this brief statement about a new discipline that has reoriented scholarship in religion, however, is quickly effaced by the editor's general introduction to the essays intended to document both the emergence of the new discipline and the major turning points in its evolution. For King speaks here not of a *discipline*, but rather of a *field* of study which "found wider recognition from the 1960s and 1970s onwards when the term 'Religious Studies' came first into general use" (15). But as a field, religious studies cannot be characterized methodologically, for fields of study involve a multiplicity of disciplinary approaches to a particular subject matter of interest. Her introduction to the essays on the institutional growth of religious studies in the universities of England, Scotland, and Wales, moreover, compromises the claim that the so-called new discipline brought about a reorientation of the study of religion already in existence prior to the 1960s. These essays, she writes, "show how much the course of Religious Studies and the history of its programmes have been intertwined with and often curtailed by earlier institutional developments in the study of theology, so that it has often been difficult to maintain the distinctiveness of Religious Studies" (16). Having acknowledged this, King then goes on to claim that religious studies cannot really "be fully understood without looking at the closely associated developments in religious education and practical issues in interfaith dialogue" (16), suggesting that religious studies is—and ought to be—more than an academic (scientific) discipline. Thus she includes in the volume essays not only on the development of the "new discipline" but also on the role of religious studies in relation to developments in religious education, interreligious dialogue, and philosophy of religion. For King, these "concerns" characterize distinct approaches to the subject matter of religious studies and are, therefore, some of the disciplines that characterize the field as multidisciplinary, but all of them clearly reflect the traditional religious and theological concerns of the scholarly study of religion which "Religious Studies" ought to have superseded. As Robert Jackson points out in his essay titled "Religious Studies and Developments in Religious Education" (1990), for example, religious education not only embodies an epistemic or scientific concern about religion but also sees religion itself as a form of knowledge and a distinct realm of experience (107), and religious education, therefore, as directed to awakening "a unique spiritual dimension of experience" in children (110). The raison d'être of religious education, therefore, is not only epistemic but also formative, aimed at helping children exercise their spiritual curiosity, and encouraging "in them an imaginative openness to the infinite possibilities of life" (110). W. Owen Cole's discussion of "The New Educational Reform Act and Worship in County Schools of England and Wales" (1990) similarly confirms the judgment that religious education is concerned not only with gaining knowledge about religion but also with nurturing religious growth and development. As Cole puts it: "Some kind of collective gathering is considered desirable by most teachers *for a number of purposes* including the collective exploration of and reflection upon values and beliefs" (129–30, emphasis added). The fact that philosophy holds the same kind of religious and theological import as one of the disciplines that make up the multidisciplinary enterprise of religious studies is clearly evident in Keith Ward's "The Study of Truth and Dialogue in Religion" (1990). For Ward, philosophy's value to religious studies is to be found in its concerns with the meaning and truth of religion:

> Religious Studies is good for philosophy, since it keeps alive the questions of ultimate meaning and value which are its lifeblood. Philosophy is good for Religious Studies, since it keeps alive the questions of truth and justification which preserve religion from complacent dogmatism. The discipline of Religious Studies now offers to philosophers a much wider and more informed basis for the investigation of meaning and truth in religion; and the most fruitful results are

to be expected from the increasingly inter-disciplinary approach which is being adopted in British universities. (230)

Interestingly (if not ironically), only Marcus Braybrooke—Chairman of the interfaith movement "World Congress of Faiths"—appears to assume that religious studies is a genuinely new approach to the study of religion. Braybrooke writes: "The underlying hope of the interfaith movement, *although not of the academic study of religions*, is that in some way religions are complementary or convergent" (1990: 138, emphasis added). He nevertheless seems to believe that a positive complementarity exists between religious studies and interfaith development. And Eleanor Nesbitt's article on Sikhism (1990) presents a similar proposal for encouraging a positive relationship between the modern student of religion and the religious devotee.

The descriptions of the emergence of religious studies in the universities in England (Adrian Cunningham), Scotland (Andrew F. Walls), and Wales (Cyril Williams), it must be noted, claim (or suggest) that it achieved status in the university as an autonomous discipline by virtue of its differentiation from religion and theology. Their claims, however, seem to be undermined by the editor of the volume in which they appear, for they are found in the context of numerous other contributions of the kind just described, as well as an essay by Smart—"Concluding Reflections on Religious Studies in Global Perspective" (1990)—that argue a contrary case. It is true that neither Smart nor the other essayists argue specifically against undertaking scientific analyses of religion and religions. Smart does argue, however, against what he calls a scientifically purist stance in religious studies. As with the other essayists, Smart insists that religious studies can only properly be understood as a polymethodic and multidisciplinary enterprise which embraces "as much as possible of the scholarship of all sorts going on in the world . . . [w]hether it is neutral and objective or religiously committed" (305, 300). As a non-purist study, religious studies, he claims, will triumph because it can "be a force for permitting deeper conversations between religions, without reverting into a simple exchange of pieties" (305). In this light, it is ironic that Cunningham should remark, as I have already noted, that even though the designation "religious studies" for the study of religion carried on in university departments has an honorable history, "perhaps 'religious' may still carry hints of its earlier usage to describe adherents, and of ambiguities of 'religious education,' and it would be better for the university area to be simply called 'religion'" (30).

Given Smart's widespread influence on the development of university studies of religion over the formative period under review here, not only in the United Kingdom but also in Canada, Australia, New Zealand, South Africa, and the United States, it may be helpful to elaborate more fully his views on the nature and structure of "religious studies." In "Some Thoughts on the Science of Religion" (1996), Smart clearly differentiates between the scientific study of religion and religious studies, with the former being associated with a multiplicity of disciplines, including history, comparative religions, and other social-scientific approaches to the study of religious phenomena (16). It is possible, Smart admits, to take "religious studies" to be fully described as the scientific study of religion, but he thinks such an understanding falls short of the view of that enterprise held by the majority of those engaged in it. Thus he argues for a broader view of "religious studies" that will include not only scientific studies but also "reflective studies" (19). By "reflective studies" Smart means the examination of philosophical questions about the meaning and value of religion, in the same sense presented by Keith Ward (1990). Smart admits that such a reflective religious studies involves itself in "presentational concerns," by which he means engagement with the questions of truth and meaning, yet he denies that this amounts to merging religious studies with theology (19). This is on two grounds: first, that which he calls "extended pluralistic theologizing" is clearly distinguishable from traditional theology; and second, that "certain reductionistic views of science are themselves ideological positions that are not clearly distinguishable from traditional theology" (20). He argues, therefore, that talk of the science of religion as the core of religious studies is wholly reasonable, but only if it remains non-reductionist. As such, the science of religion would then allow for critical reflection on the meaning, truth, and value of religion *insofar as* it is not simply identified with traditional theology, which, he claims, "is tainted by arrogance, colonialism and a usual lack of pluralism" (19). As he puts it, "If Religious Studies is to take on board reflective studies, and with that get involved with any presentational concerns with theology or ideology, it is only with Extended Pluralistic Theologizing . . . that it should blend" (19). For him, therefore, "To be genuinely scientific and objective we need to be able to steer a middle channel between the Scylla of secret theology and the Charybdis of reductionism" (20), which requires a blend of non-reductionistic scientific studies of religion with reflective, extended theology. Both traditional theology and scientific purism are excluded.

In his contribution to Jon R. Stone's *The Craft of Religious Studies* (1998b), Smart reiterates his concern about "scientific purism," even though he acknowledges that what is called modern religious studies arose only after the 1960s with the merger of the history of religions with the social sciences (18). The new discipline, he insists, must be both speculative and philosophically reflective, although he warns against its being used as mere "clothing for a religious worldview" (24). It is little wonder, therefore, that Smart characterizes religious studies here as a quest (ix). But neither should it come as a surprise, therefore, that many in the academic world, as Smart himself puts it, have categorized religious studies "as some form of tertiary Sunday School, . . . [and so] resist and despise it" (24). There is sufficient confusion about the notion of "religious studies," he judiciously notes, that "the outside world in academia may be forgiven for misunderstanding what the field of Religious Studies is all about" (24). But it does not appear to me that his own characterizations of the field have helped dispel the confusion; indeed, his own work seems to contribute to a view of religious studies as a religious exercise.

Subsequent studies on the character of "religious studies" in the UK confirm that the dominant conception of the study of religion in British universities is essentially as a religious exercise. The volume *A Century of Theological and Religious Studies in Britain* (Nicholson 2003), for example, treats essentially Christian topics from a Christian point of view, and *Fields of Faith: Theology and Religious Studies for the Twenty-first Century* (Ford, Quash, and Soskice 2005) attempts to show the interplay of the two fields in relation to a range of topics in Christian theology and thereby establish ground for a future in which theology and religious studies are pursued together.

"Religious studies" in the United States

That this kind of confusion about the nature of religious studies also exists in the American context is clearly acknowledged in the report of the Committee on "Defining Scholarly Work" of the American Academy of Religion (AAR). In a report entitled "Religious Studies and the Redefining Scholarship Project," the committee notes:

> Religious Studies, however defined or wherever located, remains suspect in the eyes of many within the rest of the academy and continually finds itself marginalized or otherwise obscured due to the fact and/or perception of blurred boundaries between studying religion and being religious, or between education about and education in religion. (Myscofski and Pilgrim et al. 1993: 7)

The suspicion in which religious studies is held in the US academic context, therefore, is due primarily to the confusion of what is proposed as an academic (and therefore scientific) enterprise with a religious or theological undertaking. As in Canada and Great Britain, scholars in the United States claim that a significant transformation in the nature of the study of religion in the university context occurred after the Second World War. In *God's People in the Ivory Tower: Religion in the Early American University* (1991), Robert S. Shepard claims that the study of religion in US colleges and universities briefly flirted with the idea of creating a science of religion but remained essentially a kind of "Christian *Religionswissenschaft*" that was essentially moralistic and apologetic in intent and practice. As such it was unable

> to separate [itself] from the theological and professional concerns of the nascent university, particularly the rising seminary within the university. A theological agenda accompanied the entrance of comparative religion in American higher education despite the arguments, some rhetorical and some sincere, that the new discipline was objective, scientific, and appropriate as a liberal arts subject. (129)

Nevertheless, claims Shepard, the academic study of religion in US colleges and universities experienced a renaissance after the Second World War and within a very short period of time gained disciplinary status within the academic context. D. G. Hart (1992) comes to a similar conclusion in his analysis of the field of religious studies. While not unaware of the fact that the rapid growth of the field was stimulated by the cultural crisis generated by the Second World War, and that such studies were aimed at ensuring college and university students received an education that included "values-training" and moral formation (209), he nonetheless insists that the development of the AAR transformed the field into a scientific discipline. These changes, he insists, constitute a watershed in the history of the study of religion in the United States because they involved the substitution of scientific explanations of religious phenomena for the earlier quest for religious, theological, and humanistic accounts of religion. "The new methods of studying religion advocated by the AAR," he writes, "signalled the demise of [the] Protestant dominance [of the field] as professors of religion became increasingly uncomfortable with their religious identification . . . . By striving to make their discipline more scientific, religion scholars not only embraced the ideals of the academy but also freed themselves from the Protestant establishment" (198). (Hart recapitulates the argument in his more recent book, *The University Gets Religion: Religious Studies in American Higher Education* (2000).)

Were this picture true, scholars would be hard-pressed to explain why the so-called new discipline is still held in suspicion by the rest of the academic and scientific community. What does account for the suspicion, however, is that the notion of religious studies is not in fact carried out within a naturalistic and scientific framework, but more nearly resembles the academic field as it first emerged in the United States— namely, as an inchoate enterprise not easily distinguishable from theology and characterized primarily by apologetic and moral concerns. This is clearly evident in the review of the field produced for the AAR by Ray Hart, entitled "Religious and Theological Studies in American Higher Education" (1991), even though he admits that the term "religious studies" is now generally used to refer to "the scholarly, neutral and non-advocative study of multiple religious traditions" (716). Hart notes that many in the AAR are extremely uncomfortable with "the nomenclature that discriminates 'religious' from 'theological studies'" (716), and points out that the members of the Academy are divided between the terms "study of religion" (gaining knowledge *about* religion) and "practice of religion" (*understanding* the truth of religion) (734, 778); he then claims, however, that by far the majority of the members favor a style of scholarship that combines the two activities, or one that at the very least eschews a clear demarcation between them. Joseph Kitagawa's essays, "The History of Religions in America" (1959) and "Humanistic and Theological History of Religion with Special Reference to the North American Scene" (1983), strengthen Hart's contention considerably. In the first essay, he maintains that the religious liberalism of the World's Parliament of Religions served as the fundamental impetus for the establishment of the study of comparative religions—which later became religious studies—in American universities, even though he acknowledges that the participants at the parliament meeting in 1893 for the most part gathered together representatives of the world's faiths rather than scholars of religion. In drawing attention to this, Kitagawa underlines the fact that the academic study of religion in the United States has more than one dimension; it has involved historical and social-scientific analysis, but it has also moved beyond what such analyses can provide. Consequently, he distinguishes the "History of Religions" (as a scientific enterprise) from the "theological History of Religions"—but with the implication that neither can do without the other. And he insists that the *Religionswissenschaft* later destined to become "religious studies" is not simply scientific but rather "religio-scientific," being obliged to "view that data 'religio-scientifically'" (1959: 21). In the second essay, Kitagawa suggests that the scientific Enlightenment principles behind the scholarship of the members of the IAHR have greatly affected the development of the field in the United States, and yet—in keeping with his earlier analysis of *Religionswissenschaft*—he refers to the discipline as "autonomous[,] situated between normative studies . . . and descriptive studies" (1983: 559). Unlike other social sciences, then, for Kitagawa this discipline does not simply seek descriptions or explanations of events and processes; rather, it enquires after the meaning of religious data and is therefore a mode of "research" linking descriptive with normative concerns (560). He contrasts this kind of study of religion with the more explicitly normative "theological History of Religions" cited in his earlier essay, but it is clear that this "humanistic History of Religions" also stands in contrast to the purely social-scientific study of religion represented by scholars affiliated to the IAHR. As one historian of the development of religious studies in the United States puts it, despite the claim of having become an independent scientific enterprise in addition to the other social sciences, it has remained haunted by religious aspirations (Reuben 1996: 142). The religious studies of the post-1960s, in particular has always been concerned with more than scientific description and explanation of religion. As D. G. Hart echoes (1992: 207–8), post-1960s religious studies in the United States is a discipline imbued with spiritual value; and the students of religion (as represented by the AAR) draw support from the humanities for their enterprise by stressing the spiritual relevance of their studies to the natural sciences.

The confusion that characterizes the postwar notion of "religious studies" in the American context is rather clearly documented in Walter H. Capps's *Religious Studies: The Making of a Discipline* (1995). Although Capps refers to religious studies as an intellectual discipline which "provides training and practice . . . in directing and conducting inquiry regarding the subject of religion" (xiv), whereby the subject of religion can be made intelligible, he also claims that "religious studies is a relatively new subject-field concerning whose intellectual composition there is as yet no consensus" (xv). He maintains that this is partly because the principal contributions to the field have been made by persons in other disciplines such as history and the social sciences, and because "convictional goals" have affected the processes of interpretation applied (xxii). He states:

> The primary differentiation within religious studies derives less from the fact that historians, sociologists, anthropologists, psychologists, philosophers, theologians, and others are intensely involved in inquiry, and raise questions from within the frame of interests that belong to their respective vantage points, and much more from the fact that representations of all these fields and disciplines are interested in uncovering certain information about the subject *and pursue it via raising fundamental questions.* (xxii, emphasis added)

Scientific inquiry, therefore, is secondary to the fundamental questions about meaning and value that provide a coherent framework within which the multiplicity of disciplines making up the field operate. Capps argues that it ought not to surprise anyone to see such a religious goal characterize this academic study. For, as he notes, not only was the historical and comparative study of religion established in the universities in the late nineteenth century and until the Second World War undertaken largely by scholars involved both in the study and the practice of religion (325) but one can also make a strong case that the subsequent flowering of the study of religion in the university context—and especially so in the United States—was due to its character as a liberal theological undertaking. According to Capps, that is, it is largely because of the Tillichian conceptualization of the theological enterprise that students of religion gained "forceful and clear access to the more inclusive cultural worlds, and in ways that could be sanctioned religiously and theologically" (290). He rejects the view that the perpetuation of theological reflection in the religious studies enterprise undermines its academic or scientific respectability (325). Instead, the student of religion must recognize that religious studies, insofar as it is merely the sum of the analytical and interpretive achievements of the various constituent fields of research, does not do full justice to the subject of religion. Furthermore, the polymethodic and multidisciplinary character of the academic study of religion today constitutes "religious studies" only if all these fields are working together to show "that religion has a necessary and proper place within the inventory of elements of which the scope of knowledge is comprised" (345). "In sum," he concludes broadly, "religious studies recognizes that religion is not fully translatable into religious studies, and this is an analytical and interpretive truth" (347).

More recent work in America concurs with Capps's conclusion. In his introduction to *Critical Terms for Religious Studies* (1998), Mark C. Taylor claims both that prior to the 1960s religious studies was essentially a Christian (Protestant) undertaking and that the raison d'être of the new religious studies since that time is still essentially religious but neither particularly Protestant nor Christian. At that time, "departments and programs in religion tended to be either extensions of the chaplain's office, which was almost always Christian and usually Protestant, or affiliated with philosophy departments, which were primarily if not exclusively concerned with Western intellectual history," whereas after the 1960s they are associated not with science, but rather with "the flowering of the 1960s counter culture" (Taylor 1998: 11). Although he admits that religious studies has been "profoundly influenced by developments dating back to the Enlightenment" (10), its new incarnation in university departments in the United States was predominantly influenced by multicultural sensibilities created by the civil rights and anti-war movements of the late 1950s and early 1960s. If the "how" of religious studies has changed because of the increased influence of the social sciences in cultural studies during this period, he avers, nevertheless, that this has not altered the essence of the discipline; that is, even if a social-scientific study of religion has somehow displaced the old theology, it has not displaced the fundamental religious concern that has always (and always will) characterized the field. Taylor notes elsewhere (1994) that it is precisely for this reason that religious studies is an academically suspect discipline in secular colleges and universities (1994: 950). Yet even though the field of religious studies became captive to other methodologies, he argues, it cannot be reduced to them (951), because the secular approach of the sciences absolutize their understanding of religion and are themselves, therefore, simply another form of theology.

For Taylor, there is no appropriate procedure for a comprehensive scientific study of religion, and religious studies must therefore be both multidisciplinary and multicultural. But if he seems to discern the complexity of his stance, he nevertheless does not assist the scholarly study under question by his fluid description. Postmodernism, he maintains, undermines all possibility of a fundamental method or comprehensive explanatory approach to the data of the field. Consequently, its quarry cannot be cognition; rather it must seek to understand religion by applying a multiplicity of notions and concepts that might act as "enabling constraints" (1998: 16) for a discourse of a different kind: "For exploring the territory of religion" (17) by means of a "dialogue between religious studies and important work going on in other areas of the arts, humanities, and social sciences" (18). Such a religious studies, he points out, properly transcends scientific reductionism and, like the study of religion antedating it, recognizes that "religion . . . is not epiphenomenal but sui generis" (6; see also 1999: 4). Stated differently, scientific theory is not not-theological, as Taylor might express it, because theory itself is theological and onto-theological in character, given that it is a search either for an "overarching or underlying unity" that will coherently frame the data. As he puts it:

> The gaze of the theorist strives to reduce differences to identity and complexity to simplicity. When understood in this way, the shift from theology to theory does not, as so many contemporary theorists think, escape God but exchanges overt faith for covert belief in the One in and through which all is understood. (1999: 76)

The new post-1960s study of religion in the American context on this reading of the situation is not new in its fundamental orientation and therefore different from the traditional study of religion in the university. The religious discourse of traditional studies is replaced not by scientific discourse but rather by a different form of religious discourse—namely, the discourse of "responsible inquiry" that "neither demands answers nor believes in progress but seeks to keep the future open by a relentless questioning that unsettles everything by settling nothing. To settle nothing is to leave nothing unanswered. Forever unanswered" (Taylor 1994: 963). This kind of "responsible discourse," it is quite apparent, is not primarily concerned with obtaining knowledge about religions and religion, but rather with the well-being of the individual.

"Religious studies" globally

That there is no general convergence of opinion about the nature of religious studies among students of religion in the Anglo-American university context is clearly demonstrated by the analyses of the various Canadian, British, and American views presented above. The same can be said about religious studies globally. Although a "thick description" of the global situation cannot be given, I will nevertheless attempt a brief sketch of similar problems raised in "religious studies" discussions elsewhere in the world. Eric J. Sharpe, for example, notes that although the study of religion in Australian universities and colleges was from its inception free from confessional attachments, "[that is] not to say . . . that those involved in teaching these various programmes were without theological interests" (1986b: 249). He continues:

> On the whole, rather few [Australian students of religion] could be regarded as "secular" scholars, and many held a form of dual citizenship, being "theological" and "scientific" at the same time. . . . All in all, the positions occupied by Australian scholars in the field by the late 1970s mirrored fairly accurately the divisions observable anywhere in the world. (249)

In an essay entitled "South Africa's Contribution to Religious Studies," Martin Prozesky claims that the discipline has made a significant contribution to society because of the peculiarity of its being both scientific and "more than" science. The student of religion, he insists, must go beyond merely seeking an explanation of religious phenomena to "a genuinely liberative practice" (Prozesky 1990: 18). According to Prozesky, the student of religion is able to do this because religion itself is a humanizing force, which, when properly understood, will have a transformative effect upon those who study it.

Another striking example is provided by Michael Pye, in his "Religious Studies in Europe: Structures and Desiderata" (1991), where he points out that the ambiguities and confusions that plague the notion of "religious studies" in the Anglo-American context also have their counterpart in Europe. He points out that in Germany, for example, "the term *Religionswissenschaft* in the singular (science of religion, which for Pye is the same as religious studies) is rivalled in some universities by the plural *Religionswissenschaften* (sciences of religion) which tends to mean religious sciences with a religious motivation, including Catholic and Protestant theology" (41). The evidence, then, regarding the diversity of perceptions, claims, and proposals about "religious studies" as an enterprise carried out in the context of the modern university cannot be ignored, and would seem to lead to only one conclusion—that "religious studies," as Pye has suggested, is "a flag of convenience" (1994: 52) used by scholars, programs, and institutions to "legitimate" the aims, methods, and procedures they adopt in their study of religions. A more recent survey of the field by a team of international scholars titled *Religious Studies: A Global View* (Alles 2008) not only attests to the versatility of the designation for the field but also confirms the continuing influence of religion and theology on it.

I do not think matters are quite as bleak as Pye paints them, however, and, in concluding this discussion, I will attempt to set out what general agreements might be reached as to the meaning and use of the term "religious studies" by those involved *in an academic study of religion in the context of the modern university*.

"Religious studies": A summary and proposal

The term "religious studies" it appears from this discussion, is used in two quite different yet not wholly unconnected ways. In one sense, as the state-of-the-art reviews of "religious studies" in universities around the world suggest, the term includes whatever study of religion and religions is undertaken in any post-secondary institution of education, whether religious or secular, and regardless of the methodology adopted. Here the term is often taken to be commensurate with "the academic study of religion" and "the scholarly study of religion," which notions themselves are often used synonymously. In this case, then, as Pye puts it, the notion of religious studies "covers a multitude of possibilities" (1991: 42), although it excludes outright confessional and apologetic studies of religion or of a particular religious tradition. Nevertheless, as the "methodological" literature in the field shows, Pye's multitude of possibilities does involve studies that have a good deal of "continuity" with such confessional studies including forms of religious education that provide an "experiential understanding" of religion (Holley 1978; Bischoff 1975; Hull 1984; Prothero 2007), as well as "revised," non-confessional forms of theology (Novak 1971; Thiemann 1990; Ford 1999) and postmodern theology (see Wiebe 2008). The second, more common use of the term, however, is as a designation for a particular kind of approach to the study of religion with a particular aim, methodology, or style that distinguishes it from the type of (religious/confessional) study of religion antedating it. And when used in this sense, it still refers to the study of religion undertaken in the academy, but now designates an enterprise legitimated by the academy—in this case the modern research university—because it measures up to the received criteria of scientific study in the other university disciplines. Identification of religious studies with the academic study of religion in this instance, therefore, does not necessarily apply to all post-secondary research carried out under that rubric. "Religious studies" as an academic undertaking, therefore, ought to connote a scientific enterprise even though it does not, as some would argue, constitute a scientific discipline (see, for example, Pye 1991). I use the notion of "enterprise" here as defined by Robert A. McCaughey (1984) as "any organized understanding of sufficient magnitude and duration to permit its participants to derive a measure of identity from it" (xiii). The religious studies literature reviewed here, unfortunately, does not reveal general agreement among those engaged in the enterprise about the nature, structure, or intent of this activity, but neither does it allow inclusion of the multitude of possibilities contained in "religious studies" merely as a designation of the institutional location in which those engaged in the study of religion are found.

Moreover, and to recall my initial thematic about the particularities of a discipline *qua* discipline, the notion of religious studies is further complicated by the fact that the very idea of disciplines in the university is under attack by postmodernist thinkers. And, as the foregoing discussion has made quite clear, religious studies is understood by many to be an enterprise involving a multiplicity of disciplines and is, therefore, polymethodical—and, consequently, without a method peculiar to itself. Nevertheless, most of those who have written on "religious studies" seem agreed upon the nature of that study of religion that religious studies either complements or displaces, namely, a confessional—and therefore engaged—study of religion (usually Christian, and, more specifically, Protestant). There appears to be agreement, then, that it is the scientific element of religious studies that constitutes the newness of the modern study of religion; but there is still radical disagreement as to whether the scientific aspect of religious studies makes the new enterprise wholly discontinuous with the traditional study of religion, or whether it allows for a degree of complementarity.

One ought also, perhaps, to acknowledge that "science" itself, like "discipline," is a seriously contested notion, which subject I might not venture to broach, did it not appear in the work of Taylor cited above. For it is obvious that such a postmodern understanding of science admits a far broader range of intellectual activities than does modern science.

As designator of a particular type of study of religion, it appears that "religious studies" is being used to refer to at least four distinct types of intellectual activity in college and university departments. Each differentiates itself from the confessional study of religion that characterized the university study of religion before the emergence of the new departments, although not all would deny at least some continuity with that earlier religio-theological study. I will provide here a brief characterization of each, moving from those that most overtly resemble the confessional approach to those that would deny all continuity with it.

The first of the activities designated "religious studies" can be described as "theology under new management." This view is succinctly presented by Schubert M. Ogden, in his "Theology in the University" (Ogden 1986 [1975]), in which he argues that theological inquiry is of the essence of the study of religion as a humanistic discipline (as distinct from a confessional undertaking) (121). If "by 'religious studies,'" he writes, "is meant *a single field-encompassing field of study*, constituted by a single question for reflection, rather than simply many studies of religion, constituted by the multiple questions of other fields of study" (129, emphasis added), then it can only be constituted by focusing on "the question as to the meaning and truth of religion as the primary way in which human beings make fully explicit the truth about ultimate reality disclosed by their spontaneous experience" (129). With the constitutive question of "religious studies," presented as indistinguishable from that of philosophical theology, Ogden insists that

> either "religious studies" designates a proper field of study constituted by the question as to the meaning of and truth of religion, and hence by the philosophical theological question as to the meaning and truth of all thinking and speaking about God or the ultimate, or else it is simply a loose way of speaking of what would be less misleadingly called "studies of religion," seeing that they are merely the several studies of religion already constituted by the constitutive questions of other fields of study such as philosophy, history, and the social sciences. (130)

Ronald F. Thiemann, in "The Future of an Illusion: An Inquiry into the Contrast Between Theological and Religious Studies" (1990), promotes a similar interpretation of the new religious studies, claiming that it, like all theologies—confessional theologies included—inquires "after the dimension of universal human experience" (74) and therefore requires reflection on the question of the meaning and truth of religion determined to be a fundamental aspect of human existence (79). Similar views are expressed in M. Novak's *Ascent of the Mountain, Flight of the Dove: An Invitation to Religious Studies* (1971):

> Religious studies are nothing more than a full articulation, through systematic, historical, and comparative reflection, of a person's way of life . . . . Religious studies—then called "theology"—used to be undertaken mainly in monasteries, seminaries, schools of divinity, [and] church colleges . . . . Today religious studies are pursued at secular universities in connection with programs of humanistic studies, with departments of the social sciences (psychology, sociology, anthropology), with institutes of African or Asian or Near Eastern studies, and even with investigations in the meaning and interpretation of the natural sciences (biology, physics, ecology). (xii-xiii)

And in *Mended Speech: The Crisis of Religious Studies and Theology* (1982), P. Joseph Cahill provides a long, intricate argument in support of the claim that the humanistic study of religion—which he equates with the history of religions—and traditional theology are "two disciplines in a coherent and intelligible field of religious studies" (5), a situation that makes possible the understanding of human religious experience by focusing attention on the element of belief and commitment central to all religions, and is used to justify his claim regarding the unity of the religious "quest" (146, 158). "'Religious studies' as theology under new management," given these accounts of it, is only marginally removed from the confessional theological studies it claims to replace. It is concerned with "religious reality," but deals with it in general philosophical and metaphysical terms rather than from a particular confessional (revelatory) point of view. An alternative theological understanding of religious studies is provided by Taylor, whose work is discussed earlier. Since for Taylor theoretical science is itself essentially theological in character, reflection on the ultimate meaning of life can hardly be excluded from a proper understanding of religious studies on the grounds that it constitutes theology. And British theologian David Ford follows a similar line of postmodern thinking in this respect. The field of the study of religion, he argues, cannot appropriately be described by using the categories "confessional" theology and "neutral" religious studies, because in light of contemporary deconstructive criticism it is no longer possible to think any intellectual enterprise can be neutral. Consequently, religious studies, no less than theology, must make sure "that questions of religious meaning, truth, practice, and beauty are given the academic significance that is due them" (1999: 12). According to Ford, therefore, "the academic study of religion" is appropriately institutionalized only in "departments of theology *and* religious studies" because religious studies, like theology, "must allow scope for intelligent faith leading to constructive and practical theologies" (18–19).

A second, distinct type of intellectual activity carried out under the banner of "religious studies" might well be called "religious studies as tertiary religious education." The primary task of religious studies here is not that of seeking explanations of religion nor that of providing the metaphysical justification for religion, but rather of providing for an "experiential understanding" of religion. In this guise, religious studies is neither the scientific debunking of religion nor the confessional promulgation of it. Rather it is a humanistic appropriation of a range of human experience lending significance to students' lives. In this sense, religious studies is not primarily directed to obtaining objective knowledge as it is concerned with the formation of the whole person. This view finds collective expression in Stephen Crites's "Liberal Learning and the Religion Major" (1990), a report written on behalf of the "AAR Task Force on the Study in Depth in Religion," undertaken in cooperation with a national review of "Majors in the Arts and Sciences" initiated by the Association of American Colleges. "The quest about religion," according to Crites,

> plunges the student into the densest and most elusive issues of value, introduces the student into an ancient and enduring conversation, not always peaceful, about ultimately serious matters, engages the imagination of the student in the most daring imaginative ventures of human experience . . . . For many students it is a disciplined encounter with an order of questioning that has affinities with their own struggles for personal identity. It is one way of joining the human race. (13)

Crites is quick to point out that the aim of the study of religion is not to convince students to join any particular religious tradition—which would be a form of sectarianism—but he nevertheless insists that the study of religion must aid students to discover that religion "makes sense" and that this "enlarges her or his own horizon of human possibility" (14).

Such a notion of religious studies really differs very little from the kind of religious education programs undertaken in modern, multicultural societies. Although religious education was at an earlier stage understood to involve the nurture of pupils in the dominant religious beliefs and traditions of a particular society, multiculturalism has forced a change of intention upon the enterprise. And although education is clearly distinguished from nurture, the educational task, with respect to religion, is still seen to involve more than simply teaching students *about* religion. As John Hull (1984) puts it, with respect to religious education in the British school system, just as schools have a responsibility to prepare pupils for participation in a political democracy, so is there "a role for the school in preparing pupils to take an informed and thoughtful part in a pluralistic society" (48), which requires a thoughtful study of the multiple religious traditions it embodies. And that "thoughtful study," he insists, involves more than the empirical and theoretical study of the traditions concerned. "Religious education," he writes,

> is a wider group of "subjects" in which things like sensitivity training, moral education, personal relations and so on are set around religious studies as the periphery around the core. Religious education may thus be thought of as helping the pupil in his own quest for meaning. Religious studies is the inquiry after other peoples' meanings. The study of non-religious lifestyles is also a study of other peoples' meanings. So the question [of religious education] concerns the relation between my search for meaning and my study of other peoples' searches for meaning. (54)

For Hull, therefore, the plurality of subjects and activities involved in religious education is held together by "the idea of informed existential dialogue" (54), which very much resembles the notion of religious studies represented in Crites's report to the AAR. And virtually the same conception of religious education holds sway in America, where scholars distinguish "religion studies" from "religious studies." "Religion studies," argues Guntrum G. Bischoff, is appropriately intended to "contribute to the student's growth in world-understanding and self-understanding" (1975: 132), an exercise clearly distinguishable from the religious instruction students receive in private religious communities. The task of such instruction is not merely to provide information about religion(s) but also to enable students to relate to a multicultural world. As Bischoff puts it:

> If we may define education generally as a process enabling a person to autonomously order his environment and himself into a meaningful world, and to relate himself to this world in a responsible way, we may define the primary educational objective of the public school as the enabling process which helps develop the young person's world-understanding and self-understanding. (129)

Religious studies, then, as Crites presents it in his report to the AAR, amounts to a rather relaxed apology for religion in general, in the same sense as in programs of religious education. And accordingly, religious studies for Crites must actively engage the student in thinking through the question of the meaning of life, with the religious studies instructor engaged as facilitator in the process. And insofar as the teacher of religious studies is involved in that process of "forming" the student, she or he takes the place of the religious educator and theologian.

The third, relatively widely held view of religious studies that can be discerned in the scholarly literature sees the enterprise to be essentially scientific. In this description, however, as noted above, I am using the concept "enterprise" as defined by McCaughey (1984)—as "any organized understanding of sufficient magnitude and duration to permit its participants to derive a measure of identity from it" (xiii). As "scientific," the enterprise is chiefly characterized by an epistemic intention, taking for granted that the natural and social sciences are the only legitimate models for the objective study of religion, but it does not itself constitute a distinct scientific discipline. The primarily epistemic focus in this version of religious studies clearly distinguishes it from the types referred to above. It is not that earlier types of religious studies wholly reject the contributions made by the natural and social sciences to their understanding of religion, but just that the epistemic intention that informs the sciences is subordinated to religious or existential commitments or theological assumptions; that it is placed in the service of other goals, such as the formation of character or the achievement of some form of religious or moral enlightenment. The earlier exercises are nevertheless "academic enterprises," because they are pursued by scholars in the context of the university, but they might be appropriately considered "mixed genre enterprises" because they attempt to blend scientific and extra-scientific goals. Religious studies as a "scientific enterprise," however, is a naturalistic study of religion carried out in several complementary disciplines. And the review of the literature above provides evidence of the widely held view that the field is polymethodic and multidisciplinary—as does the volume in which this essay appears. Religious studies, in this view, therefore, is not a separate discipline but instead a general rubric for empirical and scientific studies of religion which alone are appropriate in the context of a modern research university dedicated to the advancement of objective knowledge about the world, both natural (physical) and social.

A final type of activity designated by "religious studies" receiving some degree of general agreement among scholars in the field, is that it is a scientific discipline on a par with other scientific disciplines. There is some measure of agreement, that is, that the notion of religious studies as merely multidisciplinary and polymethodic is somehow incoherent, and that there ought to be a unifying principle guaranteeing methodological coherence and genuine complementarity in the multidisciplinary contributions to the understanding of religion. "In this situation," writes Pye,

> there may arise the temptation to enjoy the flight to our personal interests in one specific religious tradition, to disappear entirely into some specialized philological, textual study, or to pursue just one or two analytical questions to the exclusion or at least the relative disregard of others. Such anarchy may seem attractive, but then it also implies the dissolution of "religious studies" except as a flag of convenience. (1991: 52)

A search for what it is that might make of religious studies a discipline, rather than merely a disparate set of disciplines interested in one or other aspect of religion, has prompted a variety of answers, two of which I will set out briefly here. (In one sense, of course, this is simply not possible, because it would imply that religious studies is itself an autonomous discipline in addition to all the other disciplines of the so-called multidisciplinary exercise, which, it appears, would be paradoxical if not simply contradictory.) As has already been pointed out above, some scholars in the field believe the fundamental question of the truth of religion alone constitutes a unifying force among the many disciplines of the field. But this kind of approach, as I have also pointed out above, is religious and metaphysical rather than scientific, and therefore is not appropriately considered characteristic of a "discipline" as that concept is employed in the modern research university. Others, however, have suggested naturalistic alternatives that might provide the kind of coherence needed to make of the many disciplines a coherent project. Pye (1999), for example, has argued that religious studies can be understood as a disciplinary project on the basis of a judicial "clustering" of the methodologies used by the various social sciences involved in the study of religion. Instead of the miscellaneous list of disciplines usually cited in descriptions of the field, he suggests that there are disciplines that "correlate and integrate those features of academic (or in some languages 'scientific') method which are particularly necessary in the study of religions" (195), which, "clustered" together, make of religious studies a discipline. Pye lists three methodological strands, which, when integrated, make up the discipline: the relation between subject matter and method, the relation between sources and method, and the methodological requirements. And he argues (not wholly persuasively) that a complete argument about what the clustering of these strands might look like is not necessary to understanding religious studies as a discipline. An alternative view of what makes religious studies a discipline is hinted at by Eric J. Sharpe in his history of the field (Sharpe 1986a [1975]). Attention in this regard, he suggests, must be paid to the role of theory in the academic study of religion in the late nineteenth century. The early history of the academic study of religion, he writes, involved independent theological, philosophical, and other scholarly approaches to the study of religion, and therefore lacked a single guiding principle of method to provide it coherence. However, argues Sharpe, unity was brought to the field with the application of theory to the understanding of religion because, as he puts it, it made it possible for "the real focus of the study of religion . . . to be located, not in transcendental philosophy, but in . . . this-worldly categories" (24). Sharpe also points out that, as evolutionary theory became associated with simplistic notions of progress and fell into disrepute, the students of religion became interested in "close and detailed studies in a limited area rather than in vast comparison and synthetic pattern-making" (174). Thus, with the demise of theory, the study of religion once again became multidisciplinary, without focus, and therefore lost its disciplinary quality. By implication, then, the disciplinary quality of the academic study of religion can only be found in theory, for it is only theory that can provide a coherent framework that can make sense of the contributions of the various disciplines.

In providing an account of the diversity of meanings of "religious studies" alive and well in university education today, the task of this chapter has been addressed. Yet one might reasonably raise the question as to whether all these usages are appropriate to the modern university—and if not, which ones are? The answer to these questions, of course, depends upon one's conception of the nature of the modern university and, concomitantly, of the academic/scientific vocation. It is clear that, if one thinks of the academic vocation as concerned not simply with gaining objective knowledge of the world in which we live but also with edification—and therefore with the formation and cultivation of character—the first two types of religious studies are not only appropriate to the university but also necessary. If however, the raison d'être of the modern university is the search for and dissemination of knowledge for its own sake alone, and the skills involved in the process of attaining such knowledge, then the task of religious studies must be purely cognitive, committed to the advancement of objective and neutral knowledge about religion and religions. In this kind of milieu, then, only the last two types of religious studies outlined would be appropriate, for that kind of religious studies scholarship is concerned simply with what advances knowledge. If, per impossibile, one conceives of the academic vocation as involving both tasks, all the types of religious studies outlined above are acceptable, even though it is clear that the first aspect of such an academic vocation would necessarily conflict with the second. The fact of the matter, however, is that the modern Western university is generally understood as essentially a research institution dedicated to the advancement of objective knowledge about the world and we can conclude, therefore, that "religious studies" should be understood to refer to a purely scientific undertaking.

2

Secular Theology Is Still Theology

In his editorial to the volume of the *Bulletin of the Council of Societies for the Study of Religion* in which the essays on secular or postmodern theology appear, Craig Martin surmises that the "new" non-sectarian theologians who reject supernatural assumptions and traditional modes of theological thought might be less vulnerable to the criticisms that have been lodged against the role of "confessional" theology (i.e., the theology of specific religious traditions and denominations within the diverse religions) within departments of religious studies in the setting of the modern research university. Whether or not that is so depends, of course, on one's understanding of the nature and fundamental purpose of the modern research university, on why traditional/confessional theologies have been considered inappropriate in that academic setting, on what objectives of religious studies in that academic context ought to be, and how much the new secular or postmodern theologies differ from the offending "confessional" theologies. In my judgment there is an implicit postmodern critique of religious studies, and perhaps of the modern research university as a whole, in these essays that needs explicit argumentation if it is to be taken seriously, and the theology on offer, as I will try to show here, is still essentially confessional, even if it is only of a "small-c" variety compared to the "capital-c" confessionalism these theologians reject. Before proceeding with my analysis of their positions, however, I must acknowledge that theology—traditional, secular and postmodern, "capital-c" or "small-c," or any other kind—cannot simply be ignored by "students of religion" (i.e., by religious studies as an academic/scholarly/scientific approach to understanding religious thought and behavior). Theology, quite obviously, is an important aspect of religion, if not in some sense religion itself, and is, therefore, an essential "object of interest" to the field. This is not to say, however, that the student of religion ought to be engaged in the theological enterprise itself. Indeed, theology, like any other aspect of religion is, at the very least, "data" that requires understanding and explanation regardless of what else it may also be.

Although none of the four essays on which I have been asked to comment focuses direct attention on the nature of the study of religion, it seems that religious studies as an Enlightenment project is as much a problem for some of these authors as is traditional (confessional) theology, which, I think it fair to say, is seen as wholly illegitimate in the context of the modern research university. Jeffrey Robbins, for example, argues that the process of secularization not only made possible theology's emancipation from ecclesial authority but also loosened it from the hegemonic grip of secularism's adoration of reason—that is, from what he calls the master narratives superimposed on the processes of secularization, with religious studies being one such master narrative. Postmodernism's disclosure of the bankruptcy of reason, according to Robbins, shows the impossibility of an objective, scientific study of religion and he argues that secular theology (what in an earlier essay he called "re-placed theology"—a theology that is, so to speak, expropriated from the church by the university) is the only future possible for the academic study of religion. Victor Taylor, it appears, holds a similar view of religious studies, referring to it as a "discourse of control that continually threatens to impose a 'meta-narrative' on the 'language games' of the field" that is no less a constraint on the discipline than is traditional religious (ecclesial) authority. He, therefore, rejects the Enlightenment view of religious studies as the organization of the field into subject areas for dispassionate analysis. Such an approach, he intimates, simply creates disciplinary hegemonies that reflect an intellectual closed-mindedness. It is not at all clear to me, however, that identifying the master narrative(s) governing traditional theology or the academic study of religion has liberated Robbins's or Taylor's work from those narratives, or that their secular theologies escape working under similar alternative master narratives.

Unlike Robbins and Taylor, Clayton Crockett maintains that he does not reject the possibility of an empirical or scientific study of religion. In fact, he maintains that the emergence of the academic study of religion undermined the domination of organized religion in the context of the modern university. However, he also suggests (an implicit claim) that religious studies has subsequently been captivated and dominated by the social and natural sciences, which he seems to equate with a claim to the superiority (not only academically but also morally) of the scientists compared to those whom they study. John Caputo espouses a similar claim in that, as he puts it, he does not wish to contest "the legitimate place of the historical, comparative, empirical and ethnographic study of religion," but only to make room for secular theological thinking as well. However, Caputo also claims that the Enlightenment legacy is of no further value and rejects, in particular, what he calls the embedded dogmas about the contrasts between subject and object, and faith and reason, that seem to be of central importance to the natural and social sciences. And Crockett likewise rejects notions of the neutral or dispassionate observer that are still seen by many in the field of religious studies to be essential (although not in any absolutist sense) to that enterprise. Given the qualifications Crockett and Caputo attach to their espousal of an academic study of religion, I think it reasonable to conclude that all four authors are arguing not only that a new kind of non-traditional theology (under diverse rubrics) has a legitimate place in the research university setting but also for a transformation of the Enlightenment view of the *ultimate* character of religious studies in that context; for them, the only legitimate study of religion in the academy, it seems, is one that is able to accommodate the new theology. I shall return to the matter of religious studies as a modern university discipline below, but will turn now to their views on the nature of the "new theology" they argue should be acknowledged as an essential element of religious studies departments.

On my reading of the three essays, and Caputo's response to them, the "new theology" they all espouse has four main characteristics. First, all four authors characterize it as *non-dogmatic*, and therefore as involving *a rejection of traditional theological orthodoxy.* The new theology, they insist, must remain open to independent thinking and eschew both churchly confessionalism and secularist (materialist) reductionism, (although Caputo maintains that the new theology is only incompatible with confessional authority and not with confessionalism itself.) Second, following on from this, they maintain that the new theology is *an immanent theology* for, in rejecting the theology of the *ecclesia*, it rejects the supernatural and revelational and depends upon open, independent, and non-dogmatic thought. For Victor Taylor, for example, this means that it is essentially a continuation of the death-of-god theology of the 1960s and therefore constitutes a theology appropriate for a secular world, although a theology that is now aided and abetted by "a new, experimental set of powerful concepts" which, he argues, emerged with postmodern critiques of disciplinary hegemonies and closed-mindedness. As immanent, such a secular/post-secular theology, they all agree, is essentially a *political theology* that is centrally concerned with understanding what it is to be human, as Caputo puts it, and, as Robbins has it, is fundamentally concerned with the theory and practice of democracy. The third characteristic of new theology I find in their descriptions is that it, somewhat contradictorily, has to be more than immanent. According to Robbins, it must be concerned with matters of ultimacy in a fashion, as I understand his essay, that makes possible the resurgence of religion. For him, secular theology is not merely concerned to study human value but must be in the business of creating value. For Crockett, secular theology involves "an explicitly theoretical or philosophical method" that shows it to be transformative and gives it "a value beyond its value as scholarly work"; a value that derives from its engagement in reflection on our orientation to reality in an *ultimate* sense. As he puts it, the new theology is meant "to construct open systems of thought and practice that provide alternatives to the way we ordinarily live and think." For Taylor, secular theology involves a "turn to 'religious theory'" which is essentially a mode of "religious thinking" that witnesses to a more than mundane reality—to what he calls the "unrepresentable."

Finally, for Caputo, the new theology is "a theology in which eternity has come into time, God come into the world, theology conducted on and for what Deleuze calls the plane of immanence" but that nevertheless harbors what he calls an "event"— that is, "the possibility of the impossible, the end of representation, the desire to think the unthinkable, to surpass the same, to reinvent and repeat with a difference." And this, we are urged to accept, makes possible the reappearance of religion focused on "exploring" key limit experiences that get to the heart of the meaning of science, art, and philosophy. Secular theology for him, and for his co-theologians, is, as he puts it, a philosophy of religion that is essentially religious theory which in effect stands as a witness to the "unrepresentable" and as "affirming the possibility of the impossible." The fourth and final characteristic of their secular theology is the peculiar methodology it espouses; the methodology is not directed simply to gaining knowledge about religious traditions and phenomena. Rather, such a theology is self-involving and pragmatic; it is primarily meant to be *transformative*; able not only to provide knowledge but also to provide alternatives to how we ordinarily conduct our lives. Like traditional theology, therefore, it is meant to be emancipatory even if wholly on the plane of immanence, and continually open to reconsideration and reflection.

In order to respond to the claims in support of a role for a secular theology within the framework of the study of religion in the academic setting of the modern research university here, I shall try to summarize the two main issues that I consider contentious: the critique of religious studies as it is found in that academic context (and possibly, therefore, also of the modern research university itself), and the very character of secular theology itself. The following claims, it seems to me, constitute the essence of their collective critique of religious studies:

1. religious studies emerges from an Enlightenment master narrative about the secularization of society;
2. that master narrative involves the acceptance of reason as a new epistemic authority that simply replaces the authority of the church rather than transcending the grip of authority;
3. in that regard, religious studies has the very character of traditional theology which it claims to have superseded;
4. postmodernism has shown the bankruptcy of this master narrative and therefore has made possible a truly open-ended kind of thinking not hemmed in by authority;
5. this does not mean (at least according to Crockett and Caputo) a rejection of empirical and scientific studies of religion but does reject wholly subordinating the discipline to reason as an alternative authority which implies that the field must be open to a different objective from the one assigned it by the master narrative of Enlightenment—namely gaining knowledge of the world and its contents for the sake of such knowledge alone. For them, although the modern research university may seek knowledge about religions and religion, it must also make room for a new kind of theological thinking and knowledge that can transform our mundane existences.

Their understanding of the new secular theology, which they think can fit into the framework of a religious studies program/department that is not under the domination of the Enlightenment master narrative, is one that

1. rejects supernaturalism and transcendentalism as well as revelation as foundational to its thinking, thereby leaving it free from authority and open-ended;
2. is essentially non-theistic/atheistic;
3. is wholly immanent and therefore secular and essentially political in character, that is, is emancipatory/redemptive;
4. is not essentially an epistemic enterprise but rather a self-involving activity in that it is directed toward seeking/finding/creating meaning and value; and
5. is, in some sense, continuous with religion as generally understood in that it concerns our orientation to reality in some ultimate sense; that is, with a reality that is ultimately unrepresentable. It is also, therefore, a kind of "religious thinking" rather than scientific thinking, and when incorporated into religious studies takes it to a "higher plane" that transcends scientific thinking.

I trust that this summary does not misrepresent the thought of the new theologians discussed here, even though it may not capture their views with great precision. If my descriptions here are even close to the mark, however, I will be at odds with their proposal for the integration of secular theology into the academic study of religion, essentially because they have clearly misunderstood both the character of the modern research university, including the proper objectives for a study of religion in that context, and because the secular theology they espouse has the same fundamental objective of "capital-c" confessional theologies (even though in a non-dogmatic form) and is, therefore, methodologically inconsistent with the religious studies enterprise.

I am in basic agreement with these authors that religious studies is a product of the Enlightenment by virtue of its emancipation from the grip of ecclesial authority. In his *Explaining Religion: Criticism and Theory from Bodin to Freud* (1987) Samuel Preus clearly shows how this "paradigm shift" occurred by way of the development of a new ethos of thought through a persistent critique of religion that also made possible a new, non-religious way of thinking about religion. And Eric Sharpe's history of the field (1986a, 2nd ed.) provides an excellent overview of the struggle to institutionalize that way of thinking about religion—that is, a study free from ecclesiastical control—by ensconcing it in the context of the modern university. This does not mean that religious studies was ever wholly free from the admixture of theology, as I point out in *The Politics of Religious Studies* (1998), but it does show a persistent attempt on the part of nineteenth-century British and European scholars to provide a theology-free study of religion in the academic context. That Enlightenment scholars simply replaced ecclesial authority with the "authority of reason," explicitly elaborated in a new master narrative of the secularization of society, however, has not been persuasively argued either here or, to my knowledge, elsewhere. Karl Popper's notion of scientific reasoning as a process of conjectures and refutations (1963, see also his 1967 book for the role of reason in society) provides for as open-ended a mode of thinking as that adopted by the secular theologians. Ernest Gellner (1973) also provides solid evidence for the fundamental openness of scientific Enlightenment reasoning that, unlike historically earlier modes of thought, does not have simultaneously to function as the framework of social and moral order which makes impossible the production of culture-transcending knowledge of the world and its contents. As he puts it, science/reason has "diplomatic immunity" from "the social, moral, and political obligations and decencies of society" and is, therefore, free to seek the truth about the world and states of affairs in the world.

In my judgment, therefore, postmodern claims regarding the bankruptcy of reason have not been established. One need only consult here such works as Paul R. Gross and Norman Levitt (2nd ed., 1998); Alan Sokal and Jean Bricmont (1998); Alan Sokal (2008); Richard Wolin (2004); John Zammito (2004), or Susan Haack (2003), among others, to see the bankruptcy of such postmodern claims. Reason, rather, was transformed into a nonmoral instrument of inquiry (Hoopes 1962) by the Enlightenment, and encouraged a kind of theoretical curiosity that amounted to a search for knowledge for the sake of knowledge alone, free from restriction, as Hans Blumenberg puts it, by "human existential interest posited as absolute" (1983: 233). Science, that is, as Blumenberg argues, emerged as an effective form of cognition as "the result of a renunciation for the modern age . . . that lies in the separation between cognitive achievement and the production of happiness" (1983: 404). Robert Hoopes comes to the same conclusion in his analysis of the English Renaissance: "The intellectual history of the seventeenth century is marked by the gradual dissociation of knowledge and virtue as accepted and indivisible elements in the ideal structure of human reason, a shift from the tradition of right reason [which fuses in dynamic interactivity the function of knowing and being] to the new tradition of scientific reasoning" (1962: 161). And Ernest Gellner (1973) points out that a form of reason characterized by logical and epistemic permissiveness would preclude achieving any collective judgments (knowledge claims) about states of affairs in the world.

And, as Julie A. Reuben perceptively points out in her *The Making of the Modern University: Intellectual Transformation and the Marginalization of Morality* (1996), the modern research university is a purpose-designed institution created to house precisely such knowledge-achieving intellectual activities. And in that context, the only "academic study of religion" that is appropriate is one directed to obtaining public knowledge about publicly available states of (religious) affairs in the world, mediated through intersubjectively testable sets of statements that are descriptive, explanatory, and/or theoretical. And this means that the work of students of religion must be capable of being integrated structurally and methodologically with that of the other sciences; that they must adhere to the ordinary intellectual obligations pertinent to the other disciplines in the university. Religious studies, no more than the other sciences, needs to make room for a new kind of theological thinking. Its descriptive, explanatory, and theoretical accounts of religious phenomena are not exceptional (if they were, they would require housing in exceptional institutional structures); they must be accounted for within the same conceptual and causal framework used to explain all other elements and aspects of the natural and social worlds.

Crockett and Caputo explicitly acknowledge the possibility of scientific (including empirical, hermeneutical, phenomenological, and theoretical) studies of religion, and Robbins and Taylor, I believe, do so implicitly. However, none of them believe, as I do, that this constitutes the totality of the religious studies agenda. Indeed, they believe such a claim amounts to the subordination of the discipline to "another authority," namely reason, which is every bit as problematic, in their judgment, as that of the ecclesial authority that governs traditional theology. On the description I have provided here of the reasoning involved in the academic study of religion, however, revelatory, transcendent, or supernatural commitments no more characterize religious studies than they do the secular theology to which they are committed—it is no more governed by a master narrative, therefore, than is secular theology. However, the modern religious studies I describe is more circumscribed than their secular theology in that it restricts itself simply to achieving knowledge about certain states of affairs in the world rather than engaging in emancipatory projects involving something beyond the knowledge to be gained by such an academic enterprise. On the other hand, the self-involving character of their theological discourse shows it to be methodologically and structurally inconsistent with the scientific objectives and procedures that characterize the natural and the social sciences, and, therefore, inconsistent with the academic study of religion that fits seamlessly into the structure governing those sciences. The secular theology to which they subscribe—that they are trying to establish—may also concern itself with gaining knowledge about religious phenomena, and insofar as it does, it may be consistent with religious studies (and therefore with the natural and social sciences), but that is not its primary objective. Indeed, its primary objective may in effect knock religious studies (as outlined above) completely off its game by subordinating it to a different objective from its own. The primary objective of secular theology as they describe it—which, it should be noted, they see as an integral element of religious studies—is that of seeking, finding, or creating value in the world so as to provide us with meaningful ways to conduct our lives. In doing so, moreover, their theology has deep affinities with the traditional theologies they hope to supplant, especially so in that they claim that their project concerns our orientation to reality in some ultimate sense—that is, with some reality other than our ordinary, everyday reality but which is, and apparently will always remain, unrepresentable. They even insist, it appears to me, that secular theology is, therefore, a form of "religious thinking" which, if incorporated into religious studies, will take the discipline to a higher plane than that of simple scientific thinking concerned fundamentally with ordinary, mundane empirical and theoretical knowledge about religious traditions and religious phenomena. Unfortunately, these papers do not elaborate what we might call the boundary conditions of such "religious thinking" nor show how they can be integrated with the sciences upon which religious studies draws. And their claim that they are dealing with that which is unrepresentable simply calls to mind Frank Ramsey's claim that "what we can't say, we can't say, and we can't whistle it either" (1965 [1925]: 238). I suggest, therefore, that their characterization of secular theology shows it to be but another religious phenomenon in the world, not essentially different from any other (even though it is *in some sense* immanent and non-dogmatic), which makes it a fit object of analysis and explanation for religious studies as I have described it, and not an aspect of this field of scholarship that allows religious studies to transcend the concern with ordinary knowledge about religious phenomena.

After reading the essays of Robbins, Crockett, Taylor, and Caputo, then, I am still of the same mind about the intellectual (scientific) impropriety of mixing/blending theology (of any variety) and religious studies that I expressed in my essay on the "failure of nerve in the academic study of religion" nearly twenty-five years ago (Wiebe 1984). I think there might be more "intellectual room" to make a case for including "secular theology" in the political science department, given its claimed isomorphism with political theology and its immanent character; or in the department of philosophy given its rather vague, open-ended and speculative quality. That is not to say that I think such arrangements would be looked upon favorably by these departments, nor that they are actually academically justifiable—but that is not a matter to be taken up here. From my perspective, however, further clarity about the nature of the secular-theology enterprise might be gained by exploring these possibilities, or even (barring the question of funding) the possibility of the creation of a new department dedicated to secular theology alone. I for one would be interested in hearing not only what the secular theologians think about such possibilities and why but also how members of departments of political science and theology, as well as university administrators, would respond to such proposals.

3

Scientific Study of Religion and
Its Cultured Despisers

The title of this chapter may appear to assume, somewhat optimistically, the existence of a widely accepted philosophy of science capable of providing a general conception of "*the* scientific enterprise" from which the academic student of religion can generate a methodology for the field that will effortlessly produce hypotheses and theories to explain religion. I do not find this assumption wholly naive or implausible and will ultimately, therefore, attempt to set out something of the character of the scientific enterprise that explains the successes of the natural sciences in "accounting for the world," and its particular relevance to what might be called "the science of religion" (or, perhaps better, "the scientific study of religions and religious phenomena"). However, it might also be suggested, not wholly unreasonably, that there are at least two major divergent schools of philosophy of science; that we must acknowledge the existence of both a "modern" and a "postmodern" philosophy of science. The modern view of science is taken to be the product of Enlightenment thought and is associated with claims of superior epistemic authority for the sciences compared to earlier modes of thought, and the postmodern philosophy of science is seen as having emerged by way of reaction to modern science. Postmodernism, that is, maintains that the fundamental epistemic notions of the Enlightenment-inspired philosophy of science have an essentially social character and that they are, therefore, indistinguishable from simple ideological commitments and, therefore, have no greater epistemic authority than any other set of "convictions."

Whether there is a postmodern philosophy of science is, I think, open to question. There can be no question, however, that there is a postmodern understanding about the nature of science as an Enlightenment enterprise. Nor is there any question that there has been a pervasive disenchantment with science over the past quarter century or so. Postmodernist claims that science and the sciences are completely entangled in culture and therefore "nothing more than a 'narration,' a 'myth,' or [one] social construction among many others," as Alan Sokal and Jean Bricmont put it (Sokal and Bricmont 1998: 1), have, moreover, contributed to the loss of science's status in at least some segments of the academy and in society. According to the postmodernists, it is simply not possible to obtain objective knowledge about the world (i.e., states of affairs in the world), either of a factual or theoretical character. All our knowledge is perspectival and in some sense, therefore, profoundly subjective. And given the perspectival character of all so-called objective knowledge claims, the claims of neutrality on the part of scientists are hollow.

It is difficult to say much more about the postmodernist understanding of science and modern scientific rationality than is given in the brief description of it provided here. And although, at least superficially, the criticisms of science raised have some legitimacy given the embeddedness of human persons in complex sociopolitical situations, several major factors suggest that the celebration of the "end of science" by postmodernists and their supporters is premature. First, given their own sociopolitical embeddedness, their arguments against Enlightenment views of science are themselves automatically suspect; as Paul R. Gross and Norman Levitt point out in their *Higher Superstition: The Academic Left and Its Quarrels with Science* (1994), postmodernism is itself a social movement that shamelessly resorts to moral one-upmanship in argument. Second, as Ernest Gellner points out in *Postmodernism, Reason, and Religion* (1992), postmodernist argument amounts to little more than relativism and logical permissiveness and, therefore, provides no ground on which to achieve a collective judgment about matters in the world, including judgments about the nature of the scientific enterprise. And, third, as Philip Kitcher has pointed out in his *The Advancement of Science: Science Without Legend, Objectivity Without Illusion* (1993), scientists, working within a framework of critical argument and experimental research worked out collectively over centuries, have achieved a remarkable convergence of understanding on various aspects of and processes in the world. That achievement notwithstanding, the religious studies community, especially as it is represented by AAR, has to a large degree continued to espouse a form of postmodernism, largely, it appears, in order to provide room for religion and humanistically inspired sociopolitical agendas as part of the religious studies enterprise. By curtailing the scientific agenda with its search for testable hypotheses about religion, or some element or aspect thereof, the student of religion, it seems, is justified by postmodernism in seeking—or is at least permitted by it to seek—something other than mundane knowledge about religious belief and behavior.

Before elaborating on this claim, however, some response to recent histories of the field of religious studies by Hans Kippenberg and Ivan Strenski is called for, given their suggestions that the academic study of religion that emerged at the end of the nineteenth century did not give rise to an objective and neutral study of religion and religions but was essentially ideologically based. In *Discovering Religious History in the Modern Age* (2002), Kippenberg argues that the "crisis of culture" caused by modernization produced a "scholarly" study of religion that would restore religions to a significant role in society and ensure that religion would once again provide people with resources for living meaningful lives. As he puts it, these scholars set out to give "religions outdated by progress a new place and another function in modern society" (Kippenberg 2002: 193). I am not, however, persuaded by his argument, first because of his choice of representative founders of the "new study" of religions (in which I think he fails to distinguish theologically oriented scholars from those interested specifically in differentiating the new enterprise from the old), and, second, because of his treatment of them (which I think is distorted by his views on the role of philosophy of history which he understands as pervading all historiography of religion, by which he means to say that all historians of religion necessarily placed the academic study of religion in the service of a philosophy of religion). This is not to say that the nineteenth-century founders of *Religionswissenschaft* eschewed religion; it is clear, rather, that their primary concern was to obtain scientifically valid knowledge of religions and religion, although they also believed that such knowledge would ultimately, so to speak, converge with the ultimate truth/value of religion. The latter belief, it appears, ultimately proved illusory, yet played a significant role in smoothing the way for the establishment of a wholly scientific approach to the study of religion in the context of the modern university, (Wiebe 1998).

Ivan Strenski appears to adopt a similar stance to that of Kippenberg in his promotion of what he calls "ideological critique" as an essential element in the academic study of religion (2004, 2006). According to Strenski, that is, the study of religion, like religion itself, is ideologically based. He writes: "How is it possible that any self-respecting person in the study of religion could pursue academic goals in the present without some reference to underlying ideological features of what they are doing—to the social and historic contexts of the work in question, to embedded ideologies informing the agendas of the research itself?" (Strenski 2004: 290). A reasonable response to the question, it seems to me, is that it is possible because of the adoption of a self-critical objectivist stance that recognizes the possibility of ideological distortion of knowledge claims and operates in a fashion that attempts to avoid it. If Strenski thinks this impossible, then, surely, his very claim about ideological distortion of knowledge claims must itself be ideologically distorted. Strenski also maintains that even though all theories are "conditioned" or "ideologically informed," some are more determined in that fashion than others (Strenski 2004: 287) and he seems to think that we can determine which theories are better on the basis of his assessment of the greater extent of ideological influence on the authors of those theories. That, of course, presumes that his own "interpretation" of the so-called empirical record of the ideological influence is not itself ideologically informed. What lies behind his confidence in this empirical research is essentially a Western notion of science that presumes that we can transcend our "conditionedness" and arrive at an objective account of specific states of affairs in the world—precisely the same assumptions made by those who promulgated the theories in the first place. Strenski's "ideological critique," therefore, is not a new approach to religion or to the methods by which we study religion as he claims, so much as it is a strange kind of justification for attempting to understand religious theorists rather than theory or theories of religion.

In his book, *Thinking About Religion: An Historical Introduction to Theories of Religion* (2006), Strenski asks: "Once we have exposed the weakness or fatal flaw of a theory, what have we finally accomplished?" (Strenski 2006: x). Scientific students of religion, one might expect, would say that such an exercise clears the way for the production of a more cogent, testable, and fruitful theory of religion. However, Strenski suggests rather that students of religion should push on to find out why these theorists thought they were right. He writes: "Whatever else students take from this book, I at least hope they will feel that they understand how and why some remarkable folk *thought about religion*" (Strenski 2006: 6, emphasis in original). He maintains that that is why he titled the book *Thinking About Religion*, yet it is clear that religion is not his chief object of interest, nor are the theories themselves the chief objects of interest. Theorists of religion, one might reasonably assume, think they are right to hold the theories they have formulated because they believe that the theories provide a cogent, testable account of religions and religion (the data of religion) and that they, therefore, provide us with an understanding of religious behavior. Thus, whether theories of religion or theories accounting for particular religious phenomena have been influenced by idiosyncratic bias (or hidden ideological commitments) in my judgment is not of major significance to the student of religion. Indeed, it seems to me that the possibility of such distortion is generally assumed and that safeguards have been deployed in defense against it occurring. The important question is whether the theory is fruitful and testable. Strenski, however, is more interested in the biography of the scholar than in the explanatory and heuristic value of their theories.

There are other scholars in the field who have espoused a postmodern view of science for more blatantly ideological reasons; they clearly consider the postmodern critique of science as justifying the religio-theological and humanistic approaches that have long dominated departments of religious studies in our colleges and universities yet seemed, in the latter half of the twentieth century, to be threatened by the growing prestige of the sciences. If, as the postmodern critiques declare, modern science is incapable of ever obtaining its goal of providing objective empirical and theoretical knowledge about anything in the world, there is no reason why religion itself, or a religiously oriented study of religion, ought to be excluded from the university curriculum. Francis Schüssler Fiorenza in a paper on "Theology in the University" (1993) clearly attempts to reconfigure the academic study of religion in light of this kind of critique of modern science. With no justification for seeking objective explanatory accounts of religion, according to Fiorenza, he advises students of religion to be open to "the challenge of interpretive disciplines" (Schüssler Fiorenza 1993: 35) and to adopt a humanistic model for the academic study of religion. As he puts it:

> Programmes in the humanities study the classics not merely for their meaning, but also for their significance, not merely as sources of past cultures, but as challenges to present cultures. Classics raise truth claims that are legitimately discussed. Such contemporary university programmes have heeded Nietzsche's scorn of his age four score and forty years ago, when he chastised its claims to be historical with an objectivism that kills the historical. (Schüssler Fiorenza 1993: 36)

George Marsden presents a similar argument in his *The Soul of the American University: From Protestant Establishment to Established Nonbelief* (1994). With the devaluation of science, he argues, there is no reason to exclude religiously-based claims either in our teaching or in our research. Thus, he insists that scholars of religion should have the same rights as do those (like the feminists, Marxists, neoconservatives, among others) who in the context of the modern university advocate purely naturalistic moral and political views. With respect to religion in particular, he perceives the devaluation of science as clearly undermining a purely objective approach to the study of religions and rejects a wholly scientific definition of the field (Marsden 1994: 414).

The "challenge" of the interpretive disciplines advocated by Schüssler Fiorenza, moreover, constitutes what I consider a "hermeneutic methodology" which essentially generates an individualistic or "virtuoso" kind of scholarship that claims to be able to produce an understanding of cultural phenomena that is deeper and goes beyond anything that can be provided by the natural sciences. Indeed, the natural sciences, it is claimed, are to be feared because of their tendency to rationally distort reality. As Paul Feyerabend, a hero to postmodernists, has put it: "The world, including the world of science, is a complex and scattered entity that cannot be captured by theories and simple rules" (Feyerabend 1995: 142)—hence his comment about avoiding "'systematic' analysis" (Feyerabend 1995: 163) and his counsel that scholars adopt a methodology of "anything goes" (1975). Such counsel gives rise, of course, to strange, highly idiosyncratic methodologies that seem to make impossible any replicable results in the study of religious phenomena. Wendy Doniger, a historian of religions, for example, follows such advice, for she insists that the study of religion (and culture more generally) must be an art rather than a science, and as such must be "able to live comfortably with contradictions without trying to resolve them" (1984: 180). It must recognize, she argues, that ultimately "one's judgment is personal, subjective, and aesthetic" although she also insists, but without benefit of supporting argument, that such judgments "need not be solipsistic, undisciplined, or random" (Doniger 1980: 10). Her only warrant in favor of such a methodology, however, is drawn from what she calls "the *unique* form of history of religions developed by Mircea Eliade," which is founded on a "method" of "reading an enormous amount, remembering it all, and being very, very bright" (Doniger 1980: 11). According to Doniger, this will allow the scholar to recapitulate the reality one is trying to "understand" for it will allow one "to walk in the footsteps of those who made the myth" (Doniger 1980: 14, emphasis added). But replication of the event or experience is not the objective of scientific understanding. The attempt to recreate the experience the myth relates, as John Passmore pointed out more than a quarter century ago, is "to attempt what in the nature of the case, science can never do, namely, to replace the concrete and to answer the important questions of the meaning of life and the universe" (Passmore 1978: 72).

More recently, Tomoko Masuzawa also adopts a kind of "virtuoso" methodology as appropriate for scholars in religious studies. In response to an interviewer's question as to whether the study of religion has produced an increase of information/knowledge about religion, Masuzawa admits that knowledge has been obtained but claims that it is "thoroughly ideological" (Masuzawa 2004: 20). And when asked how she would "describe [her] scholarship—[her] theory or method," she replied, simply, "Read very closely" (Masuzawa 2004: 20). In an attempt to elaborate, she suggested that it is a matter of making the material that lies before you "amenable for interpretation"; but she also claims that "it's very elemental" (Masuzawa 2004: 20), which I presume means inexplicable. In another context she maintains that it is more than an advanced form of hermeneutics and she describes it as counter-conventional, involving "questioning, contesting, exposing the unavowed interests inherent in the established organization of knowledge and system of valuation, which is supposed to be objective and value free" (Masuzawa 1998: 89). In describing how she gets down to work she said:

> I can't initiate any good thought process by directly engaging some large issue, or reacting to a big question. I always begin with particular things. But it's these particulars that often end up generating a pretty big argument. . . . I suppose that's the consequence of my training in a certain school of literary criticism. At least it taught me to expect that sort of thing to happen. (Masuzawa 2004: 20, 22)

There is certainly little of the systematic here and much that is idiosyncratic; there is nothing, for example, to suggest that the results of such thinking are in any sense "testable," even though there is every possibility that someone else's "interpretation" of the data will differ radically from hers. There is, therefore, something "mystical" and "mysterious" about the "insights" she proffers. Such an approach, therefore, as Schneider points out in his *Culture and Enchantment* (1993), amounts to a process of re-enchanting the social sciences, and in this case, the humanities and especially the scientific study of religion.

Despite the pervasive disenchantment with science over the past quarter century, exemplified by the scholars discussed above, I believe the claims that science is completely entangled in culture, and therefore unable to produce objective, public knowledge of things, processes, and events in the world, is unjustified. Although postmodern criticisms of science may not be wholly without merit, they have not undermined modernist claims about the epistemic virtues of science. A brief comment on John H. Zammito's recent magisterial overview and assessment of postmodern theory and its philosophic attacks on empirical and scientific knowledge found in *A Nice Derangement of Epistemes: Post-Positivism in the Study of Science from Quine to Latour* (2004) will show why. Zammito's history reconstructs what he calls the three hyperbolic dogmas of "anti-empiricism" that have dominated postmodern theory throughout this period, namely, theory-ladenness, under-determination, and incommensurability, and he shows that "none is justified in the radical form which alone empowers the extravagances of postmodernism" (Zammito 2004: 271). Consequently, he claims, they do not justify the denigration of science (and empirical knowledge) that postmodernists have heaped upon it; and "real philosophers," he insists, "have increasingly taken a deflationary view of their authority over the empirical disciplines" (Zammito 2004: 3; see here, for example, Pierre Bourdieu's argument to this effect in his *Science of Science and Reflexivity* [2004]). Zammito contends, therefore, "that it is time to take up a more moderate [deflated] historicism" (Zammito 2004: 5) and he claims that after the extravagant postmodern claims are dispelled, what remains will be "fully assimilable into—not preemptive of—empirical inquiry" (Zammito 2004: 2). His concluding paragraph is worth quoting in full:

> There has been a derangement of epistemes. Philosophy of science pursued "semantic ascent" into a philosophy of language so "holistic" as to deny determinate purchase on the world of which we speak. History and sociology of science has

become so "reflexive" that it has plunged "all the way down" into the abîme of an almost absolute skepticism. In that light, my fears are for empirical inquiry not in the natural sciences, whose practitioners brush all this off as impertinences, but in the human sciences. Hyperbolic "theory" threatens especially the prospect for learning anything from others that we did not already presume. It is time for a hard reckoning, for a rigorous deflation. Willard Quine put it with uncharacteristic bluntness: "To disavow the very core of common sense, to require evidence for that which both the physicist and the man in the street accept as platitudinous, is no laudable perfectionism; it is a pompous confusion." (Zammito 2004: 275)

An essential element of the problem here, as Sokal and Bricmont point out, is that the postmoderns do not, for the most part, even understand scientific concepts and how they are used. Nevertheless, these scholars keep the critique of science alive in what Richard Wolin calls "the parochial climate of contemporary academe" (2004: xiii), although mostly in the humanities and social science faculties as Zammito has indicated. Wolin also claims—and I think rightly so—that this juggernaut and its "farewell to reason" has failed to take root in society.

What I wish to do here is to show how a more nuanced reading of the Enlightenment-inspired philosophy of science can help reorient the humanities and social sciences—including the science of religion—and create a climate in which it is possible to say farewell to postmodernism's "farewell to reason" in the academy; that is, to reorient the humanities and social sciences away from what the scientist/philosopher of science Roger Newton (1997) calls an egocentric mode of seeking knowledge resulting from the domination of extra-scientific goals in their research projects. Postmodernist social science theorists, students of religion, and other humanist scholars, however, often look for research to somehow "reproduce" the reality they study, or look for a science able to provide one with an experience of reality rather than simply with an explanation for objects, events, and processes in the world, or they envision science as a project of transformation of self and/or society. But, as Robin Dunbar points out in his book on *The Trouble with Science* (1995), this is in effect to interpret the world however one wishes, which, he asserts, "is intellectual laziness and doesn't deserve the name of scholarship" (Dunbar 1995: 179). And he is quite right, in my judgment, when he asserts that "we can, and should, do better than that" (Dunbar 1995: 179).

The Enlightenment-inspired philosophy of science, on the other hand, clearly presumes that scientists/scholars can distinguish and suppress non-cognitive objectives in favor of epistemic goals. As Julie Robin Solomon in *Objectivity in the Making* argues: "By the early twentieth century, the discursive pieties and rigors of scientific self-testing had permeated most intellectual fields in Western culture" (Solomon 1998: 225). Indeed, public accessibility to data and public testability of theories was seen as essential to science. As Solomon puts it: "We best legitimate knowledge not by exhibiting it as the issue of the individual mind, but by displaying its alienation from that mind and its source in the objects shared with other minds" (Solomon 1998: 156). Scientists/scholars, that is, have restricted themselves to inquiry about realities that are knowable by public intellectual operations that are subject to replication by others. Therefore, as Susan Haack puts it:

> It is false that social values are inseparable from scientific inquiry; false that the purpose of science is the achievement of social goals; false that knowledge is nothing but the product of negotiation among members of the scientific community; false that knowledge, facts, reality are nothing more than social construction; false that science should be more democratic; false that the physical sciences are subordinate to the social sciences. (Haack 1998: 104)

To put it simply, science has a distinctive epistemic authority, not in the sense that it can (or attempts to) participate in or reproduce the reality (or experience of reality) it seeks to "account for" but rather because it provides us with sets of mechanisms that explain (i.e., account for the existence and nature of) the phenomena involved. As Nicholas Rescher put it in his *The Limits of Science*, even though there are other values besides cognition, "there is no alternative but to turn to the science of the day for whatever we want to know about the furnishings of the world and their modes of comportment" (1984: 206). So also James Robert Brown in *Who Rules in Science?*: "Naturalists are motivated by the thought that the natural world is all there is and the scientific approach is the only way to comprehend it" (Brown 2001: 118).

By "science," then, to put it briefly, I mean a naturalistic approach to understanding the world, and the things, events, and processes in it, and that assumes the unity of the various disciplines which collectively provide explanations that are "part of an intellectual structure that is ultimately justified by objective public evidence obtained by observation and experimentation on Nature, rather than by divine revelation, scripture, individual experience, or authority" (Newton 1997: 47; see also Haack 2003: 266). Scientific explanation, that is, cannot take for granted the existence of nonmaterial—that is, supernatural or spiritual—entities or beings, processes or powers for which there is no publicly available evidence. This, of course, assumes a realism that, as Philip Kitcher puts it, "conceives of nature as having determinate 'joints' and mind-independent structures" (Kitcher 1993: 169–70), although, as Roger Newton notes, it must be a scale-dependent realism that recognizes that our experience and our language is adequate only at the scale of everyday life and not at the microcosmic level (Newton 1997: 175).

To say that science is a naturalistic enterprise is not, of course, to say that it is not also itself a deeply social activity—that there are no significant social factors that characterize and influence science—but rather that its social character is not wholly or even primarily determinative of the knowledge it generates. Moreover, recognizing the socially constructed character of culture and society is not to deny them some measure of independent reality (existence) having, as Kitcher puts it with respect to nature, "determinate joints." There may be no single, established, universally accepted method in science, but our scientific disciplines have systematic and methodic sets of procedures that reduce error and produce reasonably uniform research results in both the natural and (to a considerably lesser extent) the social sciences. To be sure, science does not provide us with absolute and complete knowledge, but it far exceeds the results obtained by our everyday modes of inquiry and by the kinds of "virtuoso" scholarship described above. In a sense, scientific method is very much like our methods of everyday inquiry, although in science there is a greater sophistication of reasoning because the everyday methods are greatly amplified by the use of techniques and devices, some of which Haack identifies as follows:

> [The] systematic effort to isolate one variable at a time; systematic commitment to criticism and testing; experimental contrivance of every kind; all the complex apparatus of statistical evaluation and mathematical modelling; and the engagement, cooperative and competitive, of many persons, within and across generations in the enterprise. (Haack 1998: 96–97)

Given these brief accounts of modern and postmodern views of science, I wish to echo anthropologist Marvin Harris's claim that scholars cannot avoid the conclusion that science "is not mere ethnocentric puffery . . . [but is rather] a way of knowing that has uniquely [culturally] transcendent value for all human beings" (Harris 1979: 27). Indeed, philosopher James Brown goes so far as to claim that science "is the single most important institution in our lives" (Brown 2001: 212) and urges society to wake up to this fact and seek out ways as to how it can better serve us. And for students of religion interested in maintaining academic credibility in the modern research university this means giving up extra-scientific aims and objectives and the abandonment of "virtuoso" scholarship in favor of a "science of religion"; it means recognizing that the aim of science is exclusively concerned with gaining knowledge and therefore finding a place for scientific studies of religion for scientific reasons alone. Science is not, as sociologist Robert Wuthnow has recently put it in his essay "Is There a Place for 'Scientific' Studies of Religion?," a search for the meaning of love or which moral decisions are right, or what it means to be human or to instill purpose into our students (Wuthnow 2004: 13, 32). "If the study of religion were more consistently deliberate in bringing together the realm of facts with the world of values," he writes, "then it would be harder to imagine where the objections to scientific studies would be" (Wuthnow 2004: 32). This, however, is to presume that the academic student of religion is primarily a humanist educator engaged in the service of shaping students into alert and sensitive citizens of the (nation or the) world (and therefore, in the long run, in the service of reconstructing society as a whole). For Wuthnow, then—and by far the greater number of students of religion in college and university departments today—it seems that students of religion are public intellectuals who constitute a new clerisy whose responsibility it is to provide "relevant" information about religion and spirituality that will lead people to make the right decisions with respect to "the great concerns that redound in special ways to each generation, whether those are framed in terms of such problems as violence and justice or in language of virtue and hope" (Wuthnow 2004: 32). Thus Wuthnow and his like, fail to recognize that students of religion in the context of the modern research university are scientists who, like physicists or biologists, for example, have a primary obligation to support and advance the intellectual goal of the discipline which is to show how religious phenomena can be explained in a fashion that can be fully integrated with the modes of explanation in the natural sciences. This is simply to say that the science of religion is not an autonomous discipline concerned with a subject matter that is wholly peculiar to it. Rather, the disciplinary axioms of both the natural and the social sciences constitute boundary conditions that must be satisfied by the student of religion; no conclusions about religions, that is, can be reached that are not consistent with the generally accepted conclusions of sciences like physics, chemistry, and biology.

The only "academic study of religion" that is appropriate in the context of the modern research university, therefore, is a scientific study that is wholly emancipated from religio-theological, humanistic, moral, and sociopolitical agendas. This is not to deny, however, that the results of such a study of religion are necessarily irrelevant to such agendas; the knowledge gained about religious communities and the behavior of religious individuals may be of great value to policy-makers, marketers, and a host of others in society. Just as the knowledge produced in the humanities and by social scientists may bear on human problems and public concerns, so also the knowledge produced by students of religion may bear the same relationship to such issues. I think it important in this regard, however, to note, first, that the "linkage" between the knowledge produced and the problems to be resolved is "external"; that is, it is of the same order, so to speak, as that between the natural sciences and engineering; and, second, that even though religious studies research may be relevant in that fashion, working out the policy/resolution implications of that knowledge is not the task of the student of religion. To take on that assignment is the task of policy-makers, politicians, therapists, conflict managers, and other "public intellectual" types, and it is important, I think, that the scientific character of the study of religion not be compromised in any way by bringing such tasks into the purview of religious studies itself.

4

Apologetic Modes of Theorizing

Introduction

I am both delighted to be involved in the meeting of the European Association for the Study of Religion (EASR) and grateful to the organizing committee for their kind invitation to address the association on the "decline of" and "hope for" the field of the study of religions. There are important disciplinary and institutional developments in the field that would seem to suggest growth and maturation. But when we bear in mind the original *religionswissenschaftliche* aims of the enterprise as it emerged in the last decades of the nineteenth century, there are disturbing signs that, intellectually and scientifically, the field is in decline. This is not to say, however, that there is nothing we can do to change that trajectory.

It is a quarter century since I delivered my paper, "The Failure of Nerve in the Academic Study of Religion," to the AAR. Back then I argued that although the study of religion had gained a place for itself within the academic community by distinguishing itself from the religio-theological community, by the middle of the twentieth century it had given control of the scientific and educational agenda of the field to the scholar-devotee. By the time that essay was published, the line of demarcation between religion and the study of religion had become so blurred that it was often difficult to distinguish the objectives of religious studies departments from the religious interests of liberal Protestant seminaries. Despite some positive developments since then, I nevertheless think that this "blurring" of objectives not only continues but is also getting worse both individually and institutionally. I see the theme for this conference therefore as affording me an opportunity to present a "report card" on developments in the field over the past twenty-five years.

Unfortunately, I am as pessimistic about the field today as I was in 1983. Nevertheless, my "report card" is not simply a list of "must do better" items. There have indeed been some significant positive developments since then and I shall first focus attention on them before airing my critical concerns. I shall, as they say, start with the good news. And the first item that must be acknowledged here is the incredible growth in the institutional and structural strength of the field. There are, for example, many more departments engaged in the study of religion and many more scholars engaged in research and teaching now than twenty-five years ago. There has also been a significant increase in the number of professional societies and associations dedicated to the study of religion, as well as an associated increase in the number of journals and other outlets for the dissemination of research. The most important and exciting positive development over that period of time, however, has been methodological; that is, the field has moved beyond its early and mid-twentieth-century fixation on descriptive studies of religion and religions—involving primarily textual, historical, and phenomenological analyses—to explanatory and theoretical accounts of religious phenomena.

Theory's place in the study of religion

We are all aware, of course, of the significant impact evolutionary theory has had on the academic study of religion in its earliest phase in the last quarter of the nineteenth century and the early decades of the twentieth. In her tribute to Darwin on the occasion of the fiftieth anniversary of the publication of *The Origin of Species* Jane Ellen Harrison suggested that Darwin be considered the creator of a scientific study of religion given that evolutionary theory counseled anthropologists and other social scientists to focus attention on how religious phenomena arose and developed (1909: 496) and not simply as it was then constituted. In his history of the "the history of religion," Eric Sharpe points out that research interests in the field were distributed among diverse disciplines, each "content to cultivate a limited area [of the field] intensively" until evolution emerged as a "single guiding principle of method . . . able to satisfy the demands of history and of science" (1986a [1975]: 26). That theoretical coherence, however, did not last. Not only did it fall out of favor through entanglement in moral and sociopolitical divergences that it had no business in, it did not issue in a genuinely progressive research program that allowed for the production of empirically testable theories. What we might call the scientific payload of the field from about the 1920s to the 1980s, therefore, was delivered primarily in philological, historical, and comparative work. This payload, however, was somewhat diluted by the emergence of less rigorous phenomenological studies of religion aimed at "uncovering" (or interpreting) the essential (interior) meaning of religion which, unfortunately, further obscured the line of demarcation between religion itself and the study of religion. The return to theory in the last two to three decades, for me, is a sign of hope for the possible re-establishment of the study of religion in the academic context as a proper scientific undertaking, especially so in the connections that have been forged between evolutionary psychology and the cognitive sciences, on the one hand, and the study of religion, on the other. I have in mind here scholars such as E. Thomas Lawson, Robert McCauley, Benson Saler, Pascal Boyer, Harvey Whitehouse, Ilkka Pyysiäinen, Scott Atran, Luther Martin, Armin Geertz, Aleš Chalupa, Joseph Bulbulia, Edward Slingerland, Jeppe Jensen, and Emma Cohen, to name only a few. Each attempts to provide a causal account of some religious state of affairs in hypotheses and theories that postulate the existence of evolved psychological/cognitive mechanisms that are testable in terms of historical, ethnographic, and/or experimental evidence. If the *scientific study of religion* and not just "religious studies" is to have a future, it will have to bring theory to bear on the field as have the scholars I have just noted.

A renewed call for the employment of theoretical analysis in our field was sounded by Hans Penner and Edward Yonan as early as 1972, and by H. W. J. Drijvers and others in the "Groningen School" in 1973, although little came of it until years later. I expressed my agreement for this call to theory in my 1975 article "Explanation and the Scientific Study of Religion" insisting that the field "must move beyond mere description and classification to explanation and theory" if it was to be considered a genuinely scientific enterprise. However, like many others during this period of transition, I expressed reservation about the reductionistic implications of such an approach to accounting for religion. This is what Penner and Yonan suggested was the cause of what they referred to as "theory-shyness" and Svein Bjerke called "nomothetic-anxiety." In time, however, I came to see the animus against reductionism as essentially a protectionist move on behalf of religious belief. In a subsequent general essay on "Theory in the Study of Religion," in which I provided a brief overview of support for and reaction to the role theory had played in the scholarly study of religion, I recognized the necessity of reductionism as an essential element of any scientific enterprise and, therefore, the need for a theoretical account of religion—that is, for "a set of interrelated concepts and propositions from which religious behaviour can be, in a suitably weakened sense, deduced ('made intelligible')" (1983: 298). Without espousing a metaphysical atheism, and recognizing the solid empirical work by humanist scholars in the field (1983: 305), I argued that the "determined attacks upon the reductionism of theoretical studies [were] becoming increasingly difficult to distinguish from apologies for transcendence" (1983: 287–88).

The methodological atheism I had argued for in general, however, had already been taken up in the formation and development of two new theoretical approaches to religion that had some prospect of being tested against empirical evidence: the first being a "cognitive science approach" to understanding religious phenomena represented by scholars noted above and, the second, "rational choice theory," although I shall treat them in reverse order here. Rational choice theory is best represented, I think, in Rodney Stark and William Sims Bainbridge's *A General Theory of Religion* (1987) that first appeared in the "Toronto Studies in Religion" series I edited for Peter Lang Press.

Rational choice theory

Stark and Bainbridge are sociologists (rather than religionists) who take a particular interest in religion. As social scientists they make it clear that they are committed to the undemonstrable belief "that human behavior ought to be explained" (1987: 23) and, as scientists, they set out to explain it objectively, that is, without reference to the supernatural. "We assume," they write, "that religion is a purely human phenomenon the causes of which are to be found entirely in the natural world" (22–23). Stark and Bainbridge continue: "We show that religion must emerge in human society, and we derive its existence entirely from axioms and propositions in which religion is not an original term" (39). Their theory is both objective and scientific because it is, as they put it, "rooted in a few very obvious principles about how people act and interact" and it includes a very limited number of axioms and enough definitions to derive testable propositions about religious phenomena (315). Although neither affirmed the supernatural at the time of writing, they insist that neither of them was antagonistic to religion and that they "did not write this book to 'enlighten' those who accept religion or to strike a blow for rationalism" (23). This approach to explaining religious phenomena is still very much a live option in the field of religious studies and has produced significant advances in our understanding of religion.

Cognitive science of religion

The origin of the cognitive science approach in the academic study of religion must be traced to anthropologists and archaeologists rather than to students of religion. Anthropologist Stewart Guthrie's 1980 essay "A Cognitive Theory of Religion," for example, attempted to provide a plausible way of accounting for religion in terms of a more general aspect of human cognition, namely our tendency to anthropomorphism. And archaeologist David Lewis-Williams attempts in his work *Believing and Seeing* (1981) to account for the spiritual lives of the ancient San people wholly in neuropsychological terms. It is not, however, until the 1990s that scholars of religion ever seriously considered the cognitive sciences as a framework for understanding religious thought and experience. E. Thomas Lawson and Robert N. McCauley's *Rethinking Religion: Connecting the Cognitive and the Cultural* (1990), first brought this approach to the attention of scholars in the field of religious studies, while Stewart Guthrie's *Faces in the Clouds: A New Theory of Religion* (1993), Pascal Boyer's *The Naturalness of Religious Ideas: A Cognitive Theory of Religion* (1994), Harvey Whitehouse's *Arguments and Icons: Divergent Modes of Religiosity* (2000), and Ilkka Pyysiäinen's *How Religion Works: Towards a New Cognitive Science of Religion* (2001), to name only a few, all added considerably to the credibility of this new approach. Subsequent work by these and other scholars, including collections of essays and research reports on current approaches in the cognitive science of religion, clearly show that this theoretical move has proved heuristically fruitful even though early claims to have once and for all explained religious phenomena and religions were over-optimistic.

Institutional structures

In addition to this groundbreaking work, institutional structures have appeared to underwrite and support this new research paradigm. These include the Institute of Cognition and Culture at Queen's University, Belfast; the Laboratory on Theories of Religion, University of Aarhus; the Institute of Cognitive and Evolutionary Anthropology, Oxford, and the new Emory Center for Mind, Brain, and Culture at Emory University. Publication by researchers in this subfield have found a number of outlets in established journals related to theory, such as *Method and Theory in the Study of Religion* and the *Journal of Cognition and Culture*, which is more broadly oriented to cognitive studies. The *Cognitive Science of Religion Series* (Altamira Press) has published a number of significant volumes in the area, and Equinox Press will in the near future publish a series in the cognitive science of religion in connection with the Aarhus Laboratory on Theories of Religion. Finally, 2006 saw the formation of the International Association for the Cognitive Science of Religion dedicated to promoting international collaboration in the subject.

I am very excited by these developments and regard this emphasis on the formation of testable theories as indicative of the beginnings of a renaissance in the scientific study of religion. However, this ray of hope does not, for me, offset the despair I have over other developments in society and the university negatively impacting our field. To wit, the resurgence of religion in society and its infiltration into the heart of the research university, often drawing scholars of religion away from their primary intellectual responsibilities into sociopolitical agendas involving futile metaphysical debate or encouraging scholars to engage in what I will henceforth call compatibilist and accommodationist theorizing. Such activities compromise the research we undertake, the institutions in which we undertake our research, and, ultimately, ourselves.

I will first note some recent ominous developments at my own university.

The resurgence of religion

The resurgence of religion in society at large is placing significant illegitimate demands on universities in terms of "accommodating" students from diverse religious traditions. As a consequence, many (within and without the university) are calling for a review of the role and responsibilities of the public university in light of these concerns. An entire issue of *Academic Matters*—a journal of higher education published in Canada by the Ontario Confederation of Faculty Associations—incredibly, was recently dedicated to the topic "God on Campus." C. T. McIntire, a retired member of the Department and Centre for the Study of Religion at the University of Toronto insistently claims that the university as a public institution is derelict in its responsibilities to the multicultural and multireligious society that it serves because it permits the study of religion "to act as a secular, naturalist, rationalist, objective, religiously neutral, scientific operation" (2007: 11) and thereby problematizes the practice of religion inside the university community (2007: 11). McIntire writes:

> Students have no interest in keeping their religion out of the religious studies classroom. The dichotomy "secular and religious" misses the mark of understanding the place of religion in their lives and their families' lives. They chose to study religion precisely because their religion belongs to their lives. Many find it incomprehensible that religious studies should impede them from connecting their study of religion with their experience of religion. (2007: 12)

Studying religion scientifically, for McIntire, is treating religious people as specimens when, he maintains, we have an obligation to engage them as persons (2007: 13). There is no disagreement on the matter of treating everyone respectfully, but having said that, the view McIntire puts forward here—it cannot be expressed strongly enough—is inimical to the very idea of a university.

McIntire's egregious views here emphatically do not represent the present state of affairs in the Department and Centre at Toronto; the situation there is much more nuanced than that. This is not to say, however, that such politically correct thinking is not rife within the larger academic community at the University of Toronto which has recently established a Multi-Faith Centre that, as its website announces, is meant to "accommodate a variety of spiritual and faith-based practices and [encourage] interfaith dialogue and spiritual development as part of the learning experience for all students." That the university is a secular institution is given lip-service, but the Centre nevertheless asserts that students and staff are not necessarily secular (whatever that is supposed to mean) and maintains that the university must in some ill-defined sense *accommodate* their spiritual needs. Such accommodation, in part, requires the university to provide space for religious students to engage in prayer and worship, and space for chaplains to meet with and counsel students. What is most worrying, however, is the claim that the Centre sees "the study of religion and spirituality [as] being recognized in many academic disciplines as holding the answers to some of today's most complex problems," and that they include in their vision-statement the obligation "to further our understanding of the role faith and religion play in a number of academic disciplines." Such broad public expressions of opinion and official university initiatives creates a climate of fear and intimidation for those professors who do not cooperate with the program and thereby undermines their principle of academic freedom. To require that professors not offend students (or colleagues) who bring religion to bear on their research and teaching is a constraint that effectively undermines the integrity of our teaching and research. In *History Lesson: A Race Odyssey,* Mary Lefkowitz recounts the conflicts her criticism of the "afrocentric movement" brought her way and remarks: "If the purpose of education is to instill knowledge, the feelings of individuals cannot always be protected" (2008: 89), and it seems to me that the same holds for those who study religions; while respecting cultural differences and religious diversity, individual and group religious sensitivities cannot always be protected.

Individual methodological appropriations of religious faith

A larger concern regarding the study of religion in the context of the modern university, however, is the continuing failure on the part of the majority of scholars in the field of religious studies to engage the enterprise in a *genuinely* scientific manner; in a manner that recognizes that the aim of all of the sciences is the production of knowledge—and generalized, theoretical knowledge—about the world, and in this instance, the production of empirical and theoretical knowledge about religions and religious phenomena. This is not, as philosopher of science Alan Chalmers puts it, "to adopt the naïve view that science can be practiced in isolation from other interests, nor that those other interests never, or even should never, impede the realization of the aim of science" but it does mean "that it is possible and important to distinguish the aim of producing scientific knowledge from other aims, and that the distinction is essential for an adequate explanation and appraisal of science" (1990: 94–95). This is also essential for understanding the character of the modern research university which it is widely agreed is a purpose-designed institution for the production and distribution of knowledge and training in the "tools" for the production of knowledge based on our engagement of and in the natural world.

I am no longer shocked by those scholars who adopted a dualistic methodological approach to the study of religion or those who overtly announce their religious commitments and argue the limitations of a scientific knowledge and the consequent need for a supra-scientific—generally supernatural—source of knowledge either as the basis for understanding religion or as a *necessary* complement to whatever the sciences can tell us about religion. They are legion in the field, everyone knows where they stand, and it is patently obvious that no common empirical, scientific, or philosophical ground exists on the basis of which to debate the matter with them.

The only argument possible, I think, is a "political" one that points out to them that the disciplines within the modern research university (as a purpose-designed institution) are directed to gaining a knowledge of the natural world that is intersubjectively available to all human persons and, therefore, simply involves reasoning processes as nonmoral instruments of inquiry into the empirical character and structure of that world and its contents. Thus, just as religious persons would not expect our banking system to take seriously "the promises of god" as financial instruments of commercial trade or as collateral for large-scale purchases neither should they expect our universities to take seriously their claims to supernatural (non-natural) knowledge as credible epistemic claims. Moreover, even should a fundamentalist religious believer presume that the bank *ought* to accept such promises as collateral, neither banks nor other financial institutions would do so. Following that same principle, neither should any of the disciplines in the modern university accept supernatural or non-natural claims as knowledge or the basis for knowledge. That argument, however, will have to wait another day.

Although I am not shocked by the overtly religious commitments of scholars in this group, I am nevertheless in fear of them given their numbers in academia and their collective strength in giving shape to the enterprise we most often refer to as religious studies. Their stance is inimical to the development of our field as a scientific enterprise, and our response to them ought to be unambiguous.

The scholars who do still shock me are those who believe themselves to be operating entirely scientifically yet have no hesitation in slipping religious ideas and beliefs into their work. I also fear those who, although they do not deliberately build compatibility systems between their religious and scientific beliefs, nevertheless refuse to square the methodological assumptions upon which their religious beliefs depend with the methodological assumptions they adopt in their more restrictive scientific work. I refer to them as "covert accommodationists" because they resemble religious apologists who implicitly water down the methodological requirements of the science they espouse in order to accommodate their religious beliefs, just as the liberal theologians of the nineteenth and twentieth centuries were willing to water down their religious beliefs in order to obtain scientific credibility. There may even be some in this general group of so-called scholars that one might reasonably call pseudo-accommodationists—that is, scholars who are not at all religious but will take on the appearance of being so for funding purposes. Given the ease there seems to be in confusing the scientific study of religion with religion itself, these scholars seriously subvert our enterprise. To put the matter bluntly, the intrusion of religion or religious assumptions in any form is more easily detected in the natural and biological sciences, for example, than it is in the study of religion. Knowledge about religion, that is, is not always clearly distinguished from "religious knowledge."

Unfortunately, we can find an example of such religious intrusions in the study of religion in each of the most theoretical approaches to understanding religion I have referred to as providing some ray of hope for the future of our field, namely, Rodney Stark in rational choice theory and Justin Barrett in the cognitive science of religion. I shall deal briefly with each in turn.

Rodney Stark: From methodological atheism to methodological theism

Rodney Stark has made a truly fascinating, but depressing, about-face between his *Acts of Faith* (2000, coauthored with Roger Finke) and *A Theory of Religion* (1987, republished in 1996). The history of the sociological study of religion he now maintains reveals it to be a polemical rather than a scientific exercise (2000: 13); a form of atheism intent not on explaining religion but rather on "explaining it away" (2–3). In fact, he sees it as nothing more than a form of unabashed village atheism which, he insists, cannot pass for scholarship (14). Here truly is a case of the pot calling the kettle black where he is both the kettle and the pot. A "more truly scientific approach" to studying religion, he insists, came about mainly as the result of increased participation of "persons of faith" (15) who were well trained in research methods and wholly committed to obtaining unbiased results in their work (17). It is this kind of sound scholarship that he sees as the essence of the work of the Society for the Scientific Study of Religion which, according to him, stands in stark contrast to what he considers unscientific objectives espoused by, for example, the North American Association for the Study of Religion (NAASR). The NAASR, he asserts, is made up of activist scholars who "justify aggressive atheism as the rationale of religious studies" (19) and who are "obsessed with ridding students of belief in the supernatural" (19). Stark does not, however, draw these conclusions on the basis of a study of the constitution of the NAASR, or a study of the work of members of that association. Indeed, none of the scholars to whom he refers in this diatribe against the NAASR were ever a member of the association. Furthermore, the picture he draws of the NAASR rests on an account of the dispute between it and the AAR provided by Charlotte Allen in her 1996 article in *Lingua Franca* entitled "Is Nothing Sacred: Casting Out the Gods from Religious Studies," which was a rather unfortunate way of describing NAASR's commitment to methodological, and not metaphysical, atheism (19).

The difference between Stark's approach to religion here and that of the NAASR approach, he maintains, is a difference of motive (21). As far as Stark is concerned, the methodological atheist approach concerned with explaining religion is dedicated to advancing "a religion of science" (21). He makes this claim, however, without argument or evidence. He writes: "Our fundamental quest is to apply social scientific tools to the relationship between human beings and what they experience as divine" (21), which is, by the way, precisely what scholars who adopt methodological atheism do, although they talk of the "divine," (which believers claim to have experienced) only as being "culturally postulated." Scholars of religion committed to methodological atheism, that is, do not presume to make pronouncements about what Stark refers to as the authenticity of the relationship between human persons and the divine, because there is no scientifically available—that is, intersubjectively available—evidence that can adjudicate the matter. For that reason, the scientific student must seek non-supernatural accounts of religion. By contrast, Stark's methodology "denies that secular social factors must underlie religious phenomena" (33) and he therefore clearly leaves open the possibility for supernatural explanations of religious phenomena (and, presumably, other phenomena as well). Whereas in *A Theory of Religion* Stark treats religion as "a purely human phenomenon" in the sense that methodological atheists do, in *Acts of Faith* he treats only the "human side" of what he somehow, but not scientifically, now knows to be an ultimately supernatural reality. Stark does not deny that atheists can be good scientists of religion but insists that devotees can be good scientists as well *when they study the human side of religion* (2000: 2; 2003: 197). He erroneously assumes however that this provides him a foundation for claiming that metaphysical religious propositions and science are compatible (2003: 177). And this is an "accommodation" of science to his later religious belief(s).

A further problem with the later Stark is that he invokes the notion of divine revelation to provide what he considers the fully comprehensive account of religion that eludes the methodological atheist (2007: 3–8), but seemingly does so without recognizing that this makes his "scientific study of religion" methodologically incompatible with the rest of the natural and social sciences. His recent claim that a compelling case can be made for intelligent design theory (2007: 396), moreover, suggests that his version of the scientific study is also incompatible with science on the substantive level. Stark, it seems to me, would not deny this criticism given that he finally comes to agree with Kepler "that in the most fundamental sense, science *is* theology and thereby serves as another method for the discovery of God" (399).

Justin Barrett: Methodological naturalism completed by revelation

Justin Barrett's work in the cognitive science of religion contains a similar, though less virulent, subversion of religious studies as a purely scientific undertaking in the framework of the modern research university. Barrett is a confessing Christian who nevertheless claims to espouse a fully scientific methodology capable of explaining religious phenomena, but like the later Stark, assumes that the results of such a methodology need not necessarily clash with knowledge of religion obtained from a revelational source. This, I think, is the full import of Barrett's book *Why Would Anyone Believe in God?* (2004).

Drawing on the work of cognitive anthropologists like Pascal Boyer, among others, Barret argues that many of our beliefs are nonreflective and emerge as the result of a collection of non-conscious mental tools that generate assumptions about the way things are in the world. These comprise a kind of intuitive knowledge of various aspects of the world that constitute, for example, a folk-physics, a folk-biology, a folk-psychology and so on. Consequently, most of our ordinary beliefs about our everyday environment are, in a sense, automatic, and not dependent on conscious modes of reasoning. Such nonreflective beliefs, however, become the basis for reflective beliefs as well. And, as Barrett points out, such consciously adopted beliefs that resonate with the automatic and nonreflective beliefs have a greater intuitive feel about them that gives them an increased credibility and makes them more existentially satisfying. Belief in God derives from a particular set of mental tools, such as an agency detection device, which generates a nonreflective detection of agency in one's environment. This mental tool seems to operate in a hyperactive mode (HADD), which passes on information to another device designated "theory of mind" (ToM) which in turn attributes propositional attitudes to such intuitively detected agents (referred to as counter-intuitive agents) which, in effect, are templates for conceptions of gods. As Barrett puts it: "The nonreflective beliefs generated by HADD, ToM, and other mental tools working together to make sense of unusual objects, events, or traces may become reflective beliefs when satisfactory alternative explanations fail to arise" (40). The emergence of belief in gods, and therefore the emergence of religion, requires very little in the way of peculiar inputs from the environment; they arise "naturally from the way our minds function in the ordinary world, independent of pre-existing religious systems and doctrines" (61).

Following Barrett's argument this far, one might presume that he would have concluded that religious beliefs (beliefs in god) are the result of the evolutionary "design" of our brains and are, therefore, natural, *but illusory*, phenomena. He does not, however, come to such a conclusion. But neither does he assume, as some other cognitive scientists do, that just because our brains have been designed by natural selection "we can trust them to tell us the truth" (19). He, therefore, finds it necessary to provide additional argument to prove the truth of religious beliefs—a truth which he has already, it seems, accepted on confessional grounds.

In chapter six of *Why Would Anyone Believe in God?* Barrett begins to set out an argument to the effect that the Abrahamic religious traditions have basic aspects which "give these religions further advantages over others" (75). In chapter seven he proceeds to fashion a philosophical argument of sorts for reflective belief in God, drawing on Alvin Plantinga's claim that "belief in God is as rationally justifiable as belief in other minds" (97). He writes: "People believe because such [unreflective] belief is intuitively satisfying. It matches nonreflective beliefs generated by a host of mental tools converging on the same things: minds and gods out there" (104). And he concludes that disbelief in God (which he refers to as "attacks on belief in God") arises "more from political and practical motivations, prejudice, and ethnocentrism than from a fair appraisal of the legitimacy of belief" and therefore "betrays a lack of intellectual honesty" (104). That is, why one *would not* believe in God, according to Barrett, requires special explanation because, for Barrett, such disbelief can only derive from a worldview that is "dedicated to the notion that science ultimately can answer all questions and solve all problems" (118), and is, therefore, scientistic.

In conclusion, Barrett knows that scientific studies of aspects of religion can be undertaken by those who both believe and do not believe in God. But, in the final analysis Barrett, like the later Stark, believes that a full comprehension of (explanation for) religion must go beyond that which any of the sciences can provide us. He too, ultimately, opts for a belief in intelligent design, again, it seems, based on revelatory knowledge, the rejection of which, he insists, will impede coming to a full and true understanding of religion. Thus he writes:

> God created people with the capability to know and love him but with the free will to reject him. Consequently, our God-endowed nature leads us to believe, but human endeavors apart from God's design may result in disbelief. Even if this natural tendency toward belief in God can be conclusively demonstrated to be the work of evolved capacities, Christians need not be deterred. God may have fine-tuned the cosmos to allow for life and for evolution and then orchestrated mutations and selection to produce the sort of organisms we are—evolution through "supernatural selection." (123)

Barrett seems entirely oblivious to the fact that this "philosophical move" in his argument makes his position on religion both methodologically and substantively at loggerheads with both the natural and the social sciences as they are practiced in the modern research university. He, however, does not see this as an inconsistency in his argument regarding the compatibility of science and religion, but rather sees the refusal to integrate religion and science on the part of those who approach the understanding of religion entirely on the human level as acting in a cowardly manner. According to Barrett:

> Intelligent Design reminds us that intellectual inquiry does not have to begin and end with naturalism. I happen to think that methodological naturalism is a great place to start in the sciences, and we should get as much mileage out of it as we can. But not all of intellectual discovery lies in the methods and assumptions of the contemporary natural sciences. Along with cosmology, the Intelligent Design movement also illustrates that the borders of natural science are not always clear. Refusing to do scholarship that might cross conventional borders strikes me as unfruitful and cowardly. (on GeneExpression, www.gnxp.com, "10 Questions for Justin L. Barrett" posted by Razib, 4/01/2006)

Institutional methodological appropriations of religious faith

The influence of the methodological appropriation of faith by scholars of religion on attempts to establish a truly scientific study of religion is even more problematic when it occurs at the institutional level. I have in mind here a couple of recent university-related proposals for research funds from the John Templeton Foundation that either implicitly or explicitly invoke a religious, and not simply a scientific research, agenda. The first is a 2007 grant proposal entitled "The Adaptive Logic of Religious Belief and Behavior" sponsored by ("will have an affiliative and administrative home" [2007: 3] in) the Institute of Cognitive and Evolutionary Anthropology at Oxford University, and the Institute of Cognition and Culture at Queens University, Belfast. The second is a grant awarded to the Oxford Institute for a joint proposal between it and the Ian Ramsey Centre for Science and Religion for a project entitled "Cognition, Religion, and Theology Project."

"The adaptive logic of religious belief and behavior project"

The investigators involved in the "Adaptive Logic of Religious Belief and Behavior" project set out to demonstrate that "there are powerful selective advantages of religious beliefs and practices" (2007: 5). They claim that their work will be of benefit not only to evolutionary biologists, game theorists, and neuroscientists but also to theologians (7) because, they tell us, the project will also explore "various meta-level philosophical implications of a distinctly human cognitive system" (18). As they put it, because "the human mind cannot seem to easily accommodate itself to a godless, evolutionary canon when it comes to the self's existence" (18), and because "human brains are psychologically predisposed towards religious styles of thought" (18), we must recognize that a scientific approach to understanding moral and religious behavior on its own is incomplete—that a "complete science," paradoxically, will involve going beyond the bounds of what some call "pure science." "In our view," they write, "the religious and secular approaches in moral philosophy are inseparable" (18). According to them, this is particularly so with respect to our study of human beings. There is something unique about human persons, they insist, that radically distinguishes them from other animals, and understanding them, therefore, requires moving beyond a simple set of scientific explanations. Thus, amazingly in light of the general drift of the cognitive science approaches to explaining religion, they write: *"We suggest that, by virtue of our unique social cognitive abilities, the evolution of cooperation may have been influenced more than [is] currently appreciated by the hand of God at work in the mind of man"* (19, emphasis added).

One could, in the spirit of generosity, read this statement as referring only to the "idea" of gods or God rather than indicating a belief that a form of theological theorizing is essential to a proper understanding of human behavior—that is, that human behavior can only be understood in light of the will of an actually existing god who interacts with human persons. Such an interpretation might well be indicated in the pitch they then made to the Templeton Foundation to support their grant proposal:

> This view [they write] resonates with the Templeton Foundation's vision that "scientific principles of evolution and *the idea of God* as creator are compatible" (Templeton Website). In the sense of the argument set out here, *the idea of God* is indeed inextricably linked with the biological evolution of the human mind. As E. O. Wilson once suggested, "the human mind evolved to believe in the gods. It did not evolve to believe in biology." We believe that our proposal fits solidly within the Templeton donor's mandate. We offer a set of novel linkages between science and religion, each of which impacts heavily on the other and together transforms our understanding of the origins of cooperation, ethics, and religious beliefs and behavior. (19, emphases added)

However, I think such a "generous" interpretation is unwarranted despite the ambiguity of some of the language in the passage quoted (and elsewhere in the proposal), given their insistence that the proposal "fits solidly within the Templeton donor's mandate" which is essentially religious. But if this is the case, it seems to me that they have compromised their concept of science in order to accommodate religious belief(s). They have, that is, placed religion beyond the possibility of scientific critique and explanation. Indeed, they have included "the divine" in their resources for such an explanatory account which makes sense of their intention to share this material not only with scholars of religion but also with clergy (23).

In this regard, it is important to note that the authors of the grant proposal see it as a distinct advantage that they are not theologians. This suggests to me that they believe, (or at least wish the Templeton Foundation to believe), that the "Templeton mandate" will be carried into respectable academic settings by virtue of the fact that they are "pure scientists" (33). Their thinking here is somewhat convoluted to say the least. Although they imply that they are engaged in this project as scientists, they nevertheless note that it is "hard to fund [this kind of research] in scientific departments," and "hard to justify research on religion in science departments" (24–26). If their research has a religious objective one can well understand why such research would not be justified in a science department and why they seek Templeton Foundation support. However, they also clearly believe their work to have the kind of scientific credibility to warrant support from science departments and believe that science departments have not been forthcoming in this regard because they think the subject matter is not, for whatever reason, worthy of such funding. Nevertheless, they also seem to think that should they complete this research project they would establish the research-worthiness of this subject for science departments. And given that they have pitched the project to fit Templeton parameters, it appears that they also think this an enticement to the foundation since they would be able to find university support for future research of relevance to the Templeton mandate. If that is the import of their proposal, however, that would in some sense involve deceiving the university (though it is not likely to go undetected if this Templeton proposal were made publicly available together with the research results reported from this project).

On my reading of this rather strange document I will say this. We have here a very shrewd project proposal: it is either a clever ruse to obtain funds from Templeton for a project that is structured so as to appear to fit the Templeton mandate but in fact does not (in which case they ought not to be seeking funds from it at all) or it is a genuine plea for help from the Templeton foundation in order to co-opt them into a joint venture in ultimately obtaining support from scientific funding agencies for further Templeton-type religious projects (something neither they nor Templeton should really be interested in doing). So shrewd is this document that I am not altogether sure that this ambiguity is accidental.

It is, perhaps, important here to point out that the Templeton Foundation claims that it is not a religious organization and that they do not engage in religious advocacy. Moreover, they pride themselves, as their website puts it, on having funded and employed "non-believers," and they claim that their "grantmaking history clearly demonstrates that [they] strive to find scholars and researchers who are dedicated to open-minded inquiry and rigorous scientific research." Given these protestations, one might well wonder what all the fuss is about in accepting Templeton funding. The concern, however, is that such funding from Templeton, nevertheless, places subtle pressures on grantees to tailor their research to fit the religious aims that are implicit in the "core themes" of the foundation. One of those themes is the search for "new concepts of God" which clearly indicates theistic assumptions. Even though the foundation may not, as it claims, "consider a principal investigator's personal beliefs whatsoever when reviewing the merits of a proposal" it, nevertheless, doesn't support research that does not contribute to life's "big questions" and the "spiritual quest" which it, quite clearly, sees as related to the existence of God. The Foundation, of course, has every right to distribute its funds as it see fit. The problem here lies not with the Templeton Foundation, but rather with those who seek its support in the name of pure scientific research, whether that is the individual scholar or the sponsoring university. Given the difficulty in finding sufficient funds for serious research on religion, appearing to conform to the research parameters set by Templeton may seem a small price to pay. In my judgment, however, it is too steep a price to pay, for in appearing to pursue a spiritual or religious rather than a purely scientific agenda, they compromise the prospects for establishing a genuinely scientific study of religion. Moreover, if it is claimed that the project as it will actually be carried out is nothing more than a scientific exercise, the proposal in effect is hypocritical, and in the long run, will be detrimental to the reputation of the scholars involved and to the university that sponsors the work.

Accepting the Templeton framework in good faith, on the other hand, is not a problem for those who espouse the same "religio-spiritual" agenda as the foundation, but its effect on the field and the sponsoring university is no less detrimental, for there is the same problem of the confusion of the religious with the scientific agenda, and the deception that may be perpetrated in this case is against the sponsoring university in that the grantees claim that they are engaged in purely scientific rather than religious research. The next Templeton research proposal to be discussed is, I think, of that type.

"The Cognition, Religion, and Theology Project"

The second Templeton Foundation grant proposal to come out of a research university setting was awarded jointly to the Centre for Anthropology and Mind (in the Institute of Cognition and Evolutionary Anthropology) and the Ian Ramsey Centre for Science and Religion at Oxford University. My account of this project derives from the information provided on the websites of both institutions and on an e-mail notice from Emma Cohen informing members on the COG-SCI-REL list of a cognitive science of religion small grants competition (dated March 18, 2008). Given the project's title—"Cognition, Religion, and Theology"—there is no mistaking the character of the project as one that attempts to integrate religious and theological concerns into the scientific enterprise. Indeed, the title suggests that religion and theology are not simply objects of study for science but rather partners in an altogether larger program. Moreover, given the theistic positions publicly espoused by the scholars overseeing this project—Justin Barrett of the Institute of Cognitive and Evolutionary Anthropology and Roger Trigg of the Ian Ramsey Centre—the suspicion that this larger program is an essentially religious one is hard to suppress. As I noted earlier, Barrett maintains that a full understanding of the import of the Cognitive Science of Religion will support and confirm religious belief in a transcendent reality and that such studies are entirely (both methodologically and substantively) consistent with espousing intelligent design theory. Trigg espouses similar, if not identical, views. I do not have space here to review his overall philosophical position and so refer briefly here to his "Christians-in-Science/St Edmunds" public lecture (Cambridge) "Do Science and Religion Need Each Other?" In this lecture, sponsored by the Templeton Foundation, he challenges whether scientists need always look for natural explanations. He maintains that believing this to be so would indicate a naive acceptance of a naturalistic *metaphysics* that fails to see that "there is always the possibility that science can learn from religion" (2003: 12), from intelligent design theory, for example. In his defense of intelligent design as scientific (i.e., as not repudiating any scientific knowledge), Trigg argues that intelligent design theorists are justified in "suggesting that a science closed to the possibility of non-natural explanations is itself deficient" (13). The "suspicion" that this Templeton-funded project is a religious one is confirmed in an analysis of the objectives of the proposal itself.

In a summary statement of the program announcing a "small grant competition" (2008)—which overlaps to a considerable degree with the statement found on the Ian Ramsey Centre site and will be discussed at greater length below—Barrett is primarily concerned to solicit research that will justify a negative answer to the question: "Does the naturalness of religious beliefs mean that they've been explained away and you shouldn't believe in God?" (2008: 2). His main concern here is not to find a scientifically credible explanation of religion so much as it is to justify religion and to protect it. Hence he puts religion beyond all possibility of scientific explanation in the same way that phenomenologists of religion used to put the question of the "truth of religion" beyond the pale of the comparativists and historians of religions. He writes: "If scientists can explain why people tend to believe in gods and also why other people tend to believe there are no gods, then surely the presence of a scientific explanation cannot mean that you should not believe one way or the other just on the presence or possibility of such an explanation" (2). And that, it seems, is sufficient ground for Barrett to move beyond science to a philosophical and theological exploration of "findings from the evolutionary and cognitive sciences as applied to religion." Barrett asks: "Does scientific evidence support or challenge specific theological propositions or worldviews?" That, however, is not a scientific question; rather, it invites theological and philosophical reflection.

According to Emma Cohen's e-mail to the COG-SCI-REL list regarding the small grant competition, an element of this research project includes, but without explanation as to why, "the need for enhancing the field's theological engagement." Indeed, it is not clear why anyone should think that the cognitive science of religion was ever engaged with theology. Nevertheless, the project directors call for "proposals for theoretical projects that explore philosophical and theological implications of assumptions and findings in the evolutionary and cognitive sciences as applied to religion." Questions to which they seek answers include the following: "What aspects of religion can CSR [Cognitive Science of Religion] theories hope to explain?" and "Is the cognitive science of religion 'compatible' with Christian doctrine and Christian discourse about God, including that of the compatibility of 'the findings of CSR with biological fine-tuning arguments in favour of theism'?" It is clear, therefore, that the project assumes not only a methodological compatibility between science and religion in general but also a compatibility between cognitive science theorizing and intelligent design theorizing, which amounts to a subordination of science to supernatural revelation and therefore, effectively, to a rejection of the essential character of the scientific enterprise. I find this simply astounding. There is no other scientific undertaking in the context of the modern research university that would question its most basic methodological assumptions and its place within an integrated causal model for explaining human behavior and culture.

The material on the Ian Ramsey Centre website relevant to this project, as one might expect of a theologically oriented institution, presents a similar viewpoint expressing concern as to whether the cognitive science of religion is of any benefit to philosophers and theologians. The central issue, however, seems to be whether the cognitive science of religion will undercut religious belief. Under the obligatory "FAQs" it is acknowledged that critics of religion like Richard Dawkins, Dan Dennett, and Paul Bloom have espoused a reductionistic understanding of the cognitive science of religion that has done much "to bridge the gap between strictly evolutionary or biological treatments of religion and strictly social approaches." But the only "cognitive science of religion" acceptable to the Templeton project participants will require serious modification; that is, it will have to draw on resources rejected by the reductionists. As they put it: they wish not only to undertake the kind of research these critics undertake but also "to engage theological and philosophical perspectives in a potentially mutually productive, instead of antagonistic, manner." The directors of this project, therefore, express optimism that it will maximize the scientific potential of the cognitive science approach that Dawkins, Dennett, and Bloom champion. Clearly, however, this points to the necessity for an accommodation of science to religion.

In response to the ambiguously phrased question "Is this project driven by a *particular* religious agenda" (emphasis added) they respond, equally ambiguously, by saying that they "will develop and support a scientific programme of investigation into the cognitive and evolutionary foundations of religious thinking and behaviour." Unfortunately, however, their answers to other questions suggest that their overriding concerns relate to whether the cognitive science of religion constitutes a threat to religious belief or to the practical value of religion.

In response to the question about the potential threat of the cognitive science of religion to religious beliefs, they claim that "explaining religion is not the same as explaining it away." But in taking this tack, it seems to me that they give up the claim that science (and the cognitive science of religion in particular) can fully account for religion. They confuse explaining intersubjectively available empirical data about religions with the question of the ontological existence of the agents, powers, and processes predicated by religions, which is an altogether different matter. On this score they may be entirely justified to "write off" the criticisms of the likes of Dawkins and Dennett since their atheism is an espousal of an apologetic metaphysical position with respect to the question of the existence of postulated transcendent religious beings, powers, or states. But it is crass sleight-of-hand to deny that the scientific study of religion holds no implications for the validity of religious belief. On this the early Stark is entirely correct. If we find that we can provide an explanation of religion without invoking the supernatural in doing so, there is no scientific reason or ground for believing that such a metaphysical reality actually exists, or that science even suggests something to that effect. And asserting that they will provide a similar cognitive account of the spread of atheism as of religion does little to change this and appears, therefore, to be nothing more than an attempt to placate religious devotees. It is entirely disingenuous therefore to say, as the accommodationists do, that

> it is not yet clear whether findings from CSR are generally supportive, contradictory, or neutral with regards to particular theological commitments. Nonbelievers might find satisfaction in a sound scientific explanation of why people tend to believe in God because they can now account for why people persist in believing in a fictitious being. The believer might find satisfaction in the scientific documentation of how human nature predisposes people to believe in God because it would reinforce the idea that people were divinely designed to know God. What we can more modestly say is that both believers and non-believers can agree on the scientific findings. (emphasis added)

Stark's stance, of course, is not an argument showing that the supernatural doesn't exist, but then that is not an objective either of the scientific study of religion—there is no reason to incorporate proving the existence, or likely existence, of God into a scientific project. The objective of the sciences is to explain phenomena in the world—including social phenomena like religion—in terms of causes that are wholly in the natural world. The burden of proof of such religio-theological claims as are raised in this Templeton project rests on "the believers," and that problem can only be resolved beyond the range of the sciences. Thus, in order to bring the matter to mind within the framework of an allegedly scientific project, the best the accommodationists can do is to try to obscure the issues by claiming to show that the sciences cannot distinguish between (ultimate metaphysical) reality and illusion. As Barrett puts it:

> If we could offer a social, cognitive, evolutionary, physiological, pharmacological, and neuroscientific account of your belief that your partner exists—indeed, that your partner loves you—would that undermine the truth-value of that belief? Would it support it. Where there is no incontrovertible means of independent verification, Cognitive Science of Religion is simply not equipped to distinguish whether the objects of our beliefs are real or illusory.

Unlike the first Templeton project discussed above, the grantees here openly embrace the Templeton mandate. And even though they acknowledge that "the CSR is not an ideological platform [but rather] . . . a scientific enterprise," they bracket the methodological implications of that enterprise and enter into an ideological framework which they think allows them to transcend those implications while still laying claim to being cognitive scientists of religion. Consequently, their overall project is not a scientific but rather a religio-metaphysical undertaking, for it expropriates, so to speak, the cognitive science of religion for religious and theological purposes and therefore places it beyond the integrated causal framework that governs all the other sciences within the research university. Their theorizing here, therefore, is an apologetic exercise that is but a short step away (if that) from proselytizing.

Conclusion

I must bring these comments on the present state of affairs in the academic study of religion as I see them to a close. I think that I have shown here that there is some reason to rejoice in the growth of the field of religious studies over the last three decades in that we, collectively, have moved beyond mere fact-gathering and hermeneutical and comparative analysis of the data—our theorizing, that is, has transformed our erudition into evidence with which to test explanations and theories. With the application of rational choice theory and the cognitive sciences of religion, moreover, we have also moved beyond the limitations of earlier modes of psychological and sociological theorizing. These are exciting new developments in the field that have been heuristically valuable in the generation of progressive research programs, and they are indicative of the possibility that we may soon find it possible to provide testable natural accounts of religion as a wholly human phenomenon. But I have also argued that this field of study is under severe strain given the resurgence of religious agendas, the continuing failure of nerve with respect to scientific methodology in the study of religious phenomena, and the apparent corruption of the modern research university by those who wish to accommodate what cannot be accommodated and include what cannot (and does not need to) be included, namely, metaphysical theism. Methodological atheism is sufficient for our purposes, and also necessary if we are to preserve our discipline as a legitimate branch of social science.

Given the place of religion in society at large, the scientific study of religion has little or no visibility or respectability outside the context of the modern university. And because of the "association" of religiosity with the study of religion, it has also, sadly, received little attention from colleagues in other scientific disciplines. With the resurgence of religious influence on university campuses today, what little respect the study of religion has had there may well be lost. Moreover, the integrity of our teaching in the classroom and the quality of our research could well be undermined and discredited. We must, therefore, be vigilant with respect to the increasing demands for greater religious influence on campus life and in the curriculum.

There is not much that can be done with respect to the failure of nerve on the part of individual scholars regarding scientific methodology in this field. We can, at best, point out to them that claims of access to, and the "scientific" value of, a special body of knowledge simply on the basis that it is something that cannot be disproved on naturalistic grounds is logically incoherent and methodologically problematic. Opposing the implicit theism underlying that position with an atheistic stance, however, will be of little help. I am in agreement, therefore, with the critiques of Dennett's (and possibly Dawkins's) atheism raised by Stark and Barrett. Dennett, unfortunately, espouses a metaphysical rather than a methodological atheism, and then advocates its use as a basis for making policy recommendations regarding religion for society at large. This, in my judgment, also constitutes a form of apologetic theorizing. Where students of religion do take up such a stance, it simply embroils the field in futile theological and metaphysical disputes, which is precisely what the nineteenth-century founders of the scientific study of religion set out to avoid. The only point being made in the adoption of *methodological atheism,* on the other hand, is that, as with every other science, we seek a study of religion that does not need to postulate the existence of anything supernatural which in turn implies that, (1) as an object of scientific interest, religion is comprised only of elements that are intersubjectively available to all researchers, religious or not and, (2) causes of religion can only be found within the framework of the natural world. Whether or not this also implies anything about the truth or "Truth" of religion (i.e., about the existence of religious agents, powers, or events or about the value of religion) is *not* a part of the scientific study of religion. Consequently, so far as the academic study of religion per se is concerned, there is neither ground nor need for hostility toward religion. What I think is called for then, is vigorous public criticism of those within the field who engage in apologetic theorizing (whether in a religious or an atheistic mode) or other moral or sociopolitical agendas that divert our attention from our scientific research objectives and our pedagogical role of introducing students to an important area of knowledge and training them in the techniques by which such knowledge is gained.

We can do little more regarding the problems that currently beset our institutions than to make known our criticisms and concerns about the influence religiously oriented funding agencies have on the reputations of our field and our universities. The Templeton Foundation is well known for its religious orientation: for its focus on supporting research that seeks to confirm religious belief and have a positive spiritual influence on society. The Foundation, that is, presupposes the existence of a transcendent world and only supports research consistent with such a worldview. As their website puts it, they are interested in what scientific research can "tell us about God, about the nature of divine action in the world [and] about meaning and purpose?" Consequently, acceptance of a Templeton award—with a proposal that seems tailor-made not to conflict in any obvious way with its assumptions and goals—can only indicate either a commitment to Templeton assumptions even though they clash with the methodological assumptions and procedures of normal academic and scientific activities or cast aspersion on the integrity of the scholars and institutions submitting grant proposals to the Foundation. Either way, the repercussions on our field are serious. This is particularly problematic with respect to the work being done in the Centre for Anthropology and Mind described above, and especially so with respect to the major "Explaining Religion Project" (funded by the European Commission) which shares space and administrative and research personnel with the "Cognition,

Religion, and Theology Project." Such proximity raises serious question for the broader scientific community as to the intellectual integrity of that project, as might the fact that anthropologist Harvey Whitehouse, who oversees the work of the Centre for Anthropology and Mind, actually sits on the board of the Templeton Foundation. This is a shame. The "Explaining Religion Project" is an important scientific research project wholly free of religious and/or metaphysical concerns and ought to be free from all suspicion.

I am aware that bringing these criticisms into open discussion in the academic and public realm could be seen as harmful to our field and could be regarded as inhibiting access to funding. On the other hand, it seems to me that criticism is the essence of the scientific enterprise, and, furthermore, that to withhold criticism—to say nothing— will be of even greater harm in that it will allow our scientific work to be subverted by and replaced with a religious and theological agenda, which in my judgment is far worse.

5

The Learned Practice of Religion in Canada

Introduction

The study of religion, as I have suggested elsewhere (Wiebe 2002a: xix–xxv), is probably as old as religion itself, with the earliest form of it being essentially devotional and catechetical—a kind of training in the practical and ethical requirements of religious life that provides the devotee an "understanding" of the truth, value, and meaning of life.[1] But this also presupposes that the devotee is able to provide a religious account of the world, which necessarily involves an intellectual study of religion that can afford the devotee the requisite knowledge and skills to be able to carry out that task. In addition to such a devotional and catechetical study of religion, however, religion has also inspired a more scholarly and academic study of itself that blends devotional, catechetical, and cognitive concerns in an attempt to forge a more profound understanding of religion. This development in religious thought, particularly in the West, eventually produced an elaborate structure of theological disciplines that, even though ultimately directed to the edification of the devotee, produced a more comprehensive and systematic—and therefore more "scientific"—account of the Christian faith. However, the knowledge such study generates is not fully scientific in the modern sense of the word because the "scholarship" involved in its production is constrained by religious belief and commitment—it is the product of what we might reasonably call *Glaubenswissenschaft* or "faith-imbued science."[2] Thus *Glaubenswissenschaft* is not *Religionswissenschaft*, although it did permit the development of a range of skills and methods in the study of various aspects of religion that, unlike the devotional/catechetical study of religion, escaped religio-ecclesiastical constraints, which eventually provided the basis for the emergence and growth of *Religionswissenschaft*—that is, of a genuinely secular and scientific study of religions and religion.[3]

The academic study of religion in Canada, I will argue here, has been and remains essentially of *the Glaubenswissenschaft* type, that is, confessional, although not always of the "capital-c" variety that results in denominational/sectarian control of the programs and curricula of departments of religious studies. Indeed, in the early years of those institutions the study of religion was primarily religious education of the young, dominated by "capital-c" confessionalist communities. This is indisputably the case, I contend, early in the history of our tertiary academic institutions. As Guy

Laperrière and William Westfall point out, for example, "the study of religion [during this period] was at the centre of academic life in Canada" (Laperrière and Westfall 1990: 42) and they further maintain that almost all of our colleges and universities throughout the nineteenth and early twentieth centuries "constructed their curricula around the study of religion and religiously related subjects, so that students would receive a general synthesis of knowledge and understand the relationship between the structure of the world, the course of human history, and God's plan" (Laperrière and Westfall 1990: 42). They also point out that the academic study of religion in the early history of our country was wholly dominated by denominational and ministerial (i.e., clergy training) concerns (Laperrière and Westfall 1990: 43). And as Harold Coward reads the history of this period, religion was oppressively dominant in the university curriculum in that courses pressed denominational/sectarian teaching upon students (Coward 1991: 22). The "mentality" of the religion curriculum, he maintains, was that of a Christian establishment which was tied to a missionary agenda (i.e., involving a strict religious exclusivism) (Coward 1991: 32). Coward sees this as particularly characteristic of the undergraduate department at the University of Toronto, for example, where until recently, he writes, there was an "unwillingness of University of Toronto denominational colleges to appoint specialists in non-Christian religions" (Coward 1991: 32).

The nature or character of the study of religion in more recent times cannot, I think, be as clearly delineated as in the early period of our history. Charles Anderson, for example, (in the third edition of his *Guide to Religious Studies in Canada* [1972]), claims that in the 1960s a radical change in the character of the study of religion in our colleges and universities occurred as it took its place as religious studies "alongside the study of other subjects such as art, society, literature, [and] history" (Anderson 1972: 7). This development, he claims, "indicated a clean break between the religious and the academic study of religion" (Anderson 1972: 8), and, in distinguishing the secular approach to understanding religious phenomena from the religious approach, it achieved scientific—that is, academic—legitimation.[4] However, this is not all that Anderson has to say about the new religious studies. Even though he claims that "by the mid 1960s . . . the concept of religious studies as a reputable academic enterprise had been widely accepted in the universities" (Anderson 1972: 9), he also recognizes that, for the most part, the motivation for studying religion in the academic context was still largely connected to the search for religious truth—that students saw the university as an alternative context in which to undertake their religious quests. As he put it: "Religious studies departments, insofar as they are true to their name, focus on the religious questions. Inevitably, then, appetites which found ecclesiastical fare unappealing turned to religious studies" (Anderson 1972: 10, 12). Anderson correctly claims that religious studies "has carved out an area of teaching and research recognized by the university and other institutions (Anderson 1972: 18) by eschewing an overt confessional and theological approach to understanding religion (Anderson 1972: 13) but he nevertheless also recognizes that it is not a distinctive discipline and that it shares with theology "a common commitment to academic values as well as a belief in the importance of religion" and, therefore, is "able to engage in fruitful conversation and cooperation" with theology (Anderson 1972: 18). This clearly suggests that the religious studies of which Anderson speaks is neither simply a scientific enterprise nor simply a sectarian religious exercise. A similar ambiguity, I think, is to be found in the "Call for Papers" for this conference (Gardaz 2003: 353). The opening sentence contends that a scientific study of religion has emerged on the Canadian academic scene, even if only relatively recently. However, in placing the word scientific in scare quotes, suggesting that the enterprise is at least in some respects not scientific, it simultaneously throws into doubt the academic credentials of the enterprise in which members of religious studies departments in our universities are engaged.

In one sense this ought not to be surprising given that the generation that founded religious studies in Canadian universities, as Keith Clifford points out, were a "transitional generation"—that is, scholars trained in theological institutions dominated either by neo-Thomist or neo-Orthodox outlooks that had all but disintegrated by the 1960s—who "adapted the theological disciplines of Bible, Theology and Church History to the context of the secular university" (Clifford 1991: 171). These scholars experienced little or no dissonance, claims Clifford, because for the most part, they simply "continued doing [in this context] what they had always done" (Clifford 1991: 172–73). Departments of theology in effect simply changed in name "without changing their teaching staff or their conception of what they were doing" (Clifford 1991: 172). Dissonance was experienced, Clifford maintains, only in those departments that altered the seminary pattern of courses by introducing non-Western religious traditions into the curriculum (Clifford 1991: 173). But this in itself hardly constitutes a radical transformation in the conception of the field that would require significant change in characterizing teaching and research in religious studies departments in the 1960s from that which preceded them.

Harold Coward, like Clifford, recognizes the Christian foundations upon which the so-called new religious studies departments of the 1960s were built. Moreover, Coward, like Clifford, sees the transition as still in progress. He writes: "The shift from the mentality of 'Christian establishment' and the missionary thrust that dominated the place of religion in the early history of Canadian universities to Religious Studies departments in which Christianity has no privileged position is far from complete" (Coward 1991: 32). This transition, in his judgment, has been more rapid in colleges and universities without denominational connections because they were able to create better-balanced programs, "with faculty appointments . . . and course offerings, spread over the major world religions" (Coward 1991: 32), whereas colleges with denominational connections were restricted to courses related to sectarian beliefs and concerns. Coward, therefore, like Clifford, sees the distinguishing mark of religious studies to lie in the extension of the study of religion from Christianity alone to the world's religious traditions. "The shift from Theology to Religious Studies may be thought of, from one perspective," he writes, "as paralleling the shift from dogmatic, metaphysical systems to the critical questioning and analysis of all systems by the Enlightenment" (Coward 1991: 23). And like Anderson, Coward sees the new departments of religious studies as appropriately involving not only a detached study of religious phenomena but also an *intellectual engagement with religious claims*. As he puts it:

> In Religious Studies departments, students find a place where their religious interests, and in some cases their religious commitments, can get critical examination without embarrassment or prejudice. Intellectual engagement with religious claims is encouraged, as well as detached study of religious phenomena. A sense of mental freedom is offered that is intellectually and spiritually expanding for students. (Coward 1991: 24)

One sees here, I suggest, the conception of religious studies as the learned practice of religion; a practice incorporating a "small-c" confessionalism relative to an ultimate reality experienced variously in the world's religious (and humanist) traditions. And even though one does see a kind of detached scientific study of various elements of religions involved in this larger project, it is clearly not the case, I think, that religious studies is understood as a primarily scientific undertaking directed essentially to gaining public knowledge about public religious facts. The evidence will show, rather, that religious studies on the Canadian scene is either a crypto-religious exercise based on what might be called "small-c" confessional principles or a hybrid discipline that attempts to integrate scientific and religio-theological agendas. The evidence, moreover, is voluminous, and encompasses, among other considerations, the views of "founding figures" of the field, the "founding vision" of the CSSR, the overall image of the enterprise reflected in the publications of the society's journal *Studies in Religion/Sciences Religieuses* (subsequently SR),[5] and the dominant conception of the "discipline" as it is practiced in departments of religious studies across Canada, revealed in the state-of-the-art reviews published by the Canadian Corporation for Studies in Religion/*Corporation Canadienne des Sciences Religieuses* from 1983 to 2001.

Founding figures

There are many scholars who played a major religious ideological role in the development of religious studies in Canada and exerted significant influence on students of religion who eventually took up posts in departments of religious studies in Canada. Chief among them, I think, are Wilfred Cantwell Smith, George Grant, Charles Davis, and Joseph McLelland.[6]

The clearest concise statement of Smith's approach to the study of religion in the academy is to be found in his inaugural lecture in 1949 as the first director of the McGill Institute of Islamic Studies in the then recently organized Faculty of Divinity (1948). Although Smith affirms here the value of science in understanding religion, he does not seem particularly concerned to keep the role of scientist and prophet distinct in his work. Indeed, he insists that science does not "cut one off from the truth vouchsafed through revelation" and he understands his elaboration of a science of religion in this address as "an attempt to retrieve such [religious] guidance" (Smith 1950: 56). Thus religious studies, Smith argues, like Christian theology itself, must be dedicated to gaining religious knowledge, although unlike Christian theology, it must do so within a colloquy of the world's religious traditions.

Like Smith, George Grant, in a paper delivered to the Royal Society of Canada in 1967, readily acknowledges the need for solid objective scholarship in the field of religious studies. However, despite this commitment to impartiality and science (in the broad sense of the term), Grant nevertheless also claims that more than this is needed for a proper study of religion in the academy. Whether at the undergraduate or graduate level, Grant insists, "literary and historical scholarship should not be the final object of departments of religion" (Grant 1968: 64). And because scholarship alone "cannot be the final standpoint in the study of religion" (Grant 1968: 67), Grant insists that it will inevitably have to call upon resources of theology and philosophy" (Grant 1968: 67).

Joseph McLelland of McGill University advocated a similar stance on *the true nature* of religious studies. In his 1972 essay, "The Teacher of Religion: Professor or Guru," for example, he argued that s/he must be both. To take up a strictly objective phenomenological approach to the study of religion even in the academy is unacceptable, he maintains, because that would amount to denying "the referential status of religious behaviour and statements." He writes: "If by 'phenomenology'. . . we intend some cult of objectivity that denies the humanity of both subject and object, it would seem an inappropriate discipline for the study of religion" (McLelland 1972: 232) because neither professor nor students can deny that personal commitment to a "root metaphor" orients her or his life and necessarily involves her or him in political, social, and other religio-theological obligations (McLelland 1972: 230–31). He concludes, therefore, that reductionistic scientific studies of religion are unjustifiable and that the student of religion must be willing and ready to engage in religio-theological discourse and not only in objective scientific analysis of data and the construction of theoretical explanations of religion.

In the opening presentation of the 1974 meeting of the CSSR Davis proposed "The Reconvergence of Theology and Religious Studies." Davis clearly feared that religion (and its liberal theological expression) was being pushed out of the academic realm. Davis, however, argues in this essay that a properly critical theology emerged within medieval Christendom and that it is ignorance of this fact that accounts for the tension between theology and religious studies. Davis agrees that a theology that is nothing more than an elaboration of a specific religious tradition is inappropriate in the framework of the academic study of religion because such a position amounts simply to the confession of a faith-stance. But his own so-called critical theology also constitutes a faith-stance in that, like the naive theology he subjects to critique, it too precludes all possibility of reductionistic accounts of religion—that is, accounts of religion that do not *a priori* presuppose the transcendent reality on which all theology is based. Thus Davis, like Smith, Grant, and McLelland, maintains that the academic study of religion must involve more than historical, empirical, and theoretical analysis and scholarship.

A list of other senior or established scholars during this period in the development of the field of religious studies who held nearly identical views and exerted considerable influence on the emerging "discipline" would have to include figures like William

Nicholls (University of British Columbia), Gordon Harland (University of Manitoba), and Klaus K. Klostermaier (University of Manitoba). Space does not permit comment on these scholars, or upon scholars of more junior rank in the early days like Eugene Combs (McMaster University), Michel Despland (Concordia University), Peter Slater (Carleton University), or Harold Coward (University of Calgary), who also took up very similar stances.

The founding vision of the CSSR

Looking at the nature of the field of religious studies as mediated through the activities of the CSSR provides further evidence that religious studies in Canada was, and is still, entangled in more than a scientific agenda—that it is concerned with the formation of the individual student, and, in a sense that will become clear, with the transformation of society. This certainly appears to be the case in the first decade of the society's existence as it is recounted by Combs in his essay "Learned and Learning: CSSR/SCER, 1965–1975" published in SR in 1977. Combs maintains that the work of the society in its first decade was "focused almost exclusively on demarcating the field and the methodology appropriate to [the] study [of religion]" (Combs 1977: 357), and that SR offered "a singularly appropriate context for the realization of a long-sought distinctive Canadian scholarship" (Combs 1977: 359). It is fairly clear, however, that this did not include the aim of creating a scientific framework of research and analysis that would assist students of religion in seeking explanatory accounts of religious phenomena and/or an explanation (theory) of religion in general. The society's methodological interest, as Combs indicates, was "to differentiate departments of religion and teachers of religion from catechetics" (Combs 1977: 358). Religious studies, therefore, was not to be confused with theology; it was to be an independent discipline with its own boundaries and its own "unique research needs"—not "a subdiscipline of history or philosophy" (Combs 1977: 358)—although neither the character of the boundaries nor the unique research needs are explicitly delineated by Combs. Moreover, as I will show here, they seem to be connected to the presumed peculiar transcendent character of religion.

In describing the substance of the papers presented at society meetings in the first decade, Combs suggests that religion was still very much at the center of participants' interests, with Smith (1967) discussing methodology as a religious issue (Combs 1977: 360); Joseph McLelland (1972) seeing professors of religion assuming a priestly role in secular disguise (Combs 1977: 361); Charles Davis (1974) advocating a "reconvergence of theology and religion" thesis (Combs 1977: 362); Joseph Kitagawa (1975) pressing the issue of making intelligible religious traditions in light of modern thought; and papers at the 1970 meeting constituting "a theological and philosophical inquiry *within* and about the Western religious tradition (Combs 1977: 361, emphasis added), and those at the 1972 conference being "still centrally preoccupied with religious issues as distinct from methodological issues" (Combs 1977: 362). Combs's own summary assessment of the Davis paper, moreover, reveals the fundamental thrust of the CSSR overall agenda as still religious, although not sectarian or denominational. For Combs, Davis's paper

> signified a profound conjoining of the constitutional problems which the Society had faced in 1965 with respect to demarcation of subject and method, inasmuch as it posited a plane of study that transcended the particularities both of specific religious traditions and of specific methodological insights. It eased the painful tension between religion and theology with the salvific balm of philosophy. (Combs 1977: 362)

Combs's assessment of Kitagawa's paper, moreover, suggests to him the program the society should next take up, which is essentially religious in character, namely that of "recalling, assessing, and transmitting the religious heritages of the past in the context of, and by way of, understanding and assessing the central theological, religious, and philosophical premises of the present" (Combs 1977: 363). This clearly is a (liberal, non-sectarian) religious exercise, the character of which Combs sketches out in the final section of his paper. The academic study of religion, he insists, must operate with the assumptions that both "ancient texts and traditions" and "the modern" are worth preserving, and that that can only be accomplished "by a dialectic in which the starkest moments of concord and discord of ancient and modern thought are finally exposed" (Combs 1977: 363). Only that can deliver the truth to us, because such a *practice* will make possible the creation of a new text or tradition that can contain both ancient and modern thought. Thus, he concludes his essay as follows:

> That exposure [to ancient and modern frameworks of truth] is finally itself to be wrought by human thought grounded in a *wisdom* for which there is yet no text or tradition. *To author such a text and live such a tradition is a learned task in which the learning Society must now engage.* (Combs 1977: 363, emphasis added)

Combs's essay is not an objective history of the CSSR nor do we have such a history of the society, now in its fortieth year.[7] Although a thorough analysis of papers presented at the annual programs, and a careful review of the decisions made by the executive committee of the CSSR, would need to be made to determine once and for all whether this character of the society continued for the next thirty years, my experience with the CSSR since 1975 suggests that little has changed. I provided some reasons for such an evaluation several years after the publication of Combs's article in my "Failure of Nerve in the Academic Study of Religion" article published in SR in 1984. I also think that the basic thrust of the University of Manitoba conference on "Religious Studies: Directions for the Next Two Decades" held in 1990 (organized by Klaus K. Klostermaier together with his junior colleague, Larry W. Hurtado) supports that assessment. The conference theme was concerned with "reflecting on the past of the discipline of religion, contemplating its present status, and planning for its future," and conference participants were pointedly directed "to consider the study of religion at public universities *as a continuation of the intellectual examination of religion which goes back over the ages*" (Klostermaier and Hurtado 1991: ix, emphasis added). The substance of the majority of the papers, moreover, clearly suggests that religious studies in Canada at this time was still governed by a "small-c" confessionalism. Harold Coward, for example, makes this very clear in his paper on "The Contribution of Religious Studies to Secular Universities in Canada" (1991). Of the CSSR he writes:

> It was of particular importance in translating the impact of the emerging Religious Studies into a discipline recognized within Canadian academia; [that it] achieved recognition for Religious Studies by becoming one of the recognized "Learned Societies," and helped win the acceptance of Religious Studies as a field of scholarly research suitable for support by the Canada Council and (now) the Social Sciences and Humanities Research Council of Canada (SSHRCC). (Coward 1991: 28)

But it also shows that what was established was not a scientific approach to the study of religion but rather an ecumenical scholarly religious—rather than a sectarian-pastoral—approach to "understanding" religion. Indeed, as Coward points out, the CSSR functioned as a mechanism of sorts by which non-Christian religious communities could gain the same kind of representation in our institutions of higher learning that Christianity had enjoyed in the past. As Coward puts it:

> Though Christian churches and individuals from the beginning of Canada have had their religion well recognized and represented in academic studies, the same could not be said for Jews, Muslims, Hindus, Buddhists, Native Americans and others. With the stress on the need for the presentation and study of all religions, the new departments provide a point of contact at the highest academic level for the many Canadians of religious backgrounds other than Christian. *This formal recognition within Canadian universities of the worth of these other religious traditions is a matter of genuine importance to many Canadians of non-Christian affiliation.* (Coward 1991: 31)

In other words, the formation of the society, as Combs put it, was concerned with serving the whole religious community in Canada in the search for wisdom and truth by way of a dialogue between traditions and modernity and not from within the Christian theological framework alone. And according to Coward, this ecumenical pluralism (not the scientific study of religion) became the agenda of the CSSR for the future (at least from 1975 to 1990). He is certainly joined in that judgment by Klostermaier and Hurtado who wrote in the preface to the volume of the proceedings of their conference:

> Religious Studies has by now been vindicated as reflecting a different, pluralistic approach to the study of religion and religions. Conversely, there is no longer any need to emphasize the distance between Religious Studies and traditional, largely denominational, expressions of religion. Some of these denominations have begun to see the advantages, which departments of Religious Studies at public universities can offer. They are, as a rule, open for every serious student, they strive to be scholarly and fair towards all, they often provide a meeting place for various

religions and for denominations within the same tradition. (Klostermaier and Hurtado 1991: viii–ix)

Following the vision of the philosopher of religion John Hick, Klostermaier and Hurtado advised the creation of "a field theory of religion from a religious point of view" (Klostermaier and Hurtado 1991: x). As the evidence with respect to the publications of Canadian scholars in religious studies in SR and the character of the departments of religious studies in Canadian universities spelled out in the state-of-the-art reviews to be set out below indicates, it is not likely that the CSSR has dropped the "small-c" confessionalist agenda it espoused in the first ten years of its existence.

Studies in religion/*Sciences Religieuses*

The evidence of a crypto-theological and/or general, non-sectarian, liberal religious agenda for the "academic" study of religion in Canada can readily be found in the original mandate, and continuing agenda, of SR. William Nicholls, one of the founding figures of the CSSR and first editor of SR—successor to the *Canadian Journal of Theology*—promised that SR would not abandon theological leadership of the Canadian community of scholars of religion and that it would continue to recognize "the validity of a study of religion within and for the sake of the faith communities" (Nicholls 1971: 3). Phillip B. Riley notes in his study of the first decade of SR's existence (1971–1981) that it is Smith's "work and influence perhaps more than that of any individual [that] permeates the pages of SR" (Riley 1984: 3). In Riley's assessment, normative and religio-theological concern rather than scientific interest is the distinctive contribution of SR to the study of religion in Canada (Riley 1984: 7, 20). Indeed, Riley sees the discussions of the relation of theology to religious studies as harboring a new kind of study of religion that might require of scholars in the field a new way of being religious (Riley 1984: 24). Thus, he writes: "The context for the discussions of the relationship between theology and religious studies in SR has been the need to articulate an unitive method for religious studies, a method that justifies the existence of an autonomous and distinct academic discipline or mode of inquiry that at the same time is appropriate to its object of inquiry" (Riley 1984: 23)—that is, to the ultimately transcendent aspect of human existence.

    In an unpublished paper, presented at the 1992 annual meeting of the CSSR, Barry Henaut—reviewing the first twenty years of the existence of SR—argues "that (Christian) theological and (Western) philosophical topics have continued to play a prominent role throughout [this period]" (Henaut 1992: 2), although he also maintains that there has been a significant evolution over the second decade of its life. He insists, for example, that SR moved to diversify its contents, including papers on women and religion, the sociological analysis of religion, biblical studies, and world religions, among other religious issues and themes (Henaut 1992: 3, 4). Despite these "successes" in trying to cover the full spectrum of religious studies, however, Henaut also notes that the theologico-philosophical issues of the truth of religion, the relation of theology to religious studies, and method in the study of religion lapse into theological discourse as much in the second decade of the journal as they did in the first. As he puts it: "Christianity tends, by and large, to be the hub for the journal's wheel of comparative religion" (Henaut 1992: 5). "Similarly," he claims, "there has continued to be considerable discussion in the pages of SR of the implications of various phenomena (not simply comparative religion) for . . . Christian theology" (Henaut 1992: 5). Although he admits that the line between "theology" and "religious studies" is fairly nebulous in the journal, he accounts for this continued focus on Christianity by reference to Canada's Christian past, and then insists that one must not think the second decade of the journal's print-space has been devoted exclusively to issues of Christian theology. However, his reference here to articles concerned with Marxist perspectives on social transformation and feminist programs for changing social structures reveal that they merely represent a change from "capital-c" confessionalism to "small-c" confessionalism in that they deal with religio-political matters in a less "sectarian" fashion than earlier essays related to similar political inequities. These essays, that is, are as much apologetic in character as the treatments of the "truth question" in religion, which are also to be found in the second decade of the journal's operation (Henaut 1992: 6–7).

For Henaut, then, the increased representation of articles on women and religion, sociology of religion, literature and the arts, literary critical and biblical studies suggests, "that the field has diversified and renewed itself" (Henaut 1992: 9). Yet he also acknowledges that the second decade of the journal saw an expansion of interest on the interaction of theology and religious studies. Thus, despite his comments about the renewal and diversification in the contents of the journal, he concludes that the journal "continues to show the strengths and weaknesses of its cultural context—[that] it has not fully evolved into [a] 'Religious Studies' journal with equal participation of the various sub-disciplines and fields. Its contents continue to favour Western topics, while methodologically the articles continue at times to display a Christian theological and/or apologetical element" (Henaut 1992: 9).

I know of no assessment of the contents of SR over the past fourteen years, but from a casual perusal of its contents over that period of time I have not noticed a significant change of substance or orientation of the essays it has published. This, of course, does not constitute scientific evidence of a continuing pattern. However, on the basis of a review of volume 32 (2003)—as a member of the editorial advisory board—I suspect that this is not too far off the mark. I wrote of that volume:

> There is a reasonable diversity of themes/topics presented by the papers published: dialogue of religions, women's rights, shamanism and art, ethics and social justice, theodicy, biblical scholarship, Christianity and ecology, and method in the study of religion, among others. However, on my reading, about half of the articles deal with Christianity (three papers on biblical studies, and seven on theological topics, with a couple more concerned with Muslim-Christian dialogue) which seems a little excessive. There were only four papers on [south and] East Asian religious traditions (three on India and one on China) and that seems lopsided with respect to the Western traditions (which, including Judaism and Islam, numbered about fourteen). I was also surprised by how few papers there were

that approached religious phenomena from a social scientific perspective. The scientific or theoretical perspective clearly does not show up much in Canadian studies of religion. (Wiebe 2004: 1)

The state-of-the-art-reviews

In the early 1980s, the CSSR sponsored a series of "state-of-the-art" reviews of university departments of religious studies across the country which provided an overview of this new academic enterprise in six volumes, spanning nearly two decades (1983–2001). Since I have given detailed attention to each of these reviews in Chapter 1, I will summarize their significance here. These reviews, I have shown, reveal religious studies in Canada to be an enterprise that is still fundamentally religious in orientation. The very conception under which this ambitious project of reviewing the field was carried out, in fact, suggests as much. The title of the project under which these analyses were engaged, for example, refers broadly to "the study of religion" in Canada, although it is described in the editor's introduction to each volume as a review of "religious studies," which suggests something much more restricted although, for the most part, free from ecclesiastical and sectarian control. But the overall picture provided is not that of a new kind of *scientific* enterprise; rather, it reveals it to be a continuation, in a non-sectarian form, of the religiously oriented study of religion that antedated what we might call the "religious studies" era in Canada. It is of interest to note, for example, that in a review of the Ontario study Jean-Marc Laporte is particularly sensitive to the religious character of that enterprise in Ontario's universities and colleges. As a theologian, Laporte expresses his gratitude for the authors of that state-of-the-art review for understanding the new field as a conversation partner for theology given that, in his judgment, they engage "the world and its problems" (Laporte 1993: 249). As Laporte puts it: "While the authors prize the academic objectivity of religious studies, they are far from advocating bloodless sterility. Professors of religious studies ought to respond to existential concerns and be free to disclose their own personal convictions in appropriate, non-proselytizing ways" (Laport 1993: 249). Furthermore, Laporte claims that one ought not to find this assimilation of the theological task into the religious studies agenda surprising, for the authors have shown both that "the matrix out of which religious studies emerged as a distinct reality is a theological one" and that "the pioneers of this discipline in Ontario universities by and large did not make a clean break from their origins" (Laporte 1993: 249). As I have shown in Chapter 1, much the same can be said about each of the other state-of-the-art reviews.

What is clear from the state-of-the-art reviews, then, is that although many scholars in the new departments of religious studies in Canada, since their formation in the 1960s and on, have been or are presently engaged in scholarly and scientific research, and that the departments have to all intents and purposes freed themselves from any kind of direct sectarian control or oversight, the new departments are still engaged in a "small-c" confessional (i.e., liberal religious) agendas, including the spiritual formation of students.

There is more to this story . . .

The analyses of the study of religion in Canada's colleges and universities provided so far do not exhaust the evidence relevant to the thesis I proposed in the Introduction of this chapter. There is not space here, however, to set out the various agendas and activities *of* and *in* religious studies departments in the country. In lieu of a comprehensive account, therefore, I provide a brief review of recent developments in only two universities, both in Ontario, that indicate a greater interest in a kind of "learned practice of religion" than in the scientific study of religious phenomena. The first is the recent University of Toronto's "Academic Plan: 2004–2010" for the Department and Centre for the Study of Religion, and the second, the new joint Wilfred Laurier University/University of Waterloo PhD program in Religious Studies.

The new academic plan at Toronto espouses as its aim, as it phrases it, providing "academic resources that will meet the needs of our richly diversified, multi-cultural student population . . . by developing a curriculum that will extend beyond our established concentrations in the study of Western Christianity and Judaism" (DiCenso 2004: 1). Given this statement it is clear that Coward's claim that the University of Toronto's program is dominated by the denominational colleges and has kept in place a Christian establishmentarianism is no longer true. However, whether the department and center in Toronto have transcended a crypto-religious agenda in their programs is not as clear. The academic plan, for example, places heavy emphasis on serving the needs of its multicultural and multireligious student body. The plan assumes, that is, that reorganization of the curriculum and a concomitant complement planning "*must be undertaken in relation to the distinctly diverse cultural and religious profile of the University's constituency, and the extraordinary multiculturalism and ethnic pluralism of the city of Toronto*" (DiCenso 2004: 2, emphasis in the original). It is left unclear in this document whether this desire "*to serve more students, and serve them even more effectively*" (DiCenso 2004: 6, emphasis in the original) is a matter of catering to other religious traditions as the department at one time catered to its Christian and Jewish clientele, although its concern "to enhance the student experience" suggests something of the sort, given the plan's claim that this points to "*cultural and intellectual requirements*" of its curriculum (DiCenso 2004: 4, emphasis added). The plan also refers to the department's and center's aim "*to fulfil the scholarly potential of our field*" (DiCenso 2004: 6, emphasis in the original) and to improve the faculty's participation "in the creation and dissemination of new knowledge" (DiCenso 2004: 3), but this is not explicated in terms of the creation of a scientific approach to the study of religion that would be primarily concerned with explanatory and theoretical accounts of religious phenomena. Indeed, the framework seems to be one connected to religio-political concerns that hint at the possible production of a new clerisy,[8] that is, the production of public intellectuals able to frame solutions to public crises such as the current conflict between Islam and the Christian West represented in the 9/11 attacks on the Trade Towers in New York (DiCenso 2004: 1). The department moved further in this direction in its academic plan—"Department for the Study of Religion 2010–2015"—under the chairmanship of Professor John Kloppenborg. That plan included a "Religion in the Public Sphere" program as a key strength of the department and envisaged the creation of a professional MA degree program under that rubric. The department also worked collaboratively with the University's Multi-Faith Centre to encourage engagement, sympathetic and critical, with diverse cultural and religious groups. The chair of the department, moreover, was a member of a university committee for the creation of a conjoint PhD degree program (essentially a mere renaming of the Toronto School of Theology's ThD degree program) to be awarded jointly by the university and federated and affiliated theological schools without serious consideration of the implications this might have for its own PhD degree program and graduates (see Wiebe 2015: 279–91, 2016). Though not spelled out in exactly this fashion, these documents do amount to something like Gordon Harland's justification for the creation of the Department of Religion at the University of Manitoba in 1968, although Harland was facing a period of time fraught with social turmoil and upheaval. "What we had to ask," Harland wrote, "was the relevance [of religion to self and society], what indeed, was the availability of the systems of meaning carried by the historic religious traditions?" For Harland, the need for the department was to encourage people to "become livingly aware of the resources of a deep religious heritage [and that] we engage the depths of our religious traditions as a way of laying hold of those energies and values that will enrich the present, and help us shape the future" (Harland 1991: 3). One simply does not find a deep interest in promoting a naturalistic study of religious thought and behavior at the University of Toronto.

The Laurier-Waterloo PhD program in religious studies, in my judgment, is yet another indication of religious studies departments in Canada diverting attention from a genuine scientific agenda to practical social concerns. The focus of attention in this program is not that of the discipline but rather the preparation of students for social service. As the advertisement for the program puts it, this PhD program is directed towards preparing "scholars who can effectively enter arenas of debate and withstand the heat of public intellectual life".[9] The "dissertation" is not focused on a scientific project but rather on "research" that will reach "an audience more diverse than the usual small group of specialists," which suggests that the program's primary aim is the production of "public intellectuals"—that is, leaders of society, a new, not necessarily religious, clerisy. Thus the dissertation is not, it appears, a dissertation but rather a book intended for a much broader, public audience. It also appears from the advertisement of the program that students will be coached on how to be effective in speaking to the general public—to gain broad public intelligibility. Clearly, therefore, students in this program will not be working on the cutting edge, so to speak, of problems in the field that still seek resolution.

This may not be a program of religious education as are the clergy training programs in seminaries and divinity schools, but there are, I think, some interesting analogies and parallels to such training. It is clear that "the aspirations and the tenor of the program," as the website puts it, differ from those of traditional doctoral programs, and that it is committed to "training" people for a wide array of non-academic careers in "areas of public life in which sensitivity to religious, ethnic, and other expressions of human diversity are essential".[10] The program does not exclude the possibility of candidates taking up academic careers, but it is clear that the training is not geared specifically to that end. And it is this practical/professional character of the new PhD that gives it the aura of a "divinity" program within a "small-c" confessional (or possibly wholly secular) framework.[11]

Conclusion

It is clear from the evidence presented here that the principal concerns for scholars of religion in Canadian universities—even after the founding of religious studies departments, the CSSR, and SR—have been broadly religious in character, directed to questions of truth, meaning, and purpose for the edification of students, university, and society. That is to say, the motivation for undertaking "religious studies" has been external to religious studies as a scientific discipline; it has not primarily been governed by, nor has its development been centrally concerned with, the production and dissemination of knowledge *about* religions and religion (which themselves, obviously, are engaged in activities directed to the edification of persons and society). As has been pointed out, there can be no doubt that the creation of departments of religious studies during and after the 1960s involved a shift in mentality in the study of religion in Canadian universities in that they undermined what I have referred to above as Christian establishmentarianism. The adoption of a pluralistic religious framework, however, is not the equivalent of espousing a scientific approach to understanding religion. The rejection of Christian establishmentarianism in the academic study of religion did not undermine the presumption that departments of religious studies should be engaged in civic tasks such as producing cultured, articulate individuals who in coming to understand our cultural and religious heritage will be able to sustain it (i.e., by living it in however modified form) and transmit it to the next generation or, even more generally, promote a kind of pluralistic confessionalism. Thus, for example, Harold Coward, although rejecting Christian hegemony in departments of religious studies—and insisting that "religious knowledge must not be a view from one religion or community out upon others" (Coward 1991: 33)—insists that creating a pluralistic religious stance in such departments must be the aim for the future of the discipline. Thus he writes:

> For myself, I will be more than satisfied if our departments develop a balance in which the various religions are fairly represented. Surely this is a minimum requirement for scholarship in Religious Studies. This will mean much to those citizens who are followers of the minority religions here in Canada. It could mean even more to Canadians from a Christian background, or, increasingly, from a completely secular background, for it will offer them a chance to explore their own life in relation to the richness and diversity of the totality of human religious experience. If we can achieve this, Religious Studies will make a very significant contribution to the life of the Canadian secular university. (Coward 1991: 35)

That the academic study of religion in Canada has not moved beyond this *Glaubenswissenschaftliche*-type of agenda at the time Coward wrote is not wholly surprising given the fact that the second-generation religious studies scholars had been trained by the transitional—religiously orientated—scholars who, as Clifford pointed out, founded the new religious studies departments. Clifford, however, expected the intellectualist assumptions transmitted by the transitional scholars to have only a minimal effect on religious studies scholarship in the 1990s and beyond. But this, as I have shown here, is not the case. Thus, in my judgment, there has been a relatively strong residual effect of the founding transitional religious figures on the training of the current generation of Canadian scholars in this field, although modified by the multicultural character of modern societies. Moreover, there have been several other factors that have reinforced the broadly religio-political approaches to the study of religion generated in the earliest days of the discipline: a global socio-spiritual malaise in society that has spawned a resurgence of religion and spirituality; the growth of religious violence and its import for our understanding of the future of democratic societies; and the widespread influence of identity politics on college and university campuses. These movements in society have encouraged professors and students in the field of religious studies to invoke the relevance of religion in the resolution of social and political problems and to engage the problems themselves rather than simply to engage in what is derogatorily referred to as "ivory tower" research on religions and religion. This "approach" to the field is then justified by reference to the challenges of postmodern thought to the Enlightenment conception of epistemology and the science that emerged from it. This justification, moreover, is backed up by the fact that the broader notion of knowledge now invoked by the scholar that permits him or her to become engaged in social, political, and religious issues in society finds ready acceptance in the broader community.

Clearly, therefore, the motives that provide the impetus behind the majority of students of religion in Canada today are not supplied by the inner logic of the discipline itself in the context of the modern research university, namely, the production and dissemination of knowledge about religions and religion, whether at the descriptive or the explanatory/theoretical level. I do not believe that the postmodern arguments against science are cogent, but cannot argue that matter here.[12] Of far greater significance, I believe, is the fact that the majority of scholars in the field still function in terms of a traditional conception of the role of the college and university which involved the formation of the good citizen, which requires addressing questions about the purpose and meaning of human life, and inculcating moral virtues and spiritual values that will prepare students for public service. As Ursula King has recently argued, the purpose of departments of religious studies should be different from other university departments in that they should have "a larger vision . . . than a merely academic one" (King 2002: 385); as she puts it, they should be "a means for feeding the quest for life and for enabling humans to live better, fuller lives" (King 2002: 385); that in addition to helping people "to know and understand, to analyze and explain, [it should help them] to love, to grow strong and confident, and to care and be compassionate" (King 2002: 385). And in doing so, she claims, religious studies "can help to shape the human future" (King 2002: 385). Until our present emphasis on the department as an instrument of personal and social formation is supplanted with an understanding of the student of religion as a member of an academic community with responsibilities to the discipline, we are likely to see a continuation of the pattern of religious studies outlined above in Canadian universities. The religious studies programs may not, to be sure, be controlled by denominational or sectarian religious authorities, but will in effect constitute the professors a new clerisy by virtue of the Emersonian conception of scholarship they presuppose—that is, the assumption that the scholar is/must be a Sage, a Truth-teller, a Teacher, and a Leader who will relate to students as guide and spokesperson for society. Where all semblance of religion is excluded, including "small-c" religious confessionalism, such scholars become "public intellectuals" who, no less than their religious counterparts, hope to constitute a clerisy—in this instance, the learned leaders of society. This, it seems to me, is to confuse religion and ideology with the scientific study of religion and is inappropriate in the context of the modern research university. And in "fusing" (and thereby confusing) the two types of activities, it seems to me that "religious studies" winds up simply being, as Michael Pye has put it, a flag of convenience capable of representing the multiplicity of conflicting goals and objectives espoused by virtually every "scholar of religion"—whether devotee, critic of religion, social scientist, or public intellectual—and incorporating the wide diversity of methods and approaches deployed by them in "studying" religion (Pye 1994: 52). In my judgment, therefore, the study of religion in Canada today still suffers from a failure of nerve in that, unlike the natural and social sciences, it refuses to recognize the distinction between *Glaubenswissenschaft* and *Religionswissenschaft* and proceeds as if the two can be seamlessly blended. This is not to say that there are not many in the field who approach the study of religion in a strictly academic or scientific fashion; but given the history of the field and the number of scholars committed largely to agendas that go beyond that of the discipline and the modern research university, I see little reason to believe that the future of "religious studies" will differ much from its past.

6

Affirming Religion in the History
of Religious Studies

In his *Fifty Years of Religious Studies in Canada: A Personal Retrospective* (2014), Harold Coward makes it very clear that he does not see this personal retrospective as a formal history of the development of "religious studies" in the context of Canada's universities (ix, 4, 84). Nevertheless, he thinks/hopes that the detailed information he provides about courses, student numbers, teaching staff, and so on in the formation and development of "religious studies" departments across the country will amount to "a beginning contribution toward a more formal history that remains to be written" (199–200). Since much of that information is already available in the sources on which Coward draws for his volume, his contribution to such a formal history will be simply as one "insider's" view of what "religious studies" in Canada has really amounted to.

In the first chapter of the book, Coward suggests that religious studies departments in Canada emerged as expansions from narrow theological understandings of religion to a more open, "academic" mode of study leading to an espousal of a broader non-sectarian approach to religion and a commitment to religious pluralism. Given Wilfred Cantwell Smith's focus on achieving a "humane knowledge" of religions (2) and George Grant's view that "religion is a key element in what it means to be human" (4), Coward sees them as the "founding figures" of "religious studies" in Canada. Both Smith and Grant, Coward points out, rejected not only denominationalism and sectarianism in the study of religion(s) (20) but also reductionism, insisting that "religious studies" should relate to concerns about the meaning of human existence and that it should "confront the questions of our troubled time" (7). This non-confessional, but not non-religious, approach to the study of religion is what appealed to Coward's childhood religious concerns (8) and drew him into doctoral studies in a "quest for self-understanding in this challenging, beautiful, and numinous universe" (184) with Grant at McMaster University in Ontario. The refrain about such a study having to be pursued "at the highest level of humanities and social sciences academic rigour" (20, and 30, 87, 118, 155, 176, *et passim*) clearly suggests a rather desperate need (for Coward personally, and, given his account of religious studies in Canada, for most scholars in the field) for intellectual respectability as a bona fide member of the academy (the modern university) in order to legitimate their own religious and/or theological stances (whether "large-C" or "small-c" confessional commitments).

The material in this volume that may be of assistance to the writing of a formal history of the "academic" study of religion in Canada—that is, any kind of study of religion that takes place within the university curriculum—is essentially limited to Chapters 2 and 5. According to Coward, only two types of religious studies departments emerged: those associated with already-existing departments limited to denominational theological concerns and those established de novo in modern universities without prior connections with religious institutions. Most of the material in these chapters is based on Charles Anderson's *Guide to Religious Studies in Canada* (1972) and the six-volume *State of the Art Review of Religious Studies in Canada* published over a fifteen-year period from the mid-1980s to the end of the 1990s. Chapter 2 is concerned with the period from 1966 to 1976 in which most departments of "religious studies" were founded; a period Coward refers to as the "Golden Decade" for the academic study of religion in Canada. Chapter 5 follows the growth/development of these departments from the late 1970s to the present. Chapters 3 and 4 constitute a kind of "hymn of praise" to McMaster University's Department of Religious Studies and the wonderful influence it has had on the growth of "religious studies" across Canada. In Chapter 3 he lauds the traditional *guru-sishya* style of oral study he was able to engage in with Professor T. R. V. Murti that made available to him non-conceptual levels of knowledge (63) which he thinks makes an invaluable contribution to our understanding of religion. "For those of us in religious studies, where we so often speculate about the ultimate questions of life," he writes, "something like the *guru-sishya* experience should indeed be present in our best teaching" (61). And he thinks this kind of understanding of religion sought for in McMaster's vision for a religious studies program (improved and perfected, according to him, in Calgary's department during his time there) has had "a major impact upon the development of religious studies in Canada" (67). As he puts it in the conclusion to this chapter, all of these departments, "by and large have stayed true to the vision of their founders" (143). For Wilfred Cantwell Smith, the objective for religious studies departments was the achievement of a "humane knowledge" of religious traditions in courses focused on "appreciating the other" that would lead to greater harmony in the world; and for George Grant, the objective for the field was to produce in graduates an experience of the truth of religion so that they would ultimately stem the tide of secularism in the world.

In Chapter 6 Coward focuses on the work of the Centre for Studies in Religion and Society at the University of Victoria which, strictly speaking, is not a department for the study of religion. It is an institution essentially created and funded by religious communities in Victoria, British Columbia, and approved by the University of Victoria. (This external religious influence on Victoria University has something of the flavor of the kind of influence the John Templeton Fund sought in its funding of "science/religion" courses in secular academic contexts years back and in much of its current funding of research on religion today.) As the first director of the center Coward notes that he brought his understanding of what the study of religion is all about from his department in Calgary to Victoria; his aim being to bring "religious traditions to bear on major problems facing society" (153). This chapter is essentially a lengthy catalog of the accomplishments he and his successors had in what I would call "insinuating" religion into policy matters at various levels of Canadian social and political life. This was not a concern simply for ensuring that policy decisions should be aware of religious sensitivities on a wide range of concerns, but rather to ensure that "religious wisdom" be taken into consideration in policy responses to social and ethical issues and problems in society (185); for policy-makers to be open to transcendent sources of knowledge in their decision-making. This is what, in Chapter 7 on the future of religious studies in Canada, Coward thinks is essential for the field. Referring to the work of Robert Orsi, he maintains that our focus must be on understanding the wisdom of religion in order to understand the world and respond appropriately to its problems. As he puts it: "This has been our strength in the past, providing ways to reach out to other disciplines in the humanities, social sciences, and increasingly today, in science, as we work together to make sense of our world" (180). What he means by this, is that if students of religion can engage scientists on their research projects related to social, economic, and political concerns, they in effect combine religious wisdom with scientific knowledge that will make possible a religious shaping of society. As he puts it: "It ensures that academic knowledge developed by religious studies has a place at the table alongside other disciplines and is engaged in the solving of major problems and the formation of policy recommendations valuable for today's world" (197).

It is abundantly clear that Coward believes his analysis of "religious studies" in Canada shows it to be a religious undertaking, and that, according to him, this understanding of the nature of "religious studies" dominates the work in religious studies departments across Canada. (Whether his claims is justified, however, is another matter altogether.) It is not that Coward rejects (or those working in religious studies departments in Canada reject) the importance of gaining factual knowledge about religious traditions in their formation and historical development. However, he clearly rejects the scientific study of religion that seeks to explain religious thought and practice both at the everyday level of behavior and theoretically. The idea of seeking to obtain objective theoretical knowledge about religions (religious thought and behavior) for the sake of such knowledge alone appears totally foreign to him. Indeed, at no point in the book does he indicate that this is a central focus of any of the religious studies departments he describes. Although Coward makes oblique— but incorrectly described (98)—references to International IAHR Congresses held in Canada, he ignores entirely the fact that the IAHR is committed to the scientific study of religion for the sake of achieving empirically and theoretically objective knowledge about religions. He sees no need for comment on the fact that the CSSR is a member of the IAHR which commits it to undertaking a scientific and non-religious study of religious thought and practice. Commitment to integrity would seem to require that he recommend that the CSSR withdraw from the IAHR. That may not be forthcoming, however, for, I suspect, that opting out of membership in that organization might be seen by others as undermining the "epistemic respectability" of the CSSR (and of Canada's departments of religious studies).

Coward would do well to recognize that it is not the reductionistic sciences that hold religious studies suspect. In his *Literature Lost: Social Agendas and the Corruption of the Humanities* (1997), John Ellis pointed out that "bona fide research is often not useful for political purposes: it is too full of hedged conclusions" (142), and that whereas "analysis that has political implications is one thing . . . open advocacy breaks the implicit compact with taxpayers, degrades the classroom, abolishes the possibility of free inquiry, and denies students their academic freedom" (158). Failing to see this, as Stanley Fish has put it more recently in his *Save the World on Your Own Time* (2008), is to fail to understand their duty as academics—as members of the university; that their intellectual work is one of "passing on knowledge and conferring skills" (13) and that they should not, either collectively or individually, "advocate personal, political, moral, or any other kind of views except academic views" (19), because "civic participation is a political rather than an academic role" (67). As Fish puts it:

> If what you really want to do is preach, or organize political rallies, or work for world peace, or minister to the poor and homeless, or counsel troubled youths, [or work to improve the environment, or improve health care and end-of-life care], you should either engage in those activities after hours and on weekends, or, if part-time is not enough time, you should resign from the academy . . . and take up work that speaks directly to the problems you feel compelled to address. (81)

There is nothing particularly new in this book for, as I point out above, it draws heavily on early "histories" of the field of religious studies in Canada. I find the positive light in which Coward's account presents the academic study of religion in Canada deplorable—although in substance I believe it is very nearly the whole truth. I could, of course, be wrong in this judgment. However, it seems to me that Coward's book presents a challenge to departments of religious studies in Canada to show that they have not "stayed true" to the Smith/Grant vision for the field; to show how they either were never caught up in that vision or how they have moved their departments well beyond it. As a Canadian, I am particularly interested in seeing how that case could possibly be made.

Part Two

Evidencing the Rejection of the Modern Epistemic Tradition in the Study of Religion

7

Religion Thin and Thick

D. G. Hart's stated aim in *The University Gets Religion: Religious Studies in American Higher Education* is to provide a history of the emergence and development of "Religious Studies in American Higher Education," as the subtitle of the book puts it. It is, he claims, a history that is largely hidden (xi) and very complicated (11). It is hidden, Hart maintains, because most religion scholars—for Hart that means most current members of the AAR—prefer academic (i.e., scientific) respectability whereas the majority of scholars responsible for the creation of religious studies as a discipline were religiously motivated and therefore represent something best left undisturbed. It is complicated because that hidden history is not one of institutions. Rather, it is a story of the diverse rationales for the field provided by those teaching religion in the university. Furthermore, the ideal picture of religious studies today as a coherent academic field of critical inquiry projected by the AAR cannot be seen simply as the result of a rapprochement between science and religion, even though, as Hart puts it, the university was not hostile to religion and religion was not marginal to the ethos of the early modern American university (11). The history of the field is also hidden and complicated because of Hart's extra-historical concerns that are advertised in the very title of the book which calls to mind Merrimon Cuninggim's *The College Seeks Religion* (1947), to which it is in some sense a critical response. Hart's book, that is, carries an implicit critique of Cuninggim's argument that because of the world's need for leaders "possessed of a consciousness of religious values" (222) universities ought to be contributing to the religious growth of their students. Further, the ambiguity (or irony—whether intended or not) of the identity and contrast between "religion" and "religious studies" created by Hart's choice of title and subtitle for the book leaves the reader unclear whether his concern is really with the emergence of the academic (scientific) study of religion in the modern American university or, as he puts it in the bibliographical essay (301–11), whether it is with "the study of academic religion" (301). Hart's tendency to use the notions of "religion" and "the study of religion" interchangeably creates considerable confusion and exacerbates an already confusing "history." Moreover, one becomes at least vaguely aware early in the book that Hart is interested in undermining the ideal picture of religious studies as a coherent academic field of inquiry emerging from the rapprochement between science and religion in the early modern American university, or from the ascendance of science over religion in the late twentieth-century American university. Hart correctly points out that the university was not hostile to religion nor religion marginal to its ethos for most of its history and that this made possible the development of a form of religious studies in the university under the sway of an eventually watered-down liberal Protestantism. He fails, however, to show that this is the only form in which the academic study of religion appears in the academy in America and he largely ignores all forms but that sponsored by the AAR or conflates religious and non-religious approaches to the study of religion. Nevertheless, according to Hart, the emergence and development of religious studies in America is the result of religious (Protestant) influence on the university which, he claims, reveals three distinct phases in its history, each of which Hart gives detailed attention in this book: "The Age of the University, 1870–1925" (chapters 1–3), "The Age of the Protestant Establishment, 1925–1965" (chapters 4–7), and "The Age of the American Academy of Religion, 1965–Present" (chapters 8–10).

In Part 1 Hart deals with the role of Enlightenment Christianity in the founding of the university (chapter 1), the impact of that development on seminaries and divinity schools (chapter 2), and the emergence of a pattern in the ways of sponsoring religious learning and religious activities on college and university campuses (chapter 3). The rise of interest in the natural sciences in the late nineteenth century, claims Hart, did not lead to an outright opposition to religion but rather to its reappraisal. For the university reformers science provided a universal method of knowing to which religion itself would have to conform if it was to play a continuing role in university education. Consequently, the reformers strove to free the university from sectarian (denominational) religious control and in the process created a "neutral" religion—a common faith that could serve the broader public (44)—that was consistent with the ideals of American education before the Civil War in that it provided "the glue that held together the ideology of the research university" (30–31). According to Hart, therefore, the university reformers sought to make the study of religion a legitimate discipline that would not only be faithful to the spirit of modern science but also be "publicly responsible," that is, it would serve broad social—rather than merely narrow ecclesiastical—purposes. In the process, as Hart points out, not only were seminaries and divinity schools shaped "in the image of the university" (56), the field was prevented by these "experiments in progressive divinity" (57) from creating its criteria of evaluation with scientific neutrality (55). Hart, nevertheless, claims that the development of a divinity training program compatible with the social purposes of the university in that period "was necessary if religious studies was ever to emerge as a full-blown field within American universities" (66). Given this blurring of scientific and spiritual/ social purposes, Hart shows that the study of religion proceeded in a happenstance fashion in the first three decades of the twentieth century and he provides an overview of the variety of ways found to sponsor religious learning and religious activities on university campuses from the formation of the Religious Education Association (1904) and a host of other associations and societies to the creation of university pastorates, bible chairs, and schools of religion. And he concludes: "As much as the initial efforts to professionalize the study of religion relied upon the unstable compound of academic, inspirational, and nationalistic purposes, they did help secure a greater respectability for religion in higher education . . . [but] religious studies as an academic discipline still suffered from a confusion of rationales" (88–89), so that even as late as 1925 it was still a kind of Sunday School operation and "had yet to gain a sure foothold in American higher education" (90).

In Part 2 Hart claims that in forging an alliance between religious studies and the humanities in the 1930s the Protestant establishment created the conditions that made possible a more academic orientation in the study of religion on American university campuses (chapter 4) which, however, made it possible to find a place for the teaching of theology (chapter 5), bible (chapter 6), and church history (chapter 7) in the university. The 1930s, he admits, still lacked a clear rationale for religious studies programs and made possible establishing university pastorates, chairs in biblical instruction, and schools of religion. Solving the problem of the fragmentation of life caused by secularization, however, was seen as one way of giving religious studies a greater degree of credibility. In trying to acquaint students with questions of ultimate meaning and value, religious studies, Hart points out, aligned itself with the humanities in their concern with finding a proper understanding of Western civilization and in the process acquired the mantel of academic respectability that belonged to the humanities (104). Consequently, as Hart puts it, religious studies moved "from a ragtag discipline with little departmental structure and a mixture of academic and vocational aims to [being] a partner in the humanities' effort to revive spiritual and moral values" (111). The crisis created by the Second World War and the continuation of hostilities in the period of the Cold War, he claims, constituted a period of low academic resistance to religious concerns and therefore provided religion professors great opportunity to argue for the relevance of the Bible to modern life and for a role for theology and church history in a well-rounded university education (all three areas being heavily influenced by neo-orthodoxy) (123). Biblical scholars, he concludes, tapped into a generic civic faith that was nurtured by these conditions and permitted them wide latitude in the expression of religious conviction (149). And given that "the theologian's function was to 'vindicate man's faith that this is a meaningful world'" (122), theology was able, as he puts it, to piggyback on the "humanizing mission of the humanities" (123). Moreover, by the 1960s, claims Hart, the secular academy was discovering the importance of religion to understanding American society and that, as a consequence, church historians helped give religious studies a degree of academic credibility, although church history was never as prominent in the university as either theology or biblical studies (155). As with scholars in theology and bible, church historians also felt at liberty to express freely their religious convictions yet contributed to the advance of the cause of religious studies because, insists Hart, they "demonstrated" "that religion [while complying with the intellectual standards of the academy] could contribute meaningfully to the humanistic effort of the university" (161).

Despite these developments, however, Hart acknowledges that religion scholars did not manage to shake off religious studies' "specifically Protestant orientation . . . [given that the] shape of the curriculum in most of the new departments of religion [still] resembled that of Protestant divinity schools and seminaries" (111). "While this strategy allowed the discipline to blossom," he writes, "the field could not shake its Protestant and ministerial genesis and orientation, thus leaving religious studies vulnerable when the climate of the American universities changed" (112).

Hart's analysis of "The Age of the American Academy of Religion" in Part 3 is less straightforward and more controversial than his claims in Parts 1 and 2. In chapter eight Hart claims that the impetus behind the establishment of religious studies in the university was not simply the desire to create a new discipline to be added to the university curriculum but rather—in the effort to establish an overarching purpose for higher education—the desire in effect to establish a Christian Academy. He maintains, however, that the Protestant establishment failed in the attempt; the work of Christian academics, that is, was simply not capable of creating the kind of perspective that could make a significant impact on the university. According to Hart, therefore, Christian scholars in the university were reduced to attempting to integrate their faith and learning in religious studies as a separate field "as the one place where the importance of religious convictions for scholarly endeavor made a difference" (193). To get even this they had to give over the rest of the university to secularism, but, as Hart notes, they needed to borrow "enough of the tradition of liberal education to look academically respectable" (195) in order to gain recognition as a legitimate humanistic discipline. In talking of the limits of Enlightenment rationality, then, they made sufficient room for a hermeneutics that allowed argumentation for the voice of religion being as legitimate as the voice of any other ideological perspective (188).

A clear marker of the end of the Protestant domination of the field in religious studies, Hart then argues in chapter nine, is to be found in the influence of the *Schempp v. Abington* court decision on the field in the mid-1960s which in effect forbade taking up a religious orientation in the study of religion in public institutions (201). As Hart puts it, with the *Schempp* decision "Protestants no longer had the upper hand in articulating and propagating the nations' civil religion" (201). Indeed, he claims that the professional association for teachers of religion (the National Association of Biblical Instructors [NABI]) sought to restructure itself so as to preclude further blurring of the boundary between the church and the academy. They were willing, he claims (although dubiously in my judgment), to abandon their devotional, ethical, and cultural aims and even their religious identity for identity as academics and scholars, and consequently transformed the NABI into the AAR in an "effort to provide teaching and produce scholarship about religion compatible with the public and academic character of the university" (202). Thus, he writes, after *Schempp* "the Enlightened Christianity of liberal Protestantism could no longer command the allegiance of the university's constituency" (208). Religious studies therefore usurped the place of Protestant divinity in the university—especially so after 1970—and, according to Hart, achieved an orientation in the study of religion different from theology with closer ties to scholars in the humanities and the social sciences (220). Hart claims—but incorrectly—that in the process the AAR moved away from its former affiliation (NABI) to the American Association of Theological Schools, even though he acknowledges that the AAR saw itself as concerned not only with scholarly and professional obligations but also with the commitment of faith (202). His ambiguity on this matter is even more apparent in his discussion of religious studies as "the would-be discipline" in chapter ten where he argues that "in the wake of Protestant divinity's demise" (230) this field of study lost its mission and, therefore, any coherence it had once possessed (224). The attempt to appeal to its association with the humanities, he insists, perpetuated (at least implicitly) the Protestant heritage of the field, and the attempt by historians of religion to unify the field without recourse to religion simply failed, leaving it very much an omnibus enterprise without clear direction. Thus, he maintains that religious studies after 1970 "is very little different from older liberal Protestant efforts to salvage inspiring ideals from the sordid particulars of the various world religions" (231). Thus, Hart recognizes that even after shifting its orientation from the church to the academy religious studies was still tied to its Protestant roots, and he maintains that if it had not been, it would have been an incoherent operation. As he puts it: "Without the older centripetal forces providing spiritual guidance and adding humanistic depth, religious studies lacks a center" (231). Without that older rationale, that is, religious studies could be done by scholars in a variety of other departments and, therefore, there is no rationale for its existence as an independent department in the university. Thus, he writes: "As much as religious studies had been a covert form of Protestant studies, it lacked a legitimate place in the public intellectual space of the university. But without the coherence that Protestant divinity provided, religious studies was rudderless, a discipline in search of an identity" (222).

In his conclusion to this investigation Hart attempts to answer the question "Whither Religion in the University?" As for religious studies, he concludes that it has performed well neither religiously nor academically. As he puts it, "None of the religious detractors of the university look to the academic study of religion as a positive example of religious activity in the academy" (242) and yet it is too religious "to meet the academy's standards" (243). Hart believes the detractors failed to see how religious religious studies really is, however, and argues that the "transformation" of the NABI into the AAR was really nothing more than a "facelift" that merely hid the continuing religious impulse for religious studies behind a pretense of the adoption of a naturalistic framework for that enterprise (244). For Hart, therefore, religion and religious studies are an awkward fit in the university and he believes that both religion and the university would benefit from the exclusion of religion and religious studies. This would not, he insists, contradict commitment to academic freedom because, he claims, academic freedom is not the same as "freedom of expression" and, therefore, appropriately excludes nonacademic outlooks and approaches to the subject matter. Rather, excluding religious studies from the curriculum would prevent an unwarranted politicization of the university. "By forming religion departments," he writes, "university administrators capitulated to the pressures of mainline Protestants in the same way that they later succumbed to the Afro-Americans, women, and gays, for example" (249). It is not the task of the university to heal the afflicted or to comfort the aggrieved, nor ought it to be called upon to arbitrate disputes about democracy and social justice. As for the Christian scholar who worries about being ignored in the university, Hart reminds them that their reward is not earthly but heavenly (251).

Hart's tracing of this complex, hidden history of the emergence and development of religious studies in the modern American university is an important contribution to understanding the nature of that enterprise. His assessment in many respects overlaps those of Robert S. Shepard's *God's People in the Ivory Tower: Religion in the Early American University*, Julie Reuben's *The Making of the Modern University: Intellectual Transformation and the Marginalization of Morality*, Conrad Cherry's *Hurrying toward Zion: Universities, Divinity Schools, and American Protestantism*, among others, but he draws significantly different conclusions as to the appropriate status of religious studies in the university context. Hart strikes a singular tone, for example, in his judgment that in freeing reason from revelation the early university "unwittingly liberated science from first-order considerations regarding the structure of the universe and the nature of human knowledge" (28), and naively overlooked the possibility of tensions between science and religion with the continued growth and development of the former (32). University reformers, that is, failed to recognize that with changes in the climate of the modern research university religion and the study of religion could be made vulnerable. Along with others, Hart notes that in aligning itself educationally and institutionally with the humanities in a period of social anxiety and instability, religious studies blossomed for a brief period in the middle decades of the century, but he correctly points out that the scientific orientation of the modern research university eventually brought enormous pressures to bear on the field to adopt a naturalistic framework for its operations. Hart's judgment that the field capitulated to the pressure is open to debate; that the transformation of the NABI into the AAR was an attempt to take on the mantle of science by rejecting earlier religious motivations for the discipline is not correct. Members of NABI who brought about the change of name and orientation in NABI were concerned to "desectarianize" the enterprise because of the growing plurality of religions in the country, but they did not give up their religious intentions or affiliations. Hart is right, of course, in his claim that they also hoped to gain greater academic credibility by virtue of this "broadening" of their religious mandate, but it was in no sense (except, perhaps, on a small minority of members of the NABI) a capitulation to science. Nevertheless, Hart's judgment that the transformation of the NABI into the AAR amounted to a mere "facelift," and that it therefore still left religious studies on a shaky intellectual foundation in the university setting, is wholly on the mark. That change did not really amount to shaking off the discipline's religious (liberal Protestant) orientation. But his further conclusion that a religious studies freed from such a religious orientation is rudderless and therefore does not amount to a coherent disciplinary matrix and, consequently, is without justification for its place in the university curriculum is unsubstantiated. Hart seems here to be working with a questionable essentialist notion of "discipline" as can be seen from his judgment that "without the older centripetal forces of providing spiritual guidance and adding humanistic depth, religious studies lacks a center" (231), and his peremptory rejection of pragmatic justifications for accepting research enterprises as disciplines (222). He is no doubt right to suggest that the university may not need departments of religious studies because the scientific work carried out by scholars in those institutional structures could be (and often is) carried out in other departments, but that itself reveals the reality of a naturalistic study of religion that obviously merits a place in the modern research university regardless of the specific nature of the departmental arrangements that house it.

I introduced my analysis of Hart's historical account of the study of religion in American universities with a deliberate tone of suspicion and skepticism because it seems to me that Hart's primary concern in the book is not so much to provide the reader a narrative account of the development of a new discipline in the university as it is to argue against its presence there as detrimental to religion. Hart's argument that religion's presence there is also detrimental to the university is of no consequence in this regard because for him religious studies is simply another form of religion—a very much watered-down liberal Protestantism. (Hart does, however, see the presence of religion in the university as detrimental because, as he puts it, "The environment of the modern university has never been hospitable to religion since religions depend on divine revelation, tradition and priestly authority" [232].) Indeed, Hart's conclusion to the volume suggests that the book is but one segment of an ongoing in-house argument among religiously committed scholars as to whether or not religion can legitimately play a role in research and teaching in the modern Western university—whether there are, that is, either religious, cultural, or academic warrants for its inclusion in the university—with Hart arguing for "The Blessings of Excluding Religion" (247–51). He writes: "It may be time for faithful academics to stop trying to secure a religion-friendly university while paying deference to the academic standards of the modern university" (251). It is the deference to academic standards that undermined the place of religion in the American university and this is especially evident, he argues, in the emaciated form of religion called "religious studies."

Incurably Religious: The AAR at Fifty-Five

Introduction

In this chapter I set out to review the presidential addresses to the AAR over the past fifteen years and to assess their import for the academic credibility of the field of research widely known as "religious studies" in the modern university. This chapter is a supplement to two earlier essays on this topic. In 1997 I provided an overview of the presidential addresses to the NABI, with special attention to the addresses from 1953 to 1963, and an assessment of the first thirty such addresses to the AAR, the new name under which the members of NABI continued their work (Wiebe 1997a). As one might have expected, the presidential addresses to the NABI shows that the study of religion in American universities up to the time of renaming the association was essentially a religious/confessionalist undertaking. Religious and theological concerns were the dominant aspects of the work of the NABI and its members. Several presidents, as I pointed out in that essay, argued that the change of name of the association to the AAR marked a significant change in the way religion came to be studied and taught in American universities—that it became more objective and scientific. Claude Welch's 1970 address entitled "Identity Crisis in the Study of Religion," for example, focused attention on the inability of most members in the AAR to clearly demarcate the task of the student of religion from that of the theologian and Welch urged the Academy to align itself with objective and scientific approaches to the study of religions rather than promoting them. The only other address to do the same was William A. Clebsch's "Apple, Oranges, and Manna: Comparative Religion Revisited" in 1981. However, an analysis and assessment of the first thirty presidential addresses to the AAR revealed that, like the NABI, the newly named AAR was not primarily concerned with assuring that the study of religion would conform to the scholarly practices found in other university disciplines. I concluded the essay as follows:

> The "facts" which stare us in the face, so to speak, upon analysing the presidential addresses to the Academy are: (i) that at least twenty-five of the twenty-eight published addresses are primarily theological in character and insist that the academic student of religion concerns him- or herself not only with accounting for religions and religion, but also with religious matters; (2) that at least ten of

those addresses are vigorous apologies for keeping matters that way; and (3) that the Academy, given its choices of presidents, is still essentially a religio-theological organization . . . [that refuses] to support those who take a scientific approach to the study of religions. . . . And in this the AAR is indistinguishable from the NABI out of which it was formed. (Wiebe 1997a: 371)

The only possible conclusion one can draw from this review of the first forty years of the presidential addresses of the AAR is that the Academy was not primarily committed to achieving an academic (non-religious) understanding of religions and religion but rather was engaged in supporting the teaching of religion. But it is clear that in the transition from the NABI to the AAR the "religious instruction" delivered was no longer dominated by the liberal Protestantism that characterized the NABI. The growing multicultural and multireligious character of American society from the mid-twentieth-century broadened the "religious conversation" at AAR meetings— as successive presidents described the annual meetings of the Academy. Thus, even though what we might call the "capital-c" confessionalist approach to "understanding" religion that the Protestant-dominated NABI supported was in large part rejected by the AAR, its own support of the "enlarged religious conversation" that included other "religious voices" simply replaced the "capital-c" confessionalism with a "small-c" confessionalism by way of its assumption that all religions deserve epistemic respect.

In my 2006 essay entitled "An Eternal Return All Over Again: The Religious Conversation Continues" (Wiebe 2006b), I undertook to review the presidential addresses to the AAR in the fourth decade of its existence. Robert Orsi's presidential address, entitled "A New Beginning Again" (2004)—the last of that decade—suggests that the AAR in the new millennium will not be committed simply to a continuation of "the religious conversation" approach to the study of religion in the academy. My analysis of the subsequent addresses, however, shows nine of them as primarily interested in fostering a general, non-sectarian kind of religious study of religion that will increase the role religion plays in the college and university setting and in society at large. The majority of the addresses, that is, indicate that these presidents are interested in providing a framework for an open, capacious, and inclusivist conversation about religions and religion. They were simply not interested in including a non-religious voice in that colloquy despite their clearly stated commitment to supporting academically respectable scholarship. The following analyses of the next fifteen presidential addresses to the AAR in the new millennium, I will argue, show no deviation from the promotion of a religious study of religion directed to a formation of the individual and to a transformation of society that has dominated the mission of the AAR from its beginnings in NABI. Before proceeding to that task, I provide a brief account of each of those addresses.

What the presidents said

In the conclusion to her presidential address on "Reading the Qur'ān with Fidelity and Freedom" (2005), Professor Jane Dammen McAuliffe acknowledges that "rather than raise a field-spanning question or suggest a programmatic proposal . . . [she] seized this podium for the Qur'an" (630). Since the passing of the Civil Rights Act of 1964 and the Immigration and Naturalization Act of 1965, she points out, a new religious demography has appeared in North America (618) and the "rapid expansion of the American Muslim community has been neither uneventful nor uncontested" (618)—including misrepresentation and misuse of the Qur'ān in comparison with treatments of the Christian scriptures. Given this change in the religious demography in the United States, McAuliffe argues, Americans must recognize that the Qur'ān "is now an American scripture, part of our present and a factor in our future" (630). And given that fact, she considered it essential to let "the words of the Qur'ān, and those of the Prophet, speak with operative force to current situations and issues" (623). She also thought it important to introduce American scholars to new interpretive voices in Islam who provide a nuanced understanding of the text of the Qur'ān as it is reverentially experienced within the company of the Muslim community (621). As she puts it, in its new cultural context the Qur'ān needs protection from being confined simply to "its particular historical and cultural embeddedness" because that would undermine its universality (623). She considered this particularly important since the Qur'ān has never received the kind of attention it deserves from the leadership of the AAR.

Hans J. Hillerbrand's presidential address "On Book Burnings and Book Burners" is a reflection "on the Power (and Powerlessness) of Ideas" (2006). Such reflection is essential because book burning "is the end of discourse, the end also of the exchange of ideas. It is the deathblow to the free mind" (606). This is a phenomenon, he writes, "that demonstrably has a history of millennia and is still with us today" (602). Nor is it just a Christian story. It is, rather, the story of "whatever idea is found offensive by certain people at a certain time and place . . . [and] includes not only religious ideas but a whole set of other ideas and notions as well, be they political or lascivious" (602). It is also a phenomenon both literal and figurative—committing books to the flames and the suppression of ideas found in books (594). And he sees this response to unpalatable ideas and beliefs as rising more frequently in the field of the academic study of religion since these scholars "reflect on what is a sacred subject matter and holy ground for many" (610). In this regard he considers the US government's treatment of Tariq Ramadan—in preventing him from attending the AAR meeting—as a tragic cautionary tale about "book burners" (594).

In response to his own question as to what is to be done about this phenomenon, Hillerbrand points out that we must avoid force in the determination of beliefs (acceptance or rejection of ideas) and plead for tolerance of them—especially given that fellow AAR members, as he puts it, "have been maligned and threatened over what they [have] published" (610). "I close," he writes, "with expressing my confidence that, at a time when for a variety of reasons the censors and burners of books seem to be increasing in importance, the American Academy of Religion will forever be a beacon of the free exchange of ideas" (611).

Professor Diana L. Eck's presidential address is titled "Prospect for Pluralism: Voice and Vision in the Study of Religion" (2007). Like McAuliffe, she points out that immigration since the 1960s has brought diverse peoples from all over the world to the United States and this has "made the reality of America's religious landscape ever more complex"—greatly increasing the religious and cultural "thresholds and crossing places," as she puts it (750). And this has had a significant impact on the otherwise massive presence of Christianity in the United States and changed "the dynamic life of religious America" (751), making Americans "far more aware of the forces of violence that tear communities apart than we are of those practices and movements that knit them together" (745). This new reality, she argues, constitutes a civic, theological, and academic challenge to finding "ways of living, connecting, relating, arguing, and disagreeing in a society of differences" (745) in a way that makes possible "creating a cohesive society out of all these differences" (751).

In 1991 Eck launched the "Pluralism Project" to explore this new reality—"to study [this] new phase of a multi-religious society in the making" (751), dealing seriously with the different registers of voice of this reality in the intellectual, civic, and theological arenas. As she puts it: "Because a large number of us in AAR acknowledge that these registers of voice are all ours . . . [we must] participate in scholarly, public, and theological discussion, all three" (753). The challenge to the Academy, she maintains, is to collect the myriad of microhistories in the religious transformation of the United States in order "to assess the prospects for real pluralism in the United States today" (755), to assess the prospects for peaceful interfaith activities (757), and to understand "the currents of religious history and the making of religious life in our time" (757). As a civic issue, she insists, members of the AAR must be engaged in the public discussion of religion and the shaping of "American identity" (762). She writes: "As scholars of religions we cannot sleep through this period of turbulences that has so challenged the core values of American religious freedom" (767). In the theological register, she cautions, "we and our students must be clear in recognizing and distinguishing our theological and academic voices" (769) but nevertheless insists upon taking seriously—that is, "recognizing the importance of"—theological analysis and discussion of this new religious reality in the United States (769–70).

Professor Jeffrey Stout's presidential address—"The Folly of Secularism"—is an apology for religion in the public realm. He questions those who—like Richard Rorty, Sam Harris, or Mark Lilla, among others—fear that the contemporary resurgence of religion in the United States will give way to the formation of a theocracy (2008: 533). Contrary to interpretations of the Jeffersonian position on building a wall separating church and state that insists that religion must not have a role in the public realm, Stout writes: "But the U.S. Constitution does not say that religion must be a wholly private matter, and I see no evidence that most religious citizens ever agreed, even tacitly, to treat religion as if it were" (535). Stout argues that "at this point, the religious right in the U.S. is not predominantly theocratic [and that] its theocratic strand is miniscule but vocal" (534). Stout further maintains that democratic secularists are unlikely to achieve their objectives by democratic means and that achieving them by un-democratic means can only strengthen the position of the vocal theocrats and push the moderate religious "into the arms of the extremists" (540).

Plutocracy, Stout argues, is a far greater threat to society than the possibility of the formation of a theocracy, and secularists on their own, he maintains, will not be able to undermine "the hold of billionaires and bosses on our political institutions" (541). Past reform movements in the United States such as that of the abolition of slavery or the struggle for women's suffrage he points out, could never have been won without cooperation among religious and secular individuals and groups (543–44). He argues that "if major reform is going to happen again in the United States, it will probably happen in roughly the same way as it happened before. It will not happen *because* of secularism, but in *spite* of it" (544). He is loath therefore to advise those who are excellent in citizenship, as he puts it, to keep their religious convictions to themselves for "they created coalitions of churches, synagogues, labour unions, and schools to bring about social justice—inspired by their religious convictions" (544).

Although Professor Emilie M. Townes insists in her address—"Walking on the Rim Bones of Nothingness: Scholarship and Activism" (2009)—that the scholarship of AAR members must be "rigorous [and] relentless, and responsible" (4), she also insists that it should not be an objective enterprise (10). Rather, scholarship should reflect "the quest to combine faith and intellect in the preparation of leaders for church and world" (11). "Our country," she writes, "needs those of us trained in the religious disciplines to speak up and into and with the public realm" (11). Quite simply, Townes insists that students of religion in our modern universities must recognize that religious belief and practice is essential both for the identity formation of individuals and in nation building (11–12) and "we . . . as scholars and teachers of religion [cannot] absent ourselves from public conversations about religion" (12). It is clear, therefore, that her presidential address is actually a challenge to "rigorous" and "relentless" scholarship in religious studies, because she believes that "religious studies" scholars must be "profoundly tethered to people's lives—the fullness and the incompleteness of them" (9). As she puts it, "What I am arguing against is the kind of disinterested research tact that doesn't figure in that our work is going to have a profound impact on someone's life in some way and some how" (10).

Professor Mark Juergensmeyer's presidential address to the AAR, "Beyond Words and War: The Global Future of Religion" (2010), is an account both of "the evolution of the study of religion over recent decades" (882) and, it appears, of the role of that enterprise in creating "'a universal religiosity' based on the premise that 'there is truth in all religions'" (893). The evolution of the academic study of religion in the United States, according to Juergensmeyer, falls into four distinct periods: (1) its emergence with the formation of the NABI in 1909; (2) the rapid growth of the field after the Second World War; (3) the transformation of the NABI into the AAR in 1964; and (4) its current twenty-first-century state in which "we find ourselves in a post-modern, post-national, post-secular, [and] post-Cold War era" (885). The early mission of the NABI was directed to bringing "biblical insights into the secular world" (883) by way of scholarship "free from doctrinal bias" (883). With the rapid growth of religious studies in the immediate post–Second World War period, Juergensmeyer points out, it carved out a new niche for itself in the liberal arts curriculum by adding the study of "the diversity of the world's cultures" to its curriculum (884). In the third phase of its development, he maintains that the field was influenced by the rapid pace of globalization but that the march of the secularism of the period was challenged in the 1990s by the emergence of "a strident new form of politicized religiosity" (885). In its current form, Juergensmeyer claims that scholars in the field are uncertain of what exactly they are studying because the very category of religion "has become 'a contested term'" (886) and because they are not at all clear "exactly what the distinction [between religion and secularism] demarcates" (888).

In our time, argues Juergensmeyer, there is a need to rethink the categories in the field of religious studies that he believes will lead to a rejection of the religious/secular dichotomy. This rejection will ultimately lead to a study of the variety of "ways of looking at the world" (889) which he refers to as "epistemic worldviews" (890). The task of the student of religions will then be to analyze these structures of thought, and this, he claims will involve "a fusion of social studies with theological analysis" (891) and, therefore, a "renewed appreciation for religious perceptions of reality in the study of social phenomena" (892). This analysis, he writes,

> is theological in the sense in which it incorporates the insider-oriented attempt to understand the reality of a particular worldview, and it tries to do what the field of theology has classically done, long before the advent of the modern academic disciplines: structure the social, ethical, political, and spiritual aspects of a culture's ideas and meanings into a coherent whole. (891)

This, he explains, can lead to a "global religiosity" (893) and to a new form of religiosity— "the emergence of a spiritual and ethical dimension of global civil society—a 'global higher order' of civility—that would provide the cultural basis for international order and transnational regulations" (894).

In her AAR presidential address, "'Religion' in the Humanities and the Humanities in the University" (2011), Professor Ann Taves focuses attention "on the study of religion in the context of the modern North American university" from several points of view—"as a scholar of religion and AAR president, as a historian, and as an advocate of increased collaboration between the humanities and the sciences" (288). She presents those views in three parts and a conclusion. In Part I, she deals with religious studies as a subject-oriented discipline; in Part II, she analyzes processes of valuation; and in Part III, she presents what she sees as the advantage of multilevel analysis for understanding processes of valuation.

In Part I of her address, Taves distinguishes subject-oriented disciplines from those defined by the level of analysis at which they function. The field of religious studies is clearly subject-oriented and includes for examination "religions, traditions, the sacred, magic, the occult, superstition, folk beliefs, fetishes, and so on" (291). According to Taves, this subject matter is unstable and she rejects any attempt at stipulative definitions in this field as artificial attempts to stabilize what is essentially unstable (291).What is important about these objects, claims Taves, is that they all "embed claims about what is, or ought to be, valued" (291). Taves, therefore, thinks about the objects of interest for the student of religion as both "more or less formalized, more or less coherent systems of evaluation" involving "more pragmatic, more automatic, seemingly intuitive processes of valuation" (292) that can be approached "at many different levels of analysis" (293) both diachronically and synchronically. In Part II, Taves provides a mini-history of the field of religious studies in the United States, showing how the instability of religious subjects made possible "processes of valuation" that "shaped the formation of disciplines within the modern university" (295). At the turn of the twentieth century, she asserts, the scientific study of religion was put in the service of creating a more effective form of religious education (296) which was followed in the 1920s by promoting religious studies as an extracurricular activity (296). She then maintains that "the threefold division of the university curriculum into the natural sciences, social sciences, and the humanities took final shape during the period in which the study of religion was largely exiled from the formal curriculum," with the sciences assumed to be value-free scholarship and the humanities as the promoter of values (296–97). And she insists that the influence of the "scientifically oriented scholars of religion at the turn of the century" (297) in shaping "the development of the history of religions and religious studies as it is now institutionalized in departments of religion" (299), has not been given sufficient attention by contemporary scholars in the field (297). The import of these developments, she writes, "is that 'religion' as an object of study and the disciplines that study it were constructed at the turn of the last century based on claims about what is or ought to be the case regarding 'religion'" (301). She then concludes this mini-history of religious studies with the claim that the process of creating this discipline "was shot through with valuations" because the categories used were "sites of contestation" among scholars from different disciplinary backgrounds (301–02). She concludes this section of her address with the observation that "most of us have made our careers challenging the valuations of our forebears and reclaiming what they rejected for the study of religions" (302). In Part III, Taves approaches the question of the nature of the academic study of religion from her point of view as a cognitive scientist. She understands this view to involve a rejection of what she refers to as the teleology of the Victorian era science of religion which assumed that primitive religious thought "could and should be superseded by civilized modes of thought" (304). Given that much of human thought is intuitive, she maintains, it is not possible to make sense of processes of valuation without understanding human mental processes, and that human valuations not only are biological but also have a cultural dimension and that this is essential if the contemporary student of religion is to transcend the earlier teleological mode of religious studies. This, it appears, permits us to answer in the affirmative the question Taves raises at the end of Part II: "Can [the academic study of religion] be studied like other more ordinary things"? (303). As she puts it in the conclusion: "Opening ourselves to the interplay between biology and culture at multiple levels has the potential not only to enrich the study of religion but also to build bridges between the sciences and the humanities in ways that enrich the university as a whole" (308).

In "Empire and the Study of Religion" (2012) Professor Kwok Pui-Lan argues that the institutional development of religious studies from 1600 to 1800, and its arrival in the United States early in the twentieth century, has been "shaped by the social and political forces of Empire in Europe and the United States, and by the cultural imaginary of empire" (285). She also maintains that "racism shaped the classification of religion in this new discipline in the modern university" (291). She writes: "The study of religion in U.S. colleges and universities began in the early twentieth century, shortly after the Spanish-American War [and] since then, the fortune of the discipline has been much linked to American wars and foreign interests." Pui-Lan provides virtually no evidence to support these claims. Her claim that scholars in this field "have served such imperial interests" and that if things don't change, the field of religious studies "risks becoming irrelevant" (286) is ludicrous. This is not surprising given that the goal she has in mind for the academic study of religion is to offer some suggestions for the field to change so that it can be a positive force against empire and for human flourishing (287). The objective of the study of religion and religions for Pui-Lan is not that of achieving explanatory knowledge about religion and religions but rather to change the world in order to assist greater human flourishing. She writes: "What our world desperately needs are communicators, people who have a deep knowledge of the subject and can speak to the lawyers, doctors, social policy makers, government officials, and ordinary people on the street about why religion matters" (296–297). She fears that the AAR will continue to be gripped in the cultural imaginary of empire without possible escape (294). She therefore closes her address with the following "charge" to the members of the AAR: "So go back to your institution and talk about why religion matters and how you have been changed by studying religion. But most important of all, share your dream about how the field might look like in the future. Let the conversation begin" (297–98).

The essential "message" in Professor Otto Maduro's presidential address on "Migrants' Religions under Imperial Duress" (sub-titled, "Reflections on Epistemology, Ethics, and Politics in the Study of the Religious 'Stranger'" [2013]) is that all "knowledge, including research on religions is . . . always both an ethical and a political task" (40). Invoking Weber he maintains that "it would appear as if the question of ethics in relation to research on religions in our contemporary world could hardly be disentangled from the serious epistemological and political dimensions of our lives" (43). According to him, students of religion wield "epistemological power" and that they are therefore obligated to take political action to protect undocumented workers in the United States (44). To study religion objectively, simply for the sake of knowledge about religions and religion is, for Maduro, to devalue the plight of "the undocumented." He writes:

> Scientific knowledge in general—and religious studies in particular—are nowadays carried out in a global environment where concern and compassion toward the vulnerable, the weak, and the victims of violence and marginalization are increasingly devalued as impractical weakness, whereas indifference, callousness, and insensitivity in their regard seem to become the new objectivity, the new scientificity, the new normalcy—including in religious discourse and public policy. (35)

Maduro then, like Pui-Lan, issues a call to scholars of religion "to hear the cry of the oppressed and to respond to that cry, with our power, our ethical responsibility, and our role in the production and dissemination of knowledge, in any and all forms within our reach" (46).

Much of Professor John L. Esposito's presidential address "On the Public Engagement of Religion" (2014) is focused on "the impact of the globalization of communications and global conflicts on the development of Islamic studies" and "on attitudes and behaviors toward Islam—and Muslims" (293). This is of particular importance, he points out, because the Iranian Revolution created considerable fear of Islamic fundamentalism and of the export of violence beyond the borders of Iran. Early on, he points out, Islam was seen as a political and civilizational threat but is now seen as a demographic threat as spelled out in the work of scholars like Bernard Lewis and Samuel Huntington. Esposito, however, also delivers a political message in his address by urging scholars of religion to take on the task of the public intellectual, despite having been warned by friends that he should not get involved in issues of "the public understanding of religion" (304–05). He writes: "Our scholarship of religion, all religions, and we as scholars have a special responsibility as scholars and citizens, and that's why I think that the public understanding of religion is not just something that happens out there" (304). Like Hillerbrand, he notes that the AAR has moved in this direction in its defense of Tariq Ramadan against the government's refusal to allow him to address the AAR. Thus, Esposito encourages religious studies scholars "to speak out publicly at conferences, at workshops run by domestic and international organizations, to speak to governments, NGOs, religious and civic organizations, to participate in media, to serve as expert witnesses" (305). In effect, he urges scholars of religion to become a new clerisy for the nation, writing, "whatever side we want to take, we need to be bringing to bear whatever we believe are principles that we know about the role of religion, politics, civil liberties, attitudes toward torture, and so on. *We are the ones needed to lead the way*" (306, emphasis added).

Professor Lauri Zoloth takes Otto Marduro's presidential address as model for her own AAR address entitled "Interrupting Your Life: An Ethic for the Coming Storm" (2016). With special focus on his call for action based on scriptural principles, she writes: "Scripture calls us to live as if at any moment we could be surprised, awed, ready to rise to action and to grace, ready to welcome the Messiah, ready to appear to one another, in public, because our interruption could alter what we have come to think of as 'the course of history'" (12). She sees the primary responsibility of religious studies scholars to be moral agents and moral citizens who are ready to have their scholarship be preempted by "the deep praxis of interruption," and she acknowledges that engagement in such interruption is to be engaged in doing theology (7). That is, scholars of religion must recognize that their work is "to know the story of how people struggled, spoke, wrote, and heard of the question, how are we, how am I, to live a good life? Now, how ought I to live when the world is burning?" (12). She concludes her address as follows: "Letting the danger, the power, and the endless mercy of religion be excellently told is the task of the scholar of religion. To teach religion excellently is to engage in 'the public examination of things', the task of the scholar since Socrates spoke truth to his Academy" (15).

In thinking of a theme for the AAR meeting in his presidential year Professor Thomas Tweed chose to focus his attention on the possibility of overcoming the obvious tensions among the diversity of scholars within the "Big Tent" of the AAR. As he puts it in "Valuing the Study of Religion: Improving Difficult Dialogues Within and Beyond the AAR's 'Big Tent'" (2016), he chose to focus on "our divisive internal AAR debates between humanistic and scientific approaches between scholarship alone or advocacy too, and most of all, between theology and religious studies" (288). Tweed does not consider it possible that these diverse approaches are mutually exclusive; they are just scholars "talking past each other." And he sets out to examine "the underlying values that ground our approaches to the study of religion" (288). His modus operandi was to examine how the study of religion is valued and devalued in the public arena and how scholars enact values in their professional work. After examining sixteen official AAR documents about its objectives and its procedures for attaining them, he concludes that AAR members "use value language to make normative judgments" and he maintains that "the beliefs and aspirations that ground AAR members' scholarly values and normative judgments might be religious or secular" (291). It must be recognized, he insists, that value commitments "also informed efforts to introduce the academic study of religion into private and public universities in the United States" (293) with some scholars seeking to preserve a place for the normative in the study of religion while others espoused a Weberian value neutrality as the guiding principle for the study of religious phenomena. The debates between scholars holding these positions, he argues, continued well into the 1980s after the change of name of the AAR in 1964, "when the mode of 'scientific objectivity' emerged more prominently again and some departments suggested that the study of religion should be impartial while others argued for value talk, even theology, in religious studies departments" (293–94). He admits that these debates still persist, and that some scholars insist that students of religion should be "engaged in constructive religious reflection" (294).

Tweed is aware that others in the field maintain that the study of religion in modern research universities ought to be committed wholly to seeking objective knowledge about religious thought and behavior. But he also claims that commitment to the value of knowledge for the sake of knowledge alone is a value affirmation in the same sense as are religious, moral, or political values within the field that inspire activism as an objective beyond that of seeking knowledge about religious phenomena (296). And because of this, he argues that it becomes possible to "productively reframe internal AAR debates about theology and religious studies [as well as] . . . usefully refine our defenses of religion's role in higher education" (296). He does seem to recognize, however, that AAR members work in radically different academic environments in which both modes of studying religion would not or could not be countenanced (298). He writes: "Wherever we're situated in our home institutions, and however that location shapes the conversations there, in this learned society we are in a slightly different and more inclusive setting. This setting requires something a bit different from us, I suggest, if we want to improve our conversation in the AAR" (298). In order to achieve that, he continues, we "need to commit ourselves to the two-step process of articulating and appraising the value language in which we formulate our normative judgments about what scholars ought to do" (298). But this fails to recognize the peculiar nature of the cultural value of knowledge for the sake of knowledge alone that characterizes the work of those committed to the scientific study of religion in the modern research university—an institution purpose-designed to support that goal. Whether such study can enrich students or society by answering the big questions of life, or create "the conditions for democratic citizenship, social justice, and peace building" (305), as Tweed puts it, goes beyond anything the scientific student of religion has the justification for claiming (305). However, Tweed himself confesses that he engages in activities in his classroom that might produce "that personal transformation which . . . contributes to these collective goods," with the intimation that other students of religion should do likewise. Thus, Tweed, like Jurgensmeyer, sees the AAR—that is, the collective body of religious studies scholars in that "Big Tent"—as the new clerisy for modern society (307).

This account of Professor Serene Jones's presidential address on "Revolutionary Love" (2016) is based on the video of it provided at vimeo.com.[1] Jones informs her audience that her concerns are not with the study specifically of religion but with the values scholars ought to be committed to generally at this specific time in "our" history, which she characterizes as being in the middle of a revolution. The value she considers of greatest importance is that of "revolutionary love," which she understands to be a social force that recognizes (1) that "we" are all interdependent; (2) that all of us on this planet are of equal value; and (3) that truth-telling is of the utmost importance.

Referring to the work of Edward Said and James Baldwin, among others, she argues that scholars in the AAR have a moral responsibility to speak Truth to Power for the sake of a better future, especially so since the election of Donald Trump as president of the United States. She sees the religious studies classroom—and the AAR—as "sacred sites"; like Kwok Pui-Lan, she urges scholars of religion to be both pastoral and prophetic in order, as she puts it, to "armour" students against the empire in which they will work and live; to teach them how to criticize the lies and imagine new truths that will permit genuine caring for the vulnerable members of our communities. And religion, Jones argues, is an important resource for fulfilling this responsibility in the context of an emerging fascist state, as she describes the United States under Trump. The study and teaching of religion in the modern university, therefore, must be focused on the formation of students as moral agents and cannot be limited simply to having them learn about religions or search for explanations of religious phenomena. That kind of objectivity and neutrality, she maintains, amounts to an intellectual isolationism which is indistinguishable from moral cowardice.

Professor Eddie Glaude's address to the AAR—"Religion and the Most Vulnerable" (2018)—like Jones's address, was only available on audio at the time of writing this chapter.[2] Drawing on the thought of scholars like Edward Said, Glaude insists that the study of religion in the modern university must not be engaged in an objective study of religious phenomena committed only to gaining knowledge about and explanatory understanding of religions and religion. Scholars of religion must resist being pressured—forced—to function within a framework of neutrality characteristic of the other disciplines in the university. Limited to epistemic objectives and concerns about expertise and specialization within the discipline, he insists, amounts to conformity and moral cowardice. The study of religion, that is, must be more than an academic undertaking. Inspired by such nineteenth-century figures as Mathew Arnold and Thomas Henry Huxley, Glaude encourages scholars of religion, and especially members of the AAR, to recognize that their primary task is to provide a liberal education that will produce students who will work in the service of others. What this means for Glaude is that scholars in the AAR should not be producing scholars or scientists but public intellectuals like himself who will become engaged in radical social and political causes on behalf of the poor. They, and the AAR, must be committed to enhancing the public understanding of religion and its value in creating a just society. So formed by their education, they will be enabled to contribute to the transformation of society rather than sitting on the sidelines.

Democracy has never been fully achieved, claims Glaude, and it is in a fragile state in this age of Trump. The academic study of religion in modern universities, and the AAR, Glaude admonishes his audience, should be resources for democratic society, as he puts it, by producing a different kind of scholar for the particular kind of work needed "to accomplish democracy all over again."

Professor David Gushee was already aware in 2016 that his presidential address to the AAR was likely to attract a good deal of criticism from members of the Academy who lodged complaints against the incursion of religiosity into the Academy in Serene Jones's presidential address on "Revolutionary Love."[3] He acknowledged in that posting that he shared the "religious vision" expressed in the plenary sessions in the 2016 meeting of the Academy and that he felt "the personal need for a 'thick,' resistant, religious vision after the shock of the Trump election." Gushee also acknowledged that there were "AAR constituents" who did not feel "included or comfortable" given Jones's view of the work of the Academy in her address but he does not respond to the reasons provided for the lack of "comfort," namely, the concern over "what the boundaries of the academy study [*sic*] of religion are or should be." In his own presidential address—"In the Ruins of White Evangelicalism: Interpreting a Compromised White Christian Tradition through the Witness of African-American Literature"—however, he acknowledges that concern over the election of an "evangelical" as the president of the AAR reflects less a concern about his personal religious commitments than a concern over demarcating "confessional" (religious and/or political) objectives for the field from objectives appropriate in the context of the modern research university.

"As a Christian ethicist who spent nearly 40 years of . . . [his] life and nine-tenths of [his] professional career within the white evangelical subculture," he writes, "I cannot help but engage with this moral surrender to Donald Trump. There is every evidence that this is a matter of wide interest . . . , and to address it here fits with *my* AAR theme of religious studies in public" (emphasis added). And with that said, Gushee takes up the theme of "evangelicals and racism" and, more broadly, "white American Christian racism" which he does by reading "African-American fictional works as authoritative sources" with "revelatory power" on this theme and delving into black history, theology, and ethics. He presents a moving description and powerful critique of "white Christian racism" and the fraudulence in much of white Christianity that has in the present sacrificed any credibility it might still have retained "on the altar of Donald Trump." Until the recent past, Gushee asserts, he has not sufficiently focused his attention on the deep injustice of this racism and he confesses his conviction of this as sin and sees his address as constituting, in part, his repentance of it.

The question that needs raising here is not whether Gushee's critique of "white Christian racism" or of Trump's brand of politics is on the mark or not, or whether the majority of the members of the AAR agree with it or not. The question is whether the AAR appropriately reflects what the "academic" study of religion (in the context of the modern research university) should be by allowing its presidents to choose personal religious and political themes for discussion by those who have been hired to teach "religious studies" in that context. Gushee understands that not all members of the AAR will likely be interested in his theme of "faith community." Thus he writes: "That's fine. Every AAR presidential address enters the *conversation* in our scholarly Tower of Babel as just one strange tongue among others. Forty-five minutes from now my strange tongue will cease and it will be someone else's turn." This comment not only shows the appropriateness of the Tower of Babel imagery for what the AAR is all about but also tarnishes the epistemic credibility of those universities that have approved "religious studies" programs as legitimate academic (scientific) enterprises.

Analysis and comment

In my first essay on the presidential addresses to the AAR (1997) my aim was to see whether the change in name to AAR actually involved a change in the way religion would be studied and taught in US colleges and universities, as many scholars in the field had anticipated. The change of name clearly signaled the demise of the traditional Protestant—"capital-c" confessional—dominance of the field during NABI's oversight of religious studies scholarship—a significant step in the development of a more objective approach to the study of religious phenomena but not the adoption of non-religious methodologies for the field. The AAR continued, even expanded, the religious agenda of the NABI within the framework of what might be called a religio-humanistic methodology amounting to a kind of "small-c" confessionalism that dominated the field in its first thirty years. My analysis of the next decade of presidential addresses clearly undermined Robert Orsi's claim that the AAR had approved a radical change of orientation and the adoption of new goals (Orsi 2004). The elected leadership of the AAR has made it abundantly clear that the Academy was still committed to ensuring that the religious voice would be heard in US colleges and university classrooms—precisely the aim and objective of the NABI. If my accounts of the last fifteen presidential addresses to the AAR accurately represent the positions espoused by these leaders of the Academy, it should be clear that the AAR's primary concerns are with ensuring that religious voices are heard both in the academy and in society at large, although at least one of the presidents, Taves, makes an attempt at encouraging the Academy to take the scientific study of religion seriously.

I have found several key themes on display in my reading of these presidential addresses: (1) Religious studies must make room for the "religious other" in American society, provide a public understanding of religion, and ensure a role for religion in the public realm; (2) Religious studies must provide students a liberal religious education and inspire them to become public intellectuals who bring religious values to bear on public life in their communities; and (3) Religious studies must acknowledge the value-laden character of the academic study of religion and therefore make clear the value of the humanities to its mission.

A public understanding of the social value of religion

Professors McAuliffe, Eck, Jurgensmeyer, and Esposito all attempt to make a case for recognizing the value of religions other than Christianity in the United States since the mid-twentieth century. Professors Esposito and McAuliffe focus attention on the importance of recognizing that Islam is neither a political nor a civilizational threat to America. McAuliffe, for example, argues that the Qur'ān needs protection from simply being confined to the particularities of its history and that it should be seen as another sacred scripture in America, and Esposito maintains that students of religion must include Islam in the task of providing a public understanding of religion. Professor Eck pushes the boundaries of the AAR, and American Society generally, in pushing for a political recognition of a genuine religious pluralism in the shaping of an American identity and Professor Jurgensmeyer insists that students of religion must provide a renewed appreciation for religious perceptions of reality, even if that involves the fusion of theology with social studies. And in doing so, he claims, religious studies will contribute to the creation of a universal religiosity that can unify society. As I noted in my account of Jurgensmeyer, scholars of the AAR must become the new clerisy to guide the human race into the future.

Religious studies scholars as public intellectuals

Professors Stout, Townes, Pui-Lan, Maduro, Zoloth, Jones, Glaude, and, at least indirectly, Gushee argue that religious studies ought to be involved in the making of public intellectuals who will be involved, as Townes puts it, in nation building. This is also a call for a new clerisy for America—namely, the religious intellectual. Rather than study religion objectively, she argues that religious studies must prepare leaders for the church and the world who will champion the role of religion in the shaping of the American Identity. In similar fashion, Professor Stout argues that social justice is not likely to be achieved if religious people in society keep their religious convictions to themselves. Professor Pui-Lan maintains that religious studies in the United States has been linked to American wars and foreign interests and that its epistemic and scientific objectives must be subordinated to the moral end of assisting greater human flourishing. Only with such a change, she insists, can the AAR free itself from the tendrils of empire. Professor Jones makes a similar recommendation to the AAR in suggesting that its mission ought not to be that of supporting an objective and neutral study of religion but rather the formation of students who will take seriously their moral obligations as citizens and make a positive contribution to society. Professors Maduro, Zoloth, Glaude, and, indirectly Gushee, insist that religious studies must recognize that epistemology cannot be separated from ethics and politics (Maduro) especially in the study of religion and religions (Glaude) and that the study of religion in the university cannot, and must not, be like other disciplines in the university. They all insist that the AAR must support the goal of training students of religion to be moral agents in the course of history. To support a purely objective study of religion, as Maduro puts it, is to be indifferent and callous with respect to the downtrodden in society. Consequently, for the AAR not to preempt the objective and scientific study of religion will amount to moral cowardice.

The value-laden character of religious studies and the humanities

Professors Tweed and Taves also focus their attention on value and valuation in religious studies but their understanding of this issue is not simply motivated by the condition of their vulnerable fellow citizens under Trump's "care." Hillerbrand, Tweed, and especially Taves seem ready to encourage the AAR to take a scientific study of religion seriously; that is, they appear more sympathetic to the notion of an objective and explanatory study of religion. Hillerbrand's concern about the use of force (censorship of any kind) rather than argument and evidence in the determination of knowledge claims about religion and religions grounds his advice to the AAR leadership that it must ever keep the Academy "a beacon of the free exchange of ideas." There is no clear indication, however, that his advice implies that religious studies in the context of the modern university must be scientific and objective.

Unlike Hillerbrand, however, Taves does focus attention on the twentieth-century view of science—and the science of religion in particular—as being a value-free enterprise in contrast to the widely held view of the humanities as the promoter of values. She argues that the Victorian era "science of religion," with its assumption that religious thought could and should be superseded by a civilized mode of thought, reveals that that enterprise was not objective or purely scientific but rather directed at achieving a particular goal. Taves seems to argue that such teleology still infects the academic study of religion but she, nevertheless, suggests that a cognitive science approach to explaining religion is possible and need not assume that an unbridgeable gulf exists between it and humanistic studies of religion. Such a dual approach to understanding religion, she suggests, can enrich not only the study of religion but also the university as a whole.

Professor Tweed also argues that the claim of an unbridgeable chasm between theology and religious studies—that is, between the sciences and the humanities— is indefensible because each of these enterprises rests on underlying values—not on theology or on the humanities alone. For him, the scientific value of seeking knowledge for the sake of knowledge alone is still a value affirmation and in this sense places the scientific enterprise on the same track as theology and the humanities. Recognizing this, he insists, will provide a sound foundation for cooperation between the sciences and the humanities (theology and religion) in religious studies departments.

Conclusion

If the views expressed in the annual presidential addresses to the AAR are indicative of the character of the academic study of religion in American colleges and universities, it is clear that the Academy's primary objectives are religious. The aims and objectives of the overwhelming majority of the Academy's presidents from the inception of the

Academy to the present have been limited to three: (1) The expansion of appreciation for diverse forms of religion and spirituality both in the classroom and in society at large, (2) Constructing an apology for, and contribution of, religion in the public realm, and (3) The non-denominational and interreligious formation of students as preparation for engaging in religio-political action in the public realm. None of the fifteen addresses reviewed here have given serious consideration to the objective of understanding and the explanation of religion of the type sought for the natural and social phenomena studied by every other discipline in the context of the modern research university. And this observation also applies to the analyses of the preceding forty AAR presidential addresses as I noted in my introduction to this chapter. Given this history of the AAR presidential addresses, I think it reasonable not to anticipate any significant changes in its aims and programs in the foreseeable future. The only possible answer to the question raised in the title of this chapter, therefore, is "Yes,"; the AAR, the largest professional association of college and university teachers and professors of "religious studies," is incurably religious and is involved in creating a new form of religiosity which might appropriately be called, to borrow a phrase from Robert Michaelson's 1972 AAR Presidential Address—"The Engaged Observer: Portrait of a Professor of Religion" (1973)—"classroom religion."

American Influence on the Shape of Things to Come

Introduction

I consider it a great honor to address the Korean Association for the Study of Religion on the future of "Religious Studies"—*Religionswissenschaft*—in the twenty-first century, with special focus on the trends in the discipline in the United States of America.

The overall theme for this conference is sweeping, to say the least, and tempts one to play the role of prophet or seer predicting the shape of the discipline in the twenty-first century. Although we may be able to sense developments that are likely to occur, reliable predictions about the field as a whole are beyond our capacity. Speculation may not be entirely without merit, however, for trying to read the implications of current trends in the field may provide the impetus to seek greater clarity and precision in a discipline that has since its emergence been ambiguously (and therefore problematically) related to its object of interest. With that in mind, I shall argue here that the *modern* study of religion, shaped by the likes of Friedrich Max Müller, Cornelis P. Tiele and others in the latter part of the nineteenth century, and clearly represented by the mandate of the IAHR, stands in jeopardy; to put the matter more provocatively, a decline in the global health of the discipline has already occurred and will continue because of the phenomenal growth of the study of religion in the American context since the Second World War, and particularly with the formidable power of the AAR.

At one level such a thesis may appear preposterous given the obvious strengths of the field in the United States. For there exist today more than 1,200 departments of religious studies, more than a score of societies and associations devoted to research and scholarship on religion and religions, and well over 15,000 scholars in American colleges and universities who count themselves as students of religion in some sense or other. With this vast increase in persons engaged in the field since the Second World War, there has been a concomitant increase in the volume of research, coupled with an expansion of the field's boundaries to include non-Western religious traditions. With increased numbers has come the development of specializations that have enriched the field by encouraging a depth of knowledge in a wide range of religious issues and themes. As well, the concern for academic legitimation within the university community has actually stimulated growth in methodological reflection about the field. Yet despite these achievements, I shall contend that "the academic study of religion" in the United States has advanced little in its self-definition beyond that which characterized it during the early stages of the modern research university. And it is the precise disparity between its tremendous growth in size, wealth, and power and its failure to re-conceive the field in the new setting of the research university that ought to promote serious thought to its future impact on the field globally. In order to justify my stance, of course, it will be necessary to provide a brief sketch of the history of the emergence and development of religious studies in the United States before describing the present state of affairs in the field as well as providing an analysis of its likely development and impact. It will also be useful to provide here a concise, unambiguous account of what I understand by the phrase "religious studies" as a *modern* academic enterprise.

The modern study of religion

Unfortunately, many scholars in the field use the phrase "religious studies" interchangeably—but uncritically so—with such phrases as "the academic study of religion" and "the scholarly study of religion." It is used, that is, to designate any and every approach to the study of religion found in post-secondary institutions of education, including not only colleges and universities but also university-affiliated divinity schools and schools of religion. "Religious studies" in this usage, therefore, refers indiscriminately to a variety of approaches to "understanding" religion: from reductionistic biological, psychological, and social-scientific studies, on the one hand, to implicitly religious styles of history and phenomenology of religion and explicitly confessional theologies of religion on the other. It ought to be clear, however, that no coherent theoretical understanding of religion can possibly emerge from a "religious studies" addressing so disparate a collection of enterprises. And although I will be using the terms "religious studies" and "the academic study of religion" interchangeably, it will not be in the uncritical descriptive sense above, but rather in a structural sense, applying to the style of thought that properly characterizes the modern research university.[1]

As a point of departure, I understand the enterprise of religious studies to be a *modern* phenomenon associated with the emergence of a new mode of thought in the overhaul of the notion of reason in seventeenth- and eighteenth-century Europe. As such it is clearly distinguishable from the traditional religious and theological approaches of the time. This period in European history, as Hoopes points out, "is marked by the gradual dissociation of knowledge and virtue as accepted and indivisible elements in the ideal structure of human reason, [which constitutes] a shift from the tradition of *right reason* to the new tradition of *scientific reasoning*" (Hoopes 1962: 161; emphasis added). "Right reason," that is, is derived not from the intellect alone but also from virtue and involves both thinking and doing; it "affirms that what a man knows depends upon what, as a moral being, he chooses to make of himself" (Hoopes 1962: 5).

It should be noted that the new "reason," which is nothing more "than a proximate means of rational discovery or 'a nonmoral' instrument of inquiry" (Hoopes 1962: 5) is the equivalent of today's objective "reasoning." And it is precisely this nonmoral sense of reason,[2] that constitutes the foundation of science as an objective, neutral, universalistic discourse about the world, both natural and social, because it sets out to diminish the social, political, and cultural constraints upon the thinker.[3] Advocating "knowledge for the sake of knowledge alone," this new cultural value operates with what Ernest Gellner calls "diplomatic immunity" from other cultural values (1973). Thus, religious studies, as a modern enterprise, is a purely cognitive/epistemic undertaking—a nonmoral instrument of inquiry about religious phenomena—that aims to provide explanatory (theoretical) knowledge of religion and religions rather than "wisdom" or spiritual enrichment.[4] The goal of the modern study of religion, that is, ought to be the establishing of a body of tested propositions concerning religious behavior—propositions that are neither temporally nor culturally peculiar—thereby confirming "religious studies" as part of an interdisciplinary quest for a common, underlying theory of human behavior. I want to point out, moreover, although I am not able to develop the claim here, that it is the medieval university, despite its religious origins, that first provided an institutional location within which such a new intellectual inquiry could be carried out without hindrance; for a peculiar set of legal developments established them as autonomous corporate entities and, therefore, as intellectual "neutral zones" (Huff 1993: 203, 336). This is not to deny that the medieval and early modern universities were primarily religious institutions concerned with the spiritual edification of those who studied in them. Their raison d'être was the formation and cultivation of character and the preparation of students for a productive and meaningful life. By the mid-nineteenth century, however, the growth of science and the modernization of society worked to transform the traditional, religiously founded college into the modern research university (particularly in the United States [Reuben 1996]), focused primarily on the dissemination of knowledge and the promotion of the requisite skills involved in obtaining knowledge. In such an academic context it is the *modern* study of religion alone that can be recognized as "academic."[5] And as the first institutional structure of its kind established to encourage such an objective and religiously neutral study of religions, the IAHR provided and still provides a forum for the dissemination of the results of such research.[6]

Religious studies in America: A brief history

"Religious studies" as a modern enterprise played no part in the curriculum of US colleges in the colonial period. Inspired by a medieval philosophy of education, religion virtually dominated student life, and consequently effectively determined the structure of higher education in the colonial period. New philosophies of education emerged in the nineteenth century, however, because of increasing interest in the natural sciences, which resulted in the removal of biblical and theological scholarship from college curricula to separate but college-affiliated seminaries. Although this transformed post-secondary education, it did not lead to the secularization of the antebellum college, for the integrating ideal of the unity of knowledge—that is, the belief that all knowledge is knowledge of God[7]—was retained (even though significantly modified [Reuben 1996]). Talk of "religious studies" in the sense I am using that notion here, therefore, could not have been an element of the college curriculum until the second half of the nineteenth century, when interest in specialization and professionalization, created by the continued growth of scientific knowledge, brought about a radical transformation of American higher education (Cherry 1992). This further segregated science from religion by excluding theological questions and questions of meaning from the framework of scientific inquiry (Kemeny 1998). And even with this transformation of the college into the early modern research university, the concern for achieving scientific truth (knowledge) in ever new fields of learning did not in fact bring about a wholesale secularization of religious studies in the research universities that succeeded them. As historians are quick to point out, the "university reformers"—the designation used for those who brought about this transformation in higher education in America—even though they rejected sectarianism, still believed in the ultimate harmony of scientific with religious truth, expecting that science would eventually establish that harmony as factual. Thus the "reformers" did not entirely renounce the original vision and aim of the colleges they transformed, but they nevertheless created a new educational context, an environment within which the genuinely scientific study of religion (*Religionswissenschaft*) could emerge. Whether such a study of religion did in fact emerge in that context, however, is open to debate.

Robert S. Shepard, in *God's People in the Ivory Tower: Religion in the Early American University* points out that the nineteenth-century American university provided "an academic structure for the scholarly study of religion" (Shepard 1991: 42), but in no way does he suggest that it produced a genuine science of religion. A "brief flirtation with the science of religion" (Shepard 1991: 18) at Cornell University, he notes, greatly influenced Morris Jastrow of the University of Pennsylvania to take up a scientific approach, but he acknowledges that this did not lead to the establishment of a discipline comparable to that founded by European scholars. Indeed, Shepard points out that the primary focus of students of religion in this period was the Christian faith, and he shows that they were as much concerned with the dissemination of religious knowledge as with obtaining knowledge about religion. And while admitting that this Protestant-inspired "Christian *Religionswissenschaft*" helped to raise the level of scholarship with respect to religion (in that it pushed the discourse about religion beyond ecclesiastical boundaries), he clearly stresses the "irregularity and fragility of the American university's interests in the scientific study of religion" (Shepard 1991: 9).

Julie Reuben comes to roughly the same conclusion in her book *The Making of the Modern University: Intellectual Transformation and the Marginalization of Morality*. In the final analysis, the study of religion encouraged in this new educational context was not so much secular and scientific as "desectarianized": its creation was motivated as much by religion as by science. The "scientific study of religion" for the university reformers, that is, arose naturally from their belief in the ultimate harmony between scientific and religious truth that would issue in scientifically sound religious knowledge. Interestingly, however, Reuben accounts for the decline in the fortunes of the scientific study of religion at the end of the second decade of the twentieth century in terms of the recognition by university leaders that "[the] academic study of religion was not inherently religious" (Reuben 1996: 142). She rightly notes that the number of religious studies programs in American colleges and universities grew rapidly after the Second World War but, as I shall point out below, this was not the result of a renewed interest in the non-religious study of religion. For in the intervening period it is clear that whatever the scientific influence of European developments in the field (Kitagawa 1959, 1983; Sharpe 1986a [1975]), the study of religion in America succumbed to religion, which did little to support the scientific study of religion in the academic setting.

The immediate postwar period was an age of anxiety in which university leaders in America sought ways to engage the university in the battle against fascism, communism, and the threat of a nuclear arms race, and religion was an obvious resource for the task (2001). This was an era that witnessed "a national turn to religion," as Conrad Cherry puts it (Cherry 1995: 104), and the implications of that national mood for the study of religion in the university are clearly exhibited in Merrimon Cunninggim's book *The University Needs Religion* (1947). As in the past, students of religion aligned themselves with the humanists, sharing their concerns for spirituality, morality, and the humanizing of society. And, as D. G. Hart points out (1999), this was clearly a religious revival and not an intellectual reformation, and it contributed to a reappropriation of the mainline Protestant rationale for the study of religion invoked from the 1870s to the 1920s by the university reformers (2001). The postwar leaders, as Hart indicates, "strikingly repudiated the conception of religion and higher education forged by the educational reformers who [had] led the way in creating the research university" (D. G. Hart 1999: 130). This spurred a successful theological renaissance in the university, which, in the short run, benefited the growth of "the study of religion" in American colleges and universities by appropriating humanistic values and by encouraging the creation of a "religio-scientific" study of religion (Kitagawa 1959, 1983; Capps 1995) that gave less attention to what Hart calls the "sturdier scholarly ideals" (D. G. Hart 1999: 132) of *Religionswissenschaft* than it did to the religious and moral quest. Hart writes: "From 1945 until 1970 religious studies established not only its educational but also its institutional identity as a partner with the humanities. While this strategy allowed the discipline to blossom, the field could not shake its Protestant and ministerial genesis and orientation" (D. G. Hart 1999: 112). The motive for the study of religion in this period, therefore, was primarily religious; and religion scholars, for the most part, were still playing the role of campus minister (D. G. Hart 1999: 133). This is nowhere clearer than in President Nathan Pusey's campaign to restore religion at Harvard; an act which, though "liberal and pluralistic in approach to the subject," was intended to resurrect Harvard's education for Christian ministry, understood more expansively as "unlimited in membership by formal training or ecclesiastical garb" (R. N. Smith 1986: 203, 205). I suggest there is irony in the title of Hart's analysis—*The University Gets Religion*: scholars claimed to be seeking to establish a respectable academic approach to the study of religion, but the academy merely got religion. This is an irony that seems to have escaped Hart's attention in his earlier analysis of the nature of the study of religion represented by the AAR (D. G. Hart 1992).

Religious studies in America: The contemporary scene

It has been argued by some that the study of religion in American colleges and universities today is essentially a naturalistic enterprise, and that in the mid- to late-1960s religious studies exchanged its originally Protestant religious ambitions for the scientific aspirations which still characterizes the enterprise today. Two significant developments behind this restructuring of the field have been suggested. The first is the ruling of the Supreme Court justices in the *Abington School District v. Schempp* case (1963) over the role of religion in the nation's public schools, which, according to Hart, "halted abruptly the religious and theological revival of the 1950s and early 1960s" (D. G. Hart 1999: 201). The *Schempp* decision purportedly undermined the Protestant establishment by precluding any amalgam of theology and devotion in the academic work undertaken in public colleges and universities without, however, banning the "neutral" study of religion. The second significant development in the (supposed) secularization of religious studies is the transformation of NABI into the AAR in 1964, which represented not only a reaction against the mainline Protestant influence on the study of religion in the past, but also, it is claimed, a commitment to a scientific framework for the study of religion over the pre-1960s religio-humanistic one. Hart, for example, declares that members of the Academy were concerned with establishing the field on an objective and scientific basis, and that "to be religious was no longer as important for Professors of religion as methodological sophistication and academic achievement" (D. G. Hart 1992: 213). Similarly, George Marsden maintains that with the (supposed) change of orientation represented by the AAR a "normative religious teaching of any sort has been nearly eliminated from standard university education" (Marsden 1994: 5). "While the AAR embraced both the humanistic and the social scientific impulse," Marsden writes, "the latter signalled the dominant direction for the future" (Marsden 1994: 414). Conrad Cherry echoes these claims in his insistence that the members of the AAR who now occupied the field "would gauge their work . . . by how well it conformed to the canons of the disciplinary specialties in the contemporary university" (Cherry 1995: 116). And P. C. Kemeny, following Hart and Marsden, claims that the AAR brought about a methodological revolution that gave religious studies an empirical, scientific foundation, eclipsing the non-scientific approaches of a bygone era (Kemeny 1998: 231). If these authors are to be believed, the majority of the students of religion in the United States, in the span of some five years, willingly exchanged their religious identities for the professional identity of scholar and scientist, swapping their moral and religious goals for objective knowledge about religions.

In a sense, the influence of the *Schempp* decision on the academic study of religion is surprising. For while the implications of that decision appear to exclude the study of religion directed to religious ends, they also permit the inculcation of values transmitted in and by religion; and this seems to make of the study of religion a "humanizing project" and a surrogate for religion. Students of religion in the United States focused on the obiter dicta of the justices in the case that allowed for an interpretation that would permit them to turn the "secular (objective) study of religion" that the *Schempp* decision seemed to require into a religious undertaking. Justice Clarke, for example, wrote:

> It might be said that one's education is not complete without a study of comparative religion or the history of religion and its relationship to the advancement of civilization. Nothing we have said here indicates that such a study of the Bible or of religion, when presented objectively as part of a secular program of education, may not be effected consistently with the First Amendment. (Clarke 1964: 1573)

Since the objective study of religion is regarded by many as inimical to faith, reductionist scientific studies of religion, it is argued, must be excluded from the context of public education. Thus, only that study of religion that shows the benefit of religiously derived moral values to culture and society is to be permitted.

As for the AAR, there is no doubt that some members sought to redirect the older Protestant, humanist orientation of religious studies. Others claimed that religious studies' scientific character had already been established by the freeing of the academic study of religion from sectarian interference. Claude Welch's review of graduate studies in religion and theology—under the auspices of the American Council of Learned Societies (ACLS)—gives voice to those aspirations and even suggests that the new scientific approach to the study of religion was already established in most university departments of religious studies by the late 1960s. In his presidential address to the AAR in 1970, entitled "Identity Crisis in the Study of Religion? A First Report from the ACLS Study" (1971a), Welch claims that there is no identity crisis in the field, since it had clearly differentiated religious studies from religious and theological approaches to understanding religion, confirming that religious studies as an objective, scientific pursuit was the sole concern of the university teacher of religion. In light of this internal assessment, it is not surprising that scholars such as Hart, Marsden, Cherry, and Kemeny believed a radical transformation of the study of religion in American colleges and universities had been effected. Nevertheless, there is overwhelming evidence to suggest that no such transformation of the field ever occurred, even though direct ecclesiastical influence on the study of religion in the university had to a large extent been eliminated. The fear of science and secularization, characteristic of the 1940s and 1950s, is no less present today than it was then; and the major paradigms for the study of religion created to cope with that "aftermath" of the Enlightenment still characterize religious studies today. As I shall show, there has been little or no support for those engaged in scientific studies of religious phenomena in the departments of religion or from the AAR. The change in name of NABI (which was the professional association for those engaged in teaching college and university bible and religion courses) to the AAR sprang from a dissatisfaction with the narrow Protestant orientation of the association and led to a more ecumenical approach to the study of religion, but did not signal commitment to a non-religious, scientific study of religion.

The trends in the field that for Welch indicated the emergence of a new discipline of religious studies (distinct from religion and theology) included the following: a rejection of ecclesiastical influence on college and university departments of religious studies; a rejection of the "confessional principle" and "insider theorizing"; a clear line of demarcation between the academic study of religion and the professional training of religious leaders; and the refusal to consider religious studies as a framework within which "to make sense of" the university's educational programs. (To this list he might have added the field's close association with the humanities.) Welch also pointed out that there was a complex range of problems in the study of religion, including the "legacy" of Protestant domination, that put the field at constant risk of "falling back into the aims of confessional interests" (Welch 1971a: 12). But what he did not acknowledge is that, despite the explicit rejection of the Protestant paradigm for the field, professors of religion, nevertheless, still saw their tasks, at least partly, as religious, in that sound teaching in the field required of them to remove students' indifference to religion. To be sure—given the religious pluralism that characterized American society then (as now)—they did not think it appropriate to promote one religious tradition over another; yet they still believed that a university education without a moral and transcendent dimension was incomplete.

In their effort to "humanize" and to revive spiritual and moral values in the youth of the nation, professors of religion identified their work with that of humanist scholars; and in so doing they appropriated the prestige the humanities already possessed as a "legitimate" university discipline. A little reflection, however, makes plain the circularity of the implicit argument in that political bid for credibility. The ideals taught in the humanities, that is, are virtually indistinguishable from the religious ideals of mainline, liberal Protestantism, which subverts the claim that the study of religion of the 1950s and 1960s was transformed into a bona fide science of religion in the 1970s and beyond. That simply did not occur; the motivation underlying the creation of departments of religion during this period, therefore, was, as in the past, religious rather than scientific. Given the religious origins of the values espoused, the latter were not objects of analysis so much as frames of reference within which questions about the meaning of human existence could be raised and attention to the student as a whole person, rather than simply as a knower, became possible. And it is this understanding of religious studies that was espoused by the post-1970s AAR. Stephen Crites, in a tone reminiscent of Wilfred Cantwell Smith, describes the enterprise in his "Liberal Learning and the Religion Major"—a report written on behalf of the AAR "Task Force on the Study in Depth in Religion"—as

> [a quest that] plunges the student into the densest and most elusive issues of value, introduces the student into an ancient and enduring conversation, not always peaceful, about ultimately serious matters, engages the imagination of the student in the most daring, imaginative ventures of human experience. . . . For many students it is a disciplined encounter with an order of questioning that has affinities with their own struggles for personal identity. It is one way of joining the human race. (Crites 1990: 13)

Crites is quick to point out that the aim of the study of religions is not to convince students to join any particular religious tradition, but he nevertheless insists that the study of religion must assist students in discovering that religion *makes sense* and "enlarges her or his own horizon of human possibility" (14). The report of the AAR's "Committee on Education and the Study of Religion," written by Ray L. Hart (1991) and billed as an "update on Welch," as well as the report of the "AAR Self-Study Committee" in the 1990s, also reveal the AAR to be fundamentally a religiously oriented institution. Although recognizing the deep tension between the study of religion and theological studies, Ray Hart claims it would be inappropriate to see it dissolved by subordinating either approach to the other for fear of "dishonoring the virtues the field is claimed to inculcate: tolerance, pluralism, respect for opposing positions, etc." (Ray L. Hart 1991: 790). And the AAR self-study, as Warren Frisinia reports (1993), reaffirms for the AAR the goals held by NABI, which indicates that, for the AAR, religious studies is not a science but rather a *conversation* that must include all the voices in the field, including religious voices. These reports, then, clearly show that the AAR, although desirous of intellectual respectability, and taking on, as much as possible, the appearance of a genuine academic enterprise, remained essentially a religious institution with religious aims not clearly distinguishable from those of NABI from which it sprang. And analysis of the presidential addresses of the AAR, compared with those of the NABI, confirm that conclusion (Wiebe 1997a).

The AAR as a religious enterprise reflects the situation existing today in the other institutions that support a scholarly study of religion, from departments of religious studies in colleges and universities to professional associations and journals. Religious studies departments in American colleges and universities have been, and still are, dominated by one of two major paradigms of study—even if only in modified form, adapted to more self-conscious humanities-oriented departments. Both are religious— the one little more than a broad, ecumenical extension of the mainline, liberal Protestant model (constituting an implicit world theology responsive to all the world's religions), and the other a gnostic form of religion that makes of religious studies itself an exalted vocation rather than a scientific undertaking. The first is most clearly represented by Harvard University and the Center for the Study of World Religions, best exemplified in the work of Wilfred Cantwell Smith. For Smith, even though the academic study of religion is a rational activity and involves the sciences, it is also an exercise of faith aimed at understanding not only the external aspects of religious tradition but also the interior faith of millions of ordinary religious people within that tradition. A genuine scholarly study of religion, it would seem, is the responsibility not only of the historian of religion but also of the authentic theologian who can penetrate "beyond" the data to the faith of the believer and bring to the scientific analysis of religion an awareness of ultimate reality. An unabridged, comprehensive (and therefore authentic) academic study of religion, for Smith, is one that achieves a "humane knowledge" of the religious lives of individuals, regardless of their sociohistorical contexts, in a "self-involving process of corporate critical self-consciousness" that carries them well beyond mere scientific knowledge of religious traditions. As Smith puts it in his *The Meaning and End of Religion*, "It is quite impossible to understand man's religious life if one does not understand that that life has necessarily and rightly looked different when viewed from within and when viewed from without (W. C. Smith 1962: 130-31)"; "the observer's concept of a religion is by definition constituted of what can be observed. Yet the whole pith and substance of religious life lies in the relation to what cannot be observed" (W. C. Smith 1962: 136).

The second major paradigm for the study of religion dominating contemporary higher education in America is represented by the University of Chicago and is exemplified most clearly in Mircea Eliade's approach to the study of religion.[8] Unlike the "history of religion" (written in lowercase) that emerged in European universities in the latter part of the nineteenth century, Eliade's approach to understanding religion involves, as Wasserstrom has put it, an "uncanny doubleness" of scholarship that espouses a university-based study of religion but simultaneously aims to reveal "a new form of religion after the expiration of traditional forms [of religion]" (Wasserstrom 1999: x). Wasserstrom suggests, therefore, that this "discipline" be called the "History of Religions" (capitalizing the terms used in the phrase) because, although bearing some of the marks of scholarship typical of the academy, it does not result in the academic disenchantment of religion as does its lowercase counterpart. The task of the historian of religion, then, is to create a soteriologically vibrant conversation and, therefore, involves a "knowledge" that lies beyond research. The historian of religion, consequently, is a sage, gnostic, or mystic who, as Wasserstrom puts it, has recaptured the breakthrough of the religious mystic, but in an intellectual fashion (Wasserstrom 1999: 196). Consequently, "the History of Religion, epitomized by . . . scholars [such as Eliade], epitomized the study of religion as religion" (Wasserstrom 1999: 63).

Surprising though it may seem, given the ideal of the modern research university, there is no department of religious studies in America that models an unadulterated scientific approach—a model that puts the study of religion wholly within a naturalistic framework—to the study of religion. It is no accident, therefore, that Murray G. Murphy (1989), in his discussion of the scientific study of religion in the United States from 1870 to 1980, makes no reference to departments of religious studies. Such a scientific study of religion was (and is) alive only in history and social science departments, and even there it did not achieve high profile, claims Murphy, despite the significant influence of such prominent social science theorists as Durkheim, Weber, and Freud. This is astounding in the context of the modern research university, but perhaps less so when viewed from the perspective of the broader cultural context of the study of religion and the strange history of the development of the field under the liberal Protestant hegemony described above. Nevertheless, it suggests that a *bona fide* scientific study of religion lies elsewhere than, as one scholar has put it, in "those curious academic hybrids, the departments of religious studies" (Lacey 1989: 5), whose members are neither like the scientists in regular (naturalistic) departments nor like the theologians in seminaries and divinity schools.[9]

Not only are there no departments of religious studies committed to the scientific study of religion but there are also few professional associations and societies (or journals and other means of dissemination of scientific research on religion) dedicated to the support of the academic study of religion that is purely scientific in orientation. Although institutions such as the Society for the Scientific Study of Religion and the NAASR emerged to provide support for the historical and social-scientific study of religion, the influence of most other professional associations for the development of religious studies (including the American Society for the Study of Religion), has been broadly religious in orientation from the outset. By far, the greatest number of societies and associations devoted to the field have a religious aim, intention, or affiliation, and the AAR and the Society for Biblical Literature (SBL)—the largest of the professional associations for students of religion—although not confessional in any specific sense, are nevertheless generally supportive of a religious approach to understanding religion and have clearly shown hostility to the "narrow" scientific study of religion. The SBL, it has been suggested by its chronicler, is "a fraternity of scientifically trained biblical scholars with the soul of a church" (Saunders 1982: 69), with questions of theological meaning still "su[ing] for recognition" (Saunders 1982: 102) among their members. And the AAR, with its much broader scholarly mandate, has clearly espoused an anti-scientific understanding of its responsibilities in expending its energies not in search of an explanation or theory of religion but rather in the creation of a context within which both a religious conversation and conversation about religion can take place simultaneously (Ray L. Hart 1991; De Concini 1993).[10] In an attempt to preserve their members' religious and humanistic conversation, the AAR has enthusiastically embraced recent postmodern and deconstructive movements in various humanities' disciplines, explicitly rejecting a modern notion of religious studies of the kind sketched at the beginning of this chapter. The Chicago School, a major influence in the AAR, has clearly espoused such a stance. As early as 1983, Martin E. Marty, for example, ridiculed those in the field who still "cherish a scientific ideal which other humanities and social sciences no longer seek" (Marty 1983: 83), and Frank Reynolds echoed these sentiments in 1990, claiming that a scientific perspective is structurally indistinguishable from any other kind because of the constructed character of all social reality (Reynolds 1990: 11). David Tracy, as well, in a 1995 essay, claimed that "a substantial proportion of the American academy, including the academy in religious studies, has in fact become distrustful of the epistemological and theoretical versions of the Enlightenment in favor of one or another anti-Enlightenment version of what has come to be known as postmodernity" (Tracy 1995: 328). It is not the academy generally, however, that has undergone this transformation. It is primarily the humanities that have questioned the Enlightenment model of rationality and science; and they have done so because the success of the sciences in the modern research university (in epistemic matters) is incontrovertible and thus presents a threat to the place of the humanities in that context. Unlike the nineteenth-century university reformers and their immediate successors, contemporary students of religion in America do not believe a religious appropriation of science is possible, and they reject the notion of a scientific approach to understanding religion.[11] Unless a postmodern understanding of research and scholarship is created, they insist, the sciences will proceed, unchecked, to undermine cultural and religious values.[12] And given that ideology, it is not surprising to find that the AAR has refused to work co-operatively with the IAHR which is committed to establishing and furthering the modern scientific study of religion worldwide. (The AAR eventually became a national association member of the IAHR on the occasion of its twentieth international congress in Toronto in 2010.)

In recent years the Academy's past (relative) isolationism with respect to international developments in the modern study of religion as represented by the IAHR has been replaced by hostility and open conflict with it. Since 1985, the IAHR has sought collaboration with the AAR in support of the scientific study of religion in colleges and universities around the world but has been repeatedly rebuffed. By 1990 the hostility was no longer muted; the AAR was by this time actively courting foreign scholars through its "International Connections" committee and, as Luther Martin and I have shown (1993), had in a sense declared war on the IAHR in its intention to create "a global field-spanning organization" (Ray L. Hart 1985: 791)—which Ninian Smart dubbed the World Academy of Religion (Smart 1990: 305)—to reconstruct the international scene in religious studies in its own image. In 1992 the AAR, with the assistance of the SBL (which had long been involved in annual international scholarly gatherings), sponsored its first International Congress in Melbourne, Australia. Its second such congress was held in late July of 2000 in Cape Town, South Africa, days before the quinquennial International Congress of the IAHR in Durban, South Africa, in what appears to be a direct challenge to the IAHR.[13] In the intervening years, the international connections committee of the AAR has sponsored various symposia in conjunction with international meetings of the SBL, and has covered the costs of sending several non-national participants, but has refused similar cooperation with annual regional and quinquennial international IAHR events.

The shape of things to come

Given the continuing commitment to the fundamentally religious values the AAR espoused with its Protestant heritage—tempered and modified to some extent by its interaction with "other" religious traditions—it is clear that neither it, nor the departments of religious studies it "represents," can support a modern, scientific study of religion or any organization committed to such a project. Indeed, a naturalistic study of religion would represent the triumph of science over religion and the humanities and is resisted as contributing to the dehumanization of culture and society. Consequently, it is precisely because of the expansion of the study of religion in US colleges and universities, and the successes of the AAR and the SBL in shaping the nature of that enterprise, that a modern, scientific study of religion has failed to develop fully in the United States and is unlikely to do so in the future. The "redescription" of religious studies as a postmodern—and therefore other than simply a scientific—enterprise has gained preeminent standing in the field in America. The irony of this situation is obvious: although the AAR decries the influence of the "scientistic" university for drowning out every voice but its own, it has achieved phenomenal success, whereas the plea for a scientific (naturalistic) study of religion within the structures provided by the university—namely, departments of religious studies—has fallen on deaf ears. More significantly, given the size, wealth, power, and emerging international interests of the AAR, the future for the scientific study of religion as it is represented by the IAHR, despite the latter's obvious affinity with the dominant ethos of the modern research university, stands in jeopardy. Unfortunately, the IAHR does not have access to the resources available to the AAR through its ecclesiastical/religious associations and numerous religiously inspired/oriented foundations; it is, therefore, not likely to be able to repel the American bid for "coordinating" the study of religion at the international level, which, I believe, will seriously undermine the kind of study of religion that can provide us not only with an objective understanding of the historical development and phenomenological import of particular religious traditions but also, eventually, with a natural explanation and theoretical account of religion. In my opinion, therefore, unless the IAHR can find ways and means by which to increase significantly its support for embodying the scientific study of religion, not only in professional associations, societies, and instruments for the support of research and the dissemination of scientific research on religion but also in departments of religion in modern research universities, what has been "a failure of nerve" (Wiebe 1984) in taking up the scientific attitude to that study will amount to a surrender to the religious forces that have ever been present in the field.[14]

Religious Studies in North America during the Cold War

I am grateful for the invitation to participate in this special IAHR conference on the academic study of religion during the period of the Cold War. This is not a research theme I would have picked up without some prodding. I have seldom even come across mention of the Cold War in the literature of the field, let alone serious study or analysis of the effects of Cold War values and rhetoric on students of religion in Western universities, to draw my attention to the importance of this issue. In light of the "call for papers" for this conference, this strikes me as surprising, as it seems unlikely that any academic discipline or enterprise could have emerged untouched by such "a period of bitter international recriminations between the East and the West," as the conference organizers put it, or have been deaf to the ideological justifications supporting that conflict. And I am persuaded that it is now wholly appropriate, "ten years [after] the fall of the Berlin Wall . . . to reconsider the impact of these ideological influences and how they may have impacted subject cultures and their institutions."[1]

In light of the paucity of studies on the effects of the Cold War on the academic study of religion in North America, I shall review first the literature on the general culture of the Cold War and its impact on the intellectual life in social and cultural institutions (including colleges and universities) in the United States.[2] I shall then proceed more specifically with an analysis of the impact of the Cold War on particular scientific, scholarly, and academic enterprises in American institutions of higher learning. With that survey complete and assessments made of the indirect influence of the Cold War on the academic study of religion, I shall give critical attention to the claims of Jacob Neusner and Russell McCutcheon about the direct negative impact of the Cold War on this academic discipline.

The culture of the Cold War in North America

The Cold War crusade against communism in the United States, as Stephen J. Whitfield has pointed out in his *Culture of the Cold War* (1991), gave rise in the 1950s to a national ideology that had a profound impact upon its citizens and upon virtually every American institution. Communism was seen as extremely dangerous, requiring the mobilization of every citizen in the fight against it; it was seen, that is, not simply as a body of doctrine but as a sinister political program aimed at the overthrow of America. As Whitfield describes it, "Citizens were expected to enlist in the Cold War. Neutrality was suspect, and so was a lack of enthusiasm for defining American Society as beleaguered" (10). Not only did the Cold War spawn an effort "to define and affirm a way of life, the need to express and celebrate the meaning of 'Americanism,'" (53) but it also encroached upon the civil liberties of those who did not fall in with that dominant ideology of the nation. Cold War America, that is, imposed political standards on its citizens and various government agencies applied tests of political correctness to a broad range of institutions and activities which in effect resulted in a suspension of the democratic rights of the individual. And such suspension of rights and procedures, Whitfield argues, amounted to the practice of government interference in the private sector, the film industry, the arts, colleges and universities, and a broad range of other cultural affairs. Even though Whitfield maintains that the application of such political standards and tests was not systematic, they were nevertheless sufficiently well administered to amount to a form of repression that radically affected a wide range of social institutions.[3]

Organized religion, Whitfield argues, further contributed to the repression of intellectual life in America. For the most part, he claims, it sanctified the crusade against the godless philosophy of communism and supported the ideology of Americanism; this despite the fact that it constituted a serious breach with the (until then) dominant Protestant tradition of thought in America. Consequently, "church membership and a highly favorable attitude toward religion became forms of affirming 'the American way of life' during the Cold War, especially since the Soviet Union and its allies officially subscribed to Atheism. And conspicuously active church membership became the most effective shield against the suspicion of subversiveness" (83). The increased interest in religion in America as seen, for example, in the revivals inspired by the preaching of Billy Graham or the revival of the Divinity School at Harvard University under the leadership of Nathan Pusey, Whitfield claims was not a genuine religious awakening but rather a conscription of religion in service of the fight against communism. And insofar as the study of religion on college and university campuses was of the order of that found in the revitalized Divinity School of Harvard University, it is obvious that the Cold War had a significant impact upon it. Reasonable objections can be raised, however, as to whether the so-called discipline of "religious studies" can be identified with that kind of scholarly study of religion; a scientific study of religion as opposed to a religiously oriented study, that is, only emerged in the North American scene, if at all, in the 1960s (Wiebe 1998; 2000). To talk of the "scholarly" study of religion in the American academic context before that period, as I shall point out below, is really to talk about the role of *religion* in college and university education. Ignoring this distinction, I suggest, will significantly distort one's reading of the impact of the Cold War on the field.

There can be no doubt however that Cold War politics affected the political speech and behavior of scientists and academics as much as it did that of independent intellectuals in society at large.[4] Indeed, it destroyed many scientific and academic careers, and disrupted even more for many years. More important, the intimidation of McCarthyism on college and university campuses was pervasive, bringing many scholars into alignment with the reigning nationalist ideology and so influencing what issues and topics were to receive their attention. It is not clear in Whitfield's account, however, whether—and how—that influence impinged upon disciplinary matters in the university. Nevertheless, Whitfield also points out that the impact of the Cold War on the academy was not limited to such repression. Academics could also be conscripted to the Cold War cause, as he shows with respect to the work of Conyers Read who, as president of the American Historical Association in 1949, argued that in face of totalitarian threat, if the nation is to survive, the scholar must reject the notion of a neutral, "detached," intellectual stance. Although the stance taken by Read provides a clear indication of the effect of Cold War ideology on some academics, it does not necessarily indicate the discipline's abdication of the traditional view that research and scholarship be neutral and objective. Read, as Whitfield acknowledges, explicitly rejected the implication that this required a deliberate distortion of the past in the interests of ideology.[5]

Some might claim that a comment of this sort too easily dismisses the general effect of the Cold War on academic life and its implications for the development of disciplines and areas of study in the university during this period of history. Ellen Schrecker (1986), for example, suggests that the repression of intellectuals on college and university campuses provides at least some indication that the university relinquished its commitment to objective and neutral research and scholarship. However, despite her suggestion, Schrecker provides no evidence of ideological domination in the natural or social sciences, or in any of the humanities disciplines.[6]

Schrecker's claims that the Cold War effectively repressed the civil liberties of professors finds considerable support in Lionel Lewis's analysis of the *Cold War on Campus* (1988). Many teachers and researchers, he points out, felt apprehension about their right to speak and write freely, fearing investigation by the FBI or the House Un-American Activities Committee. Such investigations, he points out, not only ruined the lives of scholars but also had serious deleterious effects on the universities themselves in creating conflicts between faculty and administrative authorities. Furthermore, the loss of diversity of perspective in some disciplines, created by the dismissal (or refusal to hire) professors considered radical, or even uncomfortably liberal, also affected the nature of the work undertaken. And given the importance of the free exchange of ideas to science and the research enterprise, the imposition of secrecy in the name of national security undoubtedly had some negative effects on various fields of study. Nevertheless, there is no indication in Lewis's work that university concerns with national security in face of the communist threat somehow deformed the disciplines themselves; somehow changed not only the focus of the disciplines but also their commitment to systematic, rational inquiry in search of knowledge of some or other aspect of the world.

The culture of the Cold War and the academic enterprise

To this point I have suggested that the Cold War pervaded all aspects of society, commenting on its general effect on both the political and intellectual life within and without the university context. I have provided some indication of its negative impact on the university community, particularly on individual scholars and professors, thus, indirectly, upon what the university is and does. Although the full significance of this for science and scholarship is not transparent, and even though interpretations of it vary widely, I think it fair to say that there is no clear indication that this indirect influence of the Cold War on scientists and other academics constituted ideological subversion of the various scientific and scholarly enterprises sponsored by the university. I shall, therefore, turn my attention in the remainder of this chapter to a brief survey of how the Cold War—and the World War that preceded it—directly shaped the academic enterprise itself; and of how it influenced the nature, number, and content of the academic disciplines in the natural and social sciences, and in the humanities. I shall begin with the general understanding of how the Second World War and the Cold War affected the conduct of research in the natural sciences.

The Cold War, and the Second World War, had an enormous effect on the natural sciences, as is the case in all wars. And although it might be argued that "no single event can be responsible for decisive transformations in the history of science" (Redner 1987: 8), it can nevertheless be argued that the impact on the natural sciences of the wars mentioned in an important sense determined their development. As Harry Redner puts it, "All in all, the mobilization of science for the purposes of war from 1914 till now, well into the Cold War, transformed all sciences, even those devoted solely to 'peaceful' or pure research" (8). The reason for this, he argues, is that such mobilization of scientific research "reinforced tendencies in science which were a long time in the making but which had been marginal till these war preparations expanded and institutionalized them" (8). Redner acknowledges that the connection between scientific research and technology, on the one hand, and the large-scale organization of research on the other, originates in the nineteenth century, but he insists that "the enormous financial and human resources made available by governments for war were necessary to amplify these trends and make them paramount throughout the sciences" (8). These conditions, he argues, involved an influence of power that transformed not only science but also the nature of the institutions that house it. He suggests, that is, that the new postwar science is a mission-oriented techno-science that is appropriately symbolized, if not inaugurated, by the Manhattan Project. This project is an appropriate symbol, according to Redner, both because of its inextricable connection to the search for "the solution of problems that arose as a consequence of the exigencies of war, armaments for the Cold War, and post-war reconstruction" (184), and because of the transfer of the main center of science from Europe to America. From this time on, he maintains, science was no longer the domain of the individual thinker and researcher, as in the classical period of the scientific revolution; rather, scientific research is socialized, and the "scientific establishment has become a political power on par with the other main agencies of the state" (16). At the same time, moreover, the state entered the process of scientific research, with the potential to dominate both scientist and scholar. He writes, "The university as the 'fountainhead of free ideas and scientific discovery' is now a mere historical relic, whose core is more or less artificially preserved in a few antiquarian localities and traditional establishments but whose outer form has almost completely decayed" (16–17). And he concludes by labeling this "Contemporary World science" (16).

R. C. Lewontin (1997) paints a similar picture of the natural sciences in postwar America, although his assessment of the role of the individual scientist within the institution is not nearly as pessimistic. He echoes Redner, however, in claiming that contemporary science is "social" in a way that classical science was not, and he agrees that very special conditions need to exist before such socialization of research and education are possible. High levels of scientific research require heavy investment that private enterprise is generally unable to provide, so that only the state can play the role of patron, determining in effect "both the cost and the conduct of research and technological education" (9). Although government control of education and scholarship was greatly feared in the United States, as was massive state intervention in the economy, Lewontin argues that it, nevertheless, came about because of the crisis of the Second World War. "Scientific research," he writes, "became a state enterprise, of which the Manhattan Project was only the most visible example, and the universities were incorporated into the training apparatus of the military" (3), and continued because the Cold War sustained such a "consciousness of . . . state national military emergency . . . continuously for 50 years" (7).[7]

Despite such attempts at control of the natural sciences by government, Lewontin surprisingly contends that there was widespread indifference to political ideology in the research supported by various government agencies, and he differs from Redner in claiming that scientists and academics involved still acted as independent entrepreneurs who were "not working *for* universities but rather *in* them" (29). Lewontin also points out that the unprecedented expansion of the academy under these conditions benefited many academic disciplines besides the natural sciences, as well as the university itself, even though the Cold War that generated it had been the cause of tragedy for a number of scientists and other scholars. The Cold War had become "the high road to professional prosperity for the great majority" (2), had contributed to a dramatic increase in the number of scientists working in the academy, and also benefited scholars in the social sciences and the humanities, even if, in many instances, only indirectly.

As Alan A. Needell (1998) points out, those "managing" the Cold War were interested in a good deal more than just the production of military weaponry. As he puts it, they sought "alternative means to prevail in the struggle against communism" (4), which directed their attention beyond the natural sciences alone. Many in the social sciences, therefore, were called upon to contribute to foreign policy planning by undertaking basic research related to other questions of national security (24–25). The struggle against communism, that is, also included engagement in "political warfare," which could be enhanced by the knowledge available to the social sciences and the humanities. A broad range of disciplines, Needell claims, were involved in this program, including anthropology, economics, psychology, sociology, political science, history, and geography. Their task was to provide some understanding of the conditions under which communism could spread in poorer, third world nations, and their work was therefore used in the control of those nations. New disciplines were also created to contribute to this end, including such fields as area studies, international studies, and development studies. Two recent collections of essays explore this aspect of the Cold War's impact: André Schiffrin's *The Cold War and the University: Toward an Intellectual History* (1997), and Christopher Simpson's *Universities and Empire: Money and Politics in the Social Sciences During the Cold War* (1998); both deserve close attention. However, since neither volume contains a contribution directly related to the effects of the Cold War on the academic study of religion, and since no unambiguous interpretation of the indirect influence upon religious studies by the other social sciences and humanities that were affected by Cold War agendas is possible, I shall not undertake an analysis of their contents here.

The academic study of religion and the Cold War

As I indicated in the introduction to this chapter, some scholars have argued that the Cold War has had a direct, negative effect on the academic study of religion and it is on these claims I now wish to focus critical attention.

In *The Price of Excellence: Universities in Conflict During the Cold War Era* (1995) Jacob Neusner, a major figure in the field of religious studies, provides a personal view of the effect of the Cold War, not only on the academy in general but also on "religious studies" in particular. Although some of his claims are dubious, as I shall argue below, these autobiographical comments, nevertheless, provide us with a helpful picture of how the Cold War influenced at least one scholar in the field in North America. (Jacob and Noam Neusner [Jacob's son] are co-authors of this book, but it is the experience of the elder Neusner that is the primary focus of my comments here.)

In the introductory material to *The Price of Excellence*, the Neusners aim at correlating "politics and academic culture, in this instance, the Cold War and the academy's golden age," a period of time in which American citizens placed their faith "in the power of universities to carry out the national will" (27). The universities, they claim, gained prominence through the Cold War as "the nation's strongest line of defense" (17), and they draw attention to the fact that this involved more than simply the scientific knowledge produced by university scientists. The knowledge brought by the university to the Cold War effort, that is, included knowledge not just of how to create better weapons but also of how to forge alliances, for it fell to them to educate those who would represent the nation in foreign affairs. As a result, government funding was made available, not only for research in science and technology "but also [for] philosophy, history, the study of religion, and the social sciences . . . [as they battled] for the country's future in the world" (29).

The Neusners interpret the influence of the Cold War on the university as a whole—and on its academic disciplines in particular—as a positive one. For it was a period in which the sciences flourished because of the massive increase of government support. The social sciences and humanities benefited as well since American commitment to world leadership obliged citizens to learn about, as they put it, "the faith and life of strangers" (23); "to make sense of other peoples' nonsense" (32); and to provide "guidance in the exotic and bizarre" (79). "Our country led the coalition of disparate nations facing Communism," they write, and

> our academicians would have to learn how to understand both allies and enemies. Their experience within the academy prepared them for leadership beyond its bounds. Used to learning from foreigners, they undertook to form a vision of one world in social science and in humanistic learning to complement the political will of national unity and international cooperation. (22)

This response on the part of the university to the Cold War challenge, they insist, was not propagandistic in nature, but rather constituted responsible scholarship, characterized by objective criticism and rigorous learning. In the Cold War, they write, the United States

> had chosen to take up intellectual arms in a long twilight struggle, meeting on battlefields of the mind, soul, and heart with the ammunition of ideas, attitudes, and deeply held convictions. [And as] vast sums of money flowed into these subjects, the best minds found a welcome, equipment, and fine laboratories for research; and all the necessities of scientific greatness came together. (23)

Despite this glowing report of the benefits brought to university research and scholarship because of the Cold War, Jacob Neusner is not entirely convinced that "buying into" the Cold War agenda was an unmitigated success. "Whether it really was a golden age," he insists, "remains to be seen" (37) for it appears that the benefits accrued to universities, disciplines, and individual scholars extended only to the decade of the 1960s. He laments the current state of affairs on college and university campuses, and he attributes this situation to the Cold War. For although Cold War mobilization initially brought prosperity and development to all, it eventually diverted universities from their unique mission of joining research to scholarship in the form of teaching and catapulted them into the realm of public policy with a mission of social justice. As he puts it, "The agenda of social amelioration has taken over, with courses aimed at indoctrination replacing instruction intending to provoke discovery" (26), and this triggered a drop in the quality of research and teaching. Thus the great age of academic learning in the 1960s waned in the 1970s and came to a halt in the 1980s (149):

> We who came to the campuses as students in the 1950s and returned as professors in the early 1960s, shaped our careers to serve three causes: scholarship, teaching, and collegial citizenship. . . . Today, the gentle virtues of learning give way to more robust values of politics and management. (150–51)

So great is the deterioration and loss of integrity in learning, and so heavy the political partisanship, in Neusner's eyes, that the final result of the influence of the Cold War on the university, its disciplines and its scholars, is that the academy in the United States has been turned "into a replica of those Latin American universities that set themselves up as fortresses of revolutionary subversion" (154).

I turn now to Jacob Neusner's understanding of the implications of all of this for the academic study of religion. Religious studies, he boldly claims, emerged as a discipline in the university because of "the political tasks of the universities of that time, which found definition in the preparation of young Americans for a long twilight struggle against the Soviet Union's quest for world hegemony: to provide the intellectual foundations for this country's encounter with world politics" (142). He is aware that religion was a recognized field of study in the university context long before the onset of the Cold War, but nevertheless insists that, like area studies, international studies, and development studies, it "re-emerged" in the academy essentially in response to the challenges to the nation brought on by the Cold War. As Neusner describes it, "The field of the academic study of religion was reinvented in the United States, the first naturally, authentically multicultural field America would produce" (23). According to him, it found a place within the university curriculum in the 1950s (74), although he later qualifies this judgment with the claim that it was only the aspiration for such a scientific study of religion that was present in the 1950s, with its realization not occurring until the 1960s (141). And whereas the pre–Cold War study of religion was primarily theological and apologetic in intent and orientation, the new "academic study of religion," committed to social description and cultural analysis was born with the assistance of various government agencies as midwives. He writes:

> Since religion then as now defined the social order for many countries and life's purpose for much of humanity, the time had come to support the study of religion, for analytical purposes and not as a medium of indoctrination, within the curriculum. That was the point at which the academic study of religion in the United States came of age. (35)

Neusner's general claims about the Cold War and its effects upon science and scholarship, and upon the university and his career, are startling to say the least, and his account of the study of religion in the university context during the Cold War period borders on astounding. His personal testimony is interesting and constitutes clear evidence that, at least for some scholars in religious studies, the Cold War agenda was a prime motivator for their decision to enter this field of research. Nevertheless, that same motivation cannot be ascribed to all who entered the field, and Neusner provides no other kinds of evidence to warrant such a general claim. Moreover, the documented development of religious studies in the university context in North America, and particularly in the United States, contradicts Neusner's assertions about its "birth," "re-establishment," "re-invention," or "coming of age." As I have attempted to show elsewhere (Wiebe; 1998), a restructuring of the study of religion on American college and university campuses took place in the mid-1960s as a result of the transformation of NABI into the AAR, and the motivation for the reconstruction came from pressures upon NABI to move beyond its Christian orientation in research and teaching. The discussions within NABI leading to the new order in the creation of the AAR, that is, provide no indication of Cold War influence, and, to my knowledge, no evidence exists that the academic study of religion was ever funded by government agencies or received major infusion of funds from foundations for Cold War purposes.[8] Cold War funding, such as that provided by the National Defense Foreign Language Act, may have indirectly benefited scholars in the field of religion, but this does not provide support for the sweeping claims Neusner makes regarding the connection between the academic study of religion and the government's Cold War agenda. Furthermore, for Neusner, the founding generations of the reinvented discipline within the university include such exemplary figures as George Thomas, Fred Berthold, J. Alfred Martin, William Clebsch, Steven Crary, Valerie Saiving, Robert Michaelson, Robert Funk, and Ray Hart—but he provides no proof of Cold War motivation in their work to establish the discipline in their respective locales.[9]

Russell T. McCutcheon's comments on the effects of the Cold War on the academic study of religion, in his *Manufacturing Religion: The Discourse on Sui Generis Religion and the Politics of Nostalgia* (1997), constitutes the only other analysis of Cold War values and the academic study of religion of which I am aware. According to McCutcheon, "One cannot help but read the texts of American-based scholars, especially those written in the late 1950s and 1960s, in [the] light of such events as the war in Korea, the war in Vietnam, the Cold War with the Soviet Union, and the increasing economic power of the United States overseas" (187). Unfortunately, McCutcheon establishes few direct links between Cold War ideology and the work of the American-based scholars of religion he has in mind in support of this claim. His claim is tied, rather, to a general attack on those who espouse a notion of religion as a sui generis cultural phenomenon that allows scholars to disconnect it from social and political concerns and prevents their recognizing that even "[claims] of intellectual and socio-cultural autonomy carry with them, and move within, political implications and relations" (5). His analysis of the representation of Vietnamese self-immolation, for example, does not clearly establish the link between religious studies and the Cold War nor does it reveal that the study of religion in the West is primarily concerned with protective strategies deployed by Western nations to ensure their continued influence over others (177). Ultimately, though, he fails to establish his claim that there is a vast number of examples of such motivation in the work of Western scholars of religion. Huston Smith's remarks on the range of motivations for understanding other religions, however, as McCutcheon points out, do clearly exemplify the political and military values of such knowledge sought by some in the field—as does the testimony of Jacob Neusner presented above[10]—but his view that Mircea Eliade's work is a rhetoric of "control and normalization" arising from the fear of "political and economic threat to the military and industrial interests of Europe and North America" (163) seems based on little more than a passing reference by Eliade in his 1989 *Journal* that we are entering an age "in which we will be not only surrounded but also dominated by 'foreigners,' the non-Occidentals" (69–70). Moreover, McCutcheon so qualifies his claim that Eliade's work can be placed "squarely within the realm of Cold War politics" (163)—by noting that this may not be so with respect to its origins but is certainly true with respect to its implications—as to nullify it; there is not much—if anything—produced in or by the academy that cannot in some way be of benefit to one or another political or military cause. McCutcheon's claims regarding the Cold War and the study of religion, therefore, seem to arise more from his general views about the intimate relations between political power and academic discourse than from direct evidence of the impact of Cold War rhetoric on religious studies scholarship in North America during this period. Finally, his views on the intimate relation between political power and academic discourse are less than clear and may in fact be incoherent given that he seems to tie them only to those who espouse a sui generis notion of religion, while intimating that those who call for the development of explicit and testable theories of religion somehow transcend that connection. That is, in wanting to unravel the Eliade-type study of religion, so as "to contribute to constructing a discursive and institutional environment where naturalist theorizing can take place" (6), he seems to be suggesting that a study of religion that transcends political influence could in fact exist.

McCutcheon's comments regarding the influence of the Cold War on the academic study of religion do not trace direct influence; rather, they are swept up as elements of an overarching claim that (1) all sui generis approaches to the study of religion are intended to aid "the worldwide spread of European culture, economics, and politics" (180), and (2) that all academic discourse on religion to date is sui generis discourse. As he puts it:

> In spite of their professed sympathies for the symbols and myths of other peoples, both Smith's and Eliade's projects—inasmuch as they are part of the larger discourse on *sui generis* religion—have much in common with the work of many of their anthropological and missiological predecessors who described and delimited the non-European, non-Christian world in preparation for the subsequent triumph of Western culture. (180)

If the comparison is extended simply to "many of their anthropological and missiological predecessors," and not to all of them, then McCutcheon's suggestion that there exists a necessary and inextricable relation between the study of religion and power politics is seriously undermined. The relationship between the study of religion and power politics, therefore, is extrinsic rather than intrinsic, and needs to be determined by detailed empirical study. And there is no reason to believe that this would be different for those who hold a sui generis view of religion from those who believe naturalistic theorizing about religion a possibility.

Although I find McCutcheon's reflections on the Cold War's effects on the study of religion interesting, I do not believe he provides an adequate framework for discussion of the relationship between the two; for the question requires a more straightforward, empirical approach rather than the "theoretical" (philosophical) one he employs. What is required but not supplied is evidence of the influence, not simply of ideas, but of the use of economic, institutional, and other inducements or constraints on the study of religion in American universities as a direct by-product of Cold War ideology. My research suggests that evidence of such encroachment does not exist. And in the final analysis, even those few scholars of religion in North America who have reflected on the "role of the Cold War" in religious studies have not been able to provide satisfactory evidence to the contrary.

Summary and conclusions

The Second World War and the Cold War profoundly affected university education and research. Its effects on the natural sciences are perhaps the most dramatic and the easiest to discern. Increased funding not only allowed intensified research and an increase in the number of scientists involved but it also led to significant changes in the structure of scientific authority and in the way research is undertaken in the natural sciences. These changes, however, in no way threatened the defining character of the sciences as cognitive enterprises committed to the generation of knowledge by means of a systematic, rational inquiry into the nature of the world. The increased government funding in the natural sciences, however, did benefit the social sciences and humanities since some of the overhead costs assessed in connection with the natural science projects was often consigned to them by university administrators. Ultimately, Lewontin notes, the increase in funding provided "the high road to professional prosperity" for the vast majority of those working in the university, including, no doubt, those who worked in the field of religion, but there is no clear connection between that prosperity and any Cold War bias in the scholars who benefited from it.

The available data does make clear that a number of disciplines and fields of study in the social sciences and humanities did receive direct funding by government agencies or foundations influenced by Cold War agendas. Those who "managed" the Cold War, obviously, had another agenda in addition to that of military preparedness. As I have indicated, the Cold War involved a variety of disciplines and fields of study—anthropology, political science, psychology, linguistics, and so on—in research that would contribute to the resolution of international problems that incidentally were threatening Western interests. Whole new fields, such as area studies, development studies, and the like, were established and funded, in the hope that they would provide the knowledge needed to win the Cold War on the fields of international relations and diplomacy and so avoid drifting into war. According to some analysts, government and foundation influence in this respect was such that one cannot but conclude that "the Cold War reshaped university structures and the context of academic disciplines, just as it penetrated the whole fabric of political and intellectual life" (Montgomery1997: xii).

These changes, however, in no way threatened the defining ideal of the sciences as cognitive enterprises committed to the generation of knowledge by means of a systematic rational inquiry into the nature of the world. The evidence available in Schiffrin (1997) and Simpson (1998), however, attests that even though there was a considerable amount of research in the social sciences and the humanities whose focus appeared to be the result of the influence of the state on the university, there is little to suggest that government involvement radically transformed the research process or diverted universities or disciplines within them to abandon their primary cognitive raison d'être of generating and disseminating knowledge. Indeed, there is considerable evidence to show that the commitment to objective science and scholarship in the university was in fact not compromised.[11] Even though some university careers were destroyed or severely affected by the anti-communist hysteria of McCarthyism, its effect on the university as institution was more muted (Geiger 1993).

As I have already noted above, the period during the Second World War and the Cold War nurtured a revival of religion in American society. It is also clear that the anxieties raised by the war made the universities themselves hospitable to religion; Merriman Cuninggim's *The University Needs Religion* (1947) provides clear indication of that. And the study of religion Cunninggim wanted ensconced in the college and university settings was, to all intents and purposes, an extension of the civic religion fostered and sustained by the wars, hot and cold. As D. G. Hart puts it in his recent *The University Gets Religion* (1999), the Second World War and the Cold War "underscored the need for understanding and preserving western culture at the nation's colleges and universities" (243–44), which, it was believed, required a renewed interest in liberal education of which the teaching of religion as one of the humanities disciplines was a central component. It must be recognized, however, that this "teaching *of* religion" was not the "teaching *about* religion" characteristic of religious studies scholars committed to the creation of an academic framework for the scientific study of religion; it was, rather, the continuation of "the efforts of mainstream Protestant ministers and educators who wanted to retain a religious influence in American higher education" (Hart 1999: 243) that had been theirs since the founding of America's institutions of higher education. The primary effect of the Cold War on the study of religion in America's colleges and universities, then, as Hart puts it, was that "for the brief period of roughly twenty years after World War II Protestants could be far more explicit in expressing religious convictions as scholarly communication" (243); the Cold War, that is, simply provided support for continuing the traditional role of *religion* in the college and university curriculum and in the process delayed somewhat the emergence and development of the scientific study of religion in the nation's colleges and universities.

There is no evidence that any direct support, whether from government agency or private foundation, is responsible for the entry of religious studies into the curriculum of colleges and universities in North America in the 1960s and no evidence that its research agendas were influenced to any great degree by specific Cold War values, despite the assertions of Jacob Neusner and Russell McCutcheon. Some scholars, to be sure, were influenced by Cold War concerns, but their influence on the field was negligible. And the fact that the favorable conditions on university campuses for the creation of new fields of study came as the result of a booming Cold War economy does not point to some sort of Cold War complicity. There is absolutely no indication that Cold War concerns with issues of national security or the protection of Western interests ever took precedence over the intellectual integrity of the research and scholarship in the field, even for those scholars who hoped that their research might have a positive bearing on the outcome of the Cold War. Jacob Neusner's comments on the study of religion and the Cold War bear clear testimony in that regard, for even though sympathetic to the American cause in the Cold War, Neusner champions the objective and neutral approach to the study of religion, free from the interference of "church and state," as is clear in his biting criticism of the politicization of the university since the 1970s.

With the evidence available to us, it appears that only one conclusion is possible with respect to the influence of the Cold War on the academic study of religion in North America (understood as a scientific rather than a religious enterprise)—namely that its encroachments on the discipline were only indirect and slight, affecting some individuals in the field, but without lasting ideological impact on it or its practitioners. This is not to say, of course, that the academic study of religion in colleges and universities in North America were altogether free from ideological influence. Religion itself has had an enormous influence on the conduct of the study of religion as an academic discipline and must, surely, be understood as ideological influence. Nevertheless, it is not primarily the religion that is closely associated with nationalism and an ideology of "Americanism" that influenced the direction the academic study of religion would take in North America, rather it is the long-standing religio-theological commitments of those in religious studies that shaped the field in the United States (and elsewhere)— commitments that helped shape, and were shaped by, what Roger Geiger (1993) refers to as, the post-1960s ideologies of egalitarianism and social responsibility.

Postscript

Two books relevant to the question of the impact of the Cold Ware on the academic study of religion have appeared since the Brno conference and merit comment here.

In *Religion after Religion: Gershom Scholem, Mircea Eliade, and Henry Corbin at Eranos* (1999) Steven Wasserstrom writes:

> It seems almost trite to observe at century's end, that the History of Religions was born in a time of crisis. Still, at the risk of banality, it is perhaps worthwhile to recall that birth did not take place during the height of wartime crisis, from 1914 to 1945. Rather, it occurred during its anxiously quiescent aftermath, at the beginning of the long stretch of peace conventionally called the Cold War. (Wasserstrom 1999: 127)

In the work of Gershom Scholem, Henry Corbin, and Eliade—whom he calls "Cold War Sages"—the history of religions, he maintains, "marched from exile to triumph . . . from the wilderness of academic life to occupying, for a time, the center of Religious Studies" (Wasserstrom 1999: 8). Although Wasserstrom does not provide a narrative of this development, he does suggest that a direct connection between the rise of the history of religions and the geopolitics of the Cold War can be seen in the support of Paul and Mary Mellon for the Eranos Conferences at Ascona, and more particularly, for the work of Henry Corbin (Wasserstrom 1999: 150–51), although just how the Mellon interests influenced these intellectual agendas is not elaborated. However, insofar as the work of Scholem, Corbin, and Eliade is fundamentally religious (Wasserstrom 1999: 63)—"a soteriologically vibrant conversation" directed to establishing "some kind of transcendent unity to world religions [and] a planetary ecumenism" (Wasserstrom 1999: 248, 142)—a Cold War impetus to their work is not altogether surprising for, as I have pointed out above, religion in general clearly benefited from the anxiety produced by the Cold War. That such a (Gnostic) history of religions (Wasserstrom 1999: 9, 258n23) became, for a time, the center of religious studies, therefore, should be no more surprising than that mainline Protestantism also regained a solid grip on departments of religion during this period. It ought also to be noted here that Wasserstrom's claims about the relationship between the Cold War and the history of religions does not entail that the intellectual concerns of the "Cold War Sages" had been directly influenced by the Cold War agenda. And Wasserstom acknowledges this when he maintains, somewhat contradictorily it seems, that the history of religions was "an immediate product of the period between the wars" and, writes: "[It] was epitomized in the older generation of Gerardus van der Leeuw and Rudolph Otto and among the Young Turks, by scholars like Henry Corbin and Mircea Eliade" (Wasserstrom 1999: 216). And from all accounts, Wasserstom's included, this (Gnostic) history of religions, as distinct from the history of religions concerned simply with historical and philological analysis of religious events and texts (*Relgionswissenschaft*), is a religious response to the general problems of modern secular society spawned by the Enlightenment that is derived from nineteenth-century romanticism and the early twentieth-century conservative revolutions (Wasserstrom 1999: 75) and so, clearly, antedates the Cold War.

Robert Ellwood's study of the work of Carl Jung, Mircea Eliade, and Joseph Campbell in his *The Politics of Myth* (1999) also connects the history of religions and study of myth with the Cold War, although more tentatively than does Wasserstrom. These scholars, Ellwood writes, were seen as living sages "on the stage of a world bound by time and history, by war and Cold War" (Ellwood 1999: xi). The study of myth and religion, as he puts it, was "enhanced by the postwar yearning to retrieve the best of the pre-modern past," and, like more traditional forms of religion, this approach to the study of religion found a secure place within the academy (Ellwood 1999: 45).

The Desire for Moral Validation

Although the evidence shows the Cold War to have had little direct ideological impact on the academic study of religion, I believe Jacob Neusner's complaint that since the 1970s American colleges and universities have been ideologically diverted from their unique mission is on target and deserves further attention here. Where I differ from Neusner, however, is in the view that this state of affairs can be directly attributed to the influence of the Cold War. Recognizing the difference between the character of the social engagement that might have characterized many scientists and scholars during the Cold War, and the projects espoused by researchers in the 1970s and beyond, will be helpful in understanding what have been the real ideological influences on the academic study of religion in the latter half of this century.

In *Research and Relevant Knowledge: American Research Universities Since World War II* (1993), Roger L. Geiger argues persuasively that it was a change of Zeitgeist that brought "challenges to the values of rational inquiry for which [the universities] ostensibly stood" (198). It was concern with government support of university research that had "enhanced the scope, vigor, and quality of graduate education and university research in the natural sciences" (199), and that eventually brought about the transformation of university education so deplored by Neusner.

Although Geiger points out that several studies of higher education in America failed to detect any major distortion of university practice in this period, many scholars, nevertheless, feel that the focus of university research was primarily on disciplinary puzzles rather than on problems of the real world, and that it was accompanied by a depreciation of teaching and a fragmentation of the curriculum that ignored student needs for personal fulfilment as well as intellectual development. Students were no longer offered the liberal education that universities still advertised; instead of courses contributing to their moral and cultural betterment they were offered "increasingly erudite and recondite specialties" (333), claims Geiger, which led to discontent, student uprisings, and eventual dissolution of the consensus that had characterized the university over the previous two decades. The university, it was felt, was dominated by dehumanizing industrial and military agendas; "service that formerly had been proudly rendered to assist in the defense of the nation were now seen as evidence of complicity in sustaining the Cold War" (236). Declining revenues—due to changes in the economy and in research funding by government agencies—and student rebellion against science and its presumed alliance with the industrial-military machine, claims Geiger, "stopped the forward momentum of research university development"

(252). The malaise caused by these developments was deepened by a new ideology of egalitarianism and social responsibility which, he writes, sent dissonant signals to the university:

> For higher education, access had eclipsed the advancement of knowledge as the nation's first priority. In research, findings applicable to immediate problems were demanded, while current rhetoric disparaged traditional scholarship in academic disciplines. This changed outlook affected the special status that research universities [had] long held. The federal government no longer felt compunction about intruding into internal university matters, and state governments increasingly denied distinctive treatment to their flagship institutions. On campus, universities had to deal with groups actively committed to engaging the institution in social and political issues. (252)

Under pressure, university leaders took steps that Geiger asserts confounded social goals with the cognitive task of the university. Its rapprochement with the real world primarily affected the social sciences and the humanities while trying to create "a fruitful interaction between social science and social praxis" (251).[1] University and scientific research were devalued, and the social sciences and humanities were structurally altered in a process that ultimately rejected the ideals of objectivity and neutrality, and the research and teaching functions of the university were effectively politicized. Geiger writes:

> The faith in basic research that had provided the underpinning for the post-Sputnik expansion was discredited, and in the process the fundamental mission of research universities was devalued. Ascendant now were values predicated on egalitarianism and social justice. This new standard affected universities obliquely: it made the operations of research universities more costly and more cumbersome, but it also made the institutions diffident about their *raison dʼêtre*. (269)

Administrative decisions, then, were taken so as to make the transformation of society the primary aim of the university. This reshaping of the university's relationship to society—in repudiating values like the objectivity and neutrality of research and scholarship that have been fundamental to the university—in essence undermined its educational mission. Cold War funding of university research, on the other hand, whether in the natural or social sciences did not in this way undermine the university disciplines or their commitment to a relentless, systematic, rational inquiry in a search for knowledge about the world.

This new kind of ideological distortion of research and scholarship in the university pointed to by Geiger is aptly illustrated by the reaction to David Stoll's recent critical examination of *I Rigoberta Menchú* (1984), an autobiographical account of the revolutionary activities and thoughts of an indigenous Guatemalan intellectual. Stoll's intention in analyzing Rigoberta's account of the revolution was to test her claims about the cause and its progress against other testimonies he had heard while working in Uspantán. He had heard a wide range of stories about land claims, membership in clandestine organizations, and responsibility for murders committed, many of which contradicted the claims made by Rigoberta, but felt pressure not to make this information public. Putting her claims to the test, he was told, would undermine the revolution of the poor Guatemalans against their oppressors and, in effect, then, provide aid to those who oppressed them. However, not testing the validity of the claims made by Rigoberta, he argues, bears too great a cost for the individuals involved in the conflict, and sacrifices genuine understanding of the revolutionary situation. "Refusing to judge whose story was more reliable," he writes, "would . . . mean giving equal credibility to an army collaborator and the widow of the man he killed" (217). Without testing claims made about the revolution and its benefits, moreover, it is impossible to tell whether the effect of violence in the particular situation might have been misconstrued, or whether stories of guerrilla warfare might have prolonged hardship for the people rather than resolving the problems causing the hardship. The outsider can be constructive in such matters, he claims, precisely "by stepping back from victimization narratives and weighing their reliability," and preventing a text such as *I, Rigoberta Menchú* from being misused to the detriment of those caught in the conflict. A scholarly assessment of how the violence might have been misconstrued by Rigoberta, or of how myths about guerrilla warfare propagated by her may have misguided individuals and groups, Stoll argues, might well provide important knowledge that could help prevent similar tragic events from occurring in the future. It is simply unacceptable for the scholar, therefore, to protect the book from criticism and verification for that would, in effect, make of it a proof-text for purposes quite contrary to its original intent. He then proceeds to show how the triumph of the political over the scholarly agenda in the university with respect to Rigoberta's story may well have produced just such a result.

Rigoberta's story differed from that of other Mayas caught up in the conflict, so that seeing how her story "mobilized international support for a defeated insurgence long after most peasants wanted peace" (231), Stoll writes, is crucially important. He admits that many of the peasants in Uspantán had reacted to the atrocities of the government forces in the way Rigoberta did but claims that they did so only so long as they held the belief that the guerrillas could win. But "once that was impossible," he writes,

> they began to think differently about how the killing started. Blame that they had focused exclusively on the army, for the obvious reason that it murdered their relatives, they now extended to the guerillas for luring indígenas into a hopeless cause. (133)

Rigoberta's account of the conflict gained international support for what had become an unpopular war. And it did so, claims Stoll, by means of distortion—in simplifying the issues involved, in the use of melodramatic descriptions of events without provision of verifying evidence, and in the use of images and symbols that had little to do with the actual lives of the indígenas. Rigoberta seems to have been well aware, he suggests, that "what [foreigners] are most likely to embrace is a well-defined cause with moral credibility, whose contradictions have been shoved under the table" (233). Her use of human rights imagery "met the needs of the revolutionary movement but discouraged reporting what many peasants had to say" (231). Thus, Stoll concludes that

> Rigoberta's story may have given voice to the dead in the early 1980s, but by the late 1980s, it had become so sacrosanct that it was drowning out the voices of other Guatemalans who, every time I visited, told me they wanted the war to end. (278)

Stoll challenges not only Rigoberta's account of events and their causes but also the assumptions of many academics who support her claim "that guerrilla warfare is an inevitable response by the poor [and] their way of defending themselves from exploitation" (278). However, their defense, he points out, is not based on carefully collected data and sociohistorical analysis, but rather on the indefensible moral ground that responsible scholars must identify with the oppressed; and he shows how this position, tied to an ideology of egalitarianism and social responsibility, devalues the traditional cognitive aims of the university. "In the 1960s," he writes, "many North American academics began to justify their careers by identifying with the oppressed" (242), for in counteracting the atrocities described by Rigoberta, they insist, factual issues lose their significance. What was important, if the poor were to overcome their oppression, was not the objective understanding of the situation, but rather the scholarly community's identification and solidarity with them. And such a stance, Stoll points out, shows that a desire for moral validation has supplanted empirical investigation and theoretical analysis in the legitimation of the social sciences. Those who seek knowledge and understanding, therefore, stand against the oppressed and must, consequently, be operating out of racist or imperialist motivation. As Stoll puts it:

> The premise of the new orthodoxy [in science and scholarship] is that Western forms of knowledge such as the empirical approach adopted [in my book] are fatally compromised by racism and other forms of domination. Responsible scholars must therefore identify with the oppressed, relegating much of what we think we know about them to the dustbin of colonialism. (xv)

For the guardians of the new orthodoxy the important question is simply whether victims deserve support and not the question of victimhood—to define who they are, why they find themselves in that condition, or what needs to be done; debate on such matters is discouraged as debilitating to the cause. Consequently, "authority to speak is reduced to membership in an oppressed group, or solidarity with it, restricting what can be said to what will be inoffensive" (245)—hardly what one would expect in the context of the modern university.

Stoll objects to this redefinition of the task of scholars in the university, insisting that the testing of claims through empirical research and sociohistorical analysis is the essence of solid, critical research and scholarship. Contrary to the claims of his critics, he insists that it is legitimate to question Rigoberta's story of the revolution in light of supplementary data. His astonishment at the iconic, semi-sacred status achieved by Rigoberta is understandable, as he queries "how a human being [could] achieve godlike status in an American research university" (232). His answer to that query is, I think, credible, and in fact implied by Stoll himself: it was desire for moral validation that made this possible. In supporting Rigoberta, scholars were affirming themselves as "caring human beings" involved in something of far greater significance than the mere search for knowledge.

Whether Stoll's criticisms of Rigoberta are on the mark or not is not at issue here. The fact that raising critical questions of her claims is interpreted as racist, colonialist, or imperialist is, for this implies that the university's essential agenda is neither epistemic nor educational, but rather moral, social, and political. And this suggests that the subversion of the traditional tasks of the university on North American campuses, as Jacob Neusner complains, may resemble in some pale sense the conditions that emerged at San Carlos University in Guatemala where "the elections for university authorities allowed guerrilla supporters to take over the university" (84).[2]

Part Three

In Search of a
Culture-Transcending Knowledge
of Religions and Religion

12

Removing Religion from the Study of Religion: A Nineteenth-Century Innovation

I am grateful to the organizing committee for the invitation to participate in the final event of this series of lectures on "Religion in the Academic Arena" in honor of C. P. Tiele that marks the occasion of the centenary of his death.

I am particularly excited to be involved in this Tiele event because Tiele's thought has had an enormous impact on my understanding of religion and the religious studies enterprise. Although I did my doctoral work in the philosophy of science and the philosophy of religion with Professor Ninian Smart, I was drawn into the field of the historian of religion and comparative religionist thirty years ago when Professor Smart asked me to teach a course on "Theories of Religion," at the University of Lancaster. I accepted the offer, seeing it as providing me a license to inquire into the nature of the academic study of religion in the context of the modern research university. This was something that the would-be philosopher of science in me thought a worthy topic for consideration and I looked for guidance from those whom I took to be the earliest spokespersons for the scientific study of religion. I turned first to C. P. Tiele's Gifford Lectures on *Elements of the Science of Religion* and Friedrich Max Müller's *Introduction to the Science of Religion* to gain some orientation in the field, and over the years each has been a formative influence in shaping my understanding of what the "religious studies enterprise" in the modern university ought to be—notwithstanding the fact that I found neither scholar persuasive with respect to their views about religion itself, or about how the study of religion ultimately relates to religion itself. Even though I completed my doctoral studies in England on the question of the relationship of religion to modern Western science, the nature of the new academic study of religion subsequently became a primary focus of interest for me.

This ought not to be surprising for Tiele's tireless campaign for a separate embodiment of the scientific study of religion in the university resulted in the passing of the Act in Higher Education in 1876 that clearly distinguished the new enterprise from religious and theological studies, already ensconced in the Dutch university curriculum, which made possible a broad dissemination of this new approach to the study of religion in a fashion not found in most other Western nations. I am aware of Arie Molendijk's recent assessment that the Dutch Act of Higher Education did not actually underwrite "a gradual emancipation [of the scientific study of religion] from the patronizing power of theology," but I am not convinced he is right in this judgment. The contrast between Britain and Holland with respect to the development of the scientific study of religion is not something that can be ignored. Müller—as much a champion on behalf of the scientific study of religion as Tiele—did not succeed in institutionalizing "the science of religion" in British academic life, and it was not until the mid-1960s that Britain saw the establishment of its first department of religious studies free from ecclesiastical control (or at least relatively free from such interference). Furthermore, even though interest in a non-theological study of religion has grown in the UK since then, there has been little interest in a purely scientific study of religion; in fact, there has been considerable opposition to the establishment of the scientific study of religion in British universities.

A few comments here about religious studies in North America, and especially in the United States, will, I think, reinforce the claim I am making on behalf of the science of religion in Holland since Tiele. American and Canadian scholars in this field have been even less assiduous in distinguishing religious studies from religious and theological modes of "inquiry," with the consequence that religious studies departments in American and Canadian colleges and universities have been, and still are, dominated by one of two major paradigms of study, and both are religious. The first might well be called the "traditional paradigm" for it is little more than a broad, ecumenical extension of the mainline, liberal Protestant theology that dominated the study of religion in North America until roughly the 1960s. Speaking plainly, it amounts to being essentially a kind of "world theology" that is sensitive and responsive to the world's major religious traditions, and its methodology is primarily that of phenomenology and "inter-religious dialogue." This paradigm is best represented by Harvard University's Center for the Study of World Religions and is exemplified in the work of scholars like Robert Lawson Slater, Wilfred Cantwell Smith (both Canadians), and John B. Carman. The second paradigm is best designated the "gnostic paradigm" for it makes of religious studies an exalted vocation concerned with recovering esoteric religious truth that far exceeds science and scholarship, yet does so, paradoxically, through scholarly and scientific means. It is clearly exemplified in the work of scholars like Mircea Eliade, Henry Corbin, and Gershom Schoelm and best represented by the Divinity School of the University of Chicago. Unlike the "history of religions" that emerged in European universities in the late nineteenth and early twentieth centuries, Eliade's gnostic understanding of religion, as Steven Wasserstrom has demonstrated (1999), involves an "uncanny doubleness of scholarship" that espouses a university-based study of religion while it simultaneously aims to create a "soteriologically vibrant conversation" that provides a "knowledge" of religion that lies beyond the realm of scientific research. Surprisingly—given the ideal of the modern research university—there is no department of religious studies in North America that models an unadulterated scientific and naturalistic approach to the study of religious phenomena. Such a model, in my judgment however, is represented in the Dutch tradition of the study of religion—as it is in the work of the IAHR, which has been strongly supported by the Dutch since the first of the international congresses of the association was held in Paris in 1900.

Given this view of Tiele and his influence on the academic study of religion in the Netherlands and beyond, you can see that I feel academically and intellectually at home here, and you will understand the extraordinary pleasure I take in being involved in this Tiele celebration. I do not mean to imply by saying all of this that everyone in Holland is likely to agree with my understanding of the history of the development of the scientific study of religion in this country, or, even if they do, that they will have the same appreciation for the naturalistic study of religion that I have expressed here. I mean only to say that I think this a reasonable interpretation of Tiele's influence on the growth of the academic study of religion as a distinctive element in the curriculum of the public university in Holland and on the field more generally as a scientific, rather than a religious or theological, enterprise.

I find the general theme announced for this afternoon's panel discussion—"The Future of Religion and of the Science of Religion"—particularly intriguing in light of the rubric under which the lectures themselves were presented—"Religion in the Academic Arena." On one reading of the phrase it appears that, in contrast to Dr. Molendijk's assessment, religion's place in the curriculum of the university is being contested by the very existence of the scientific study of religions; the continuation of religion's influence in the university, that is, seems to be inversely related to the success of the scientific study of religion in the university. On the other hand, the future of religion in society at large (including, paradoxically, the university campus), I suspect, is not at all—or only very slightly—tied to the success of the scientific study of religion in a nation's institutions of higher education; on this score I have no doubt that Rodney Stark and Roger Finke have some justification for their dissatisfaction with the secularization thesis in their recent book, *Acts of Faith: Explaining the Human Side of Religion* (2000). And as I have just indicated, the question of the future of religion on college and university campuses is not without its ambiguities. George Marsden's *The Soul of the American University: From Protestant Establishment to Established Nonbelief* (1994), Kieran Flanagan's *The Enchantment of Sociology: A Study of Theology and Culture* (1996), and Paul J. Griffiths's *Religious Reading: The Place of Reading in the Practice of Religion* (1999) on the one hand, provide clear indication that the scientific study of religion has had a strong negative impact on the place of religion in the academy. On the other hand, however, the recent volume *Religion on Campus* by Conrad Cherry, Betty DeBerg, and Amanda Porterfield (2001), Porterfield's earlier *The Transformation of American Religion: The Story of a Late Twentieth-Century Awakening* (2001), and D. G. Hart's *The University Gets Religion: Religious Studies in American Higher Education* (1999) argue that religion in the academy is alive and well, (although for Hart—even though deference to science in one sense has undermined the place of religion in the university—departments of religious studies nevertheless provided at least a watered-down liberal Protestantism and therefore religion continues on in the university even if only in an emaciated form).

Our theme, however, need not restrict us simply to the broad questions of the future of religion or of the science of religion; there is sufficient freedom under this rubric to pursue related concerns that I have been informed have emerged over the course of these lectures but without sufficient time to engage them in discussion with the audience. Dr. Wiegers, for example, in his introductory lecture raised the issue of whether human beings are religious by nature, and if so, what implications that fact holds for the academic study of religion. Other closely related questions raised in the lectures, I have been told, include the questions of the specific character of the "science of religion" and how that enterprise is related to the social-scientific studies of religion and religions by anthropologists, sociologists, psychologists, and others, as well as questions as to whether any or all of these sciences are necessarily reductionistic. The latter question in itself, moreover, requires that we first determine whether the reductionism that is objectionable to many students of religion is of the same order as the reductionism spoken of in a discussion of the natural or social sciences. On the other hand, as Dr. Jenner's lecture in this series might suggests, the issue of reductionism ought also to be viewed from a quite different, more practical, angle in connection with the treatment of patients with "disorders" involving auditory forms of religious experience. Another matter that has emerged over the past few weeks that might also be raised for discussion is that of the public responsibility of the student of religion; the responsibility the student of religion has, if any, not simply to the university and the profession, but to the broader community. Ought the scientific student of religion, it might be asked, also take on the role of the public intellectual, and can this be done without detriment to the field itself?

The answers these questions receive will depend in large part upon the point of departure taken up by the scholar providing the answer. And I want to suggest here that for the student of religion *qua* scientist, that the point of departure ought to be a clear understanding of the notion of "religion" determined by the nature of the academic enterprise we call religious studies. I am well aware, however, that there is considerable dispute over that matter but shall argue that the issue can only be determined by the nature of the institution in which the enterprise is situated. In my judgment there are at least two, and possibly three, distinct approaches to the intellectual or scholarly study of religion within the university context that must be given consideration. I note them here in chronological order of their emergence within the university curriculum, and since each is still a live option, I speak of them in the present tense. The first is the premodern study of religion that blends devotional, catechetical, moral, *and* intellectual/scientific concerns; it might well be designated *Glaubenswissenschaft* or "faith-imbued science," and is fundamentally concerned with providing one an in-depth (personal) *understanding* rather than a (public) explanation of religion. The second approach emerged with the modern university and is a strictly scientific study of religions which espouses reason as a nonmoral instrument of inquiry in an attempt to diminish as much as possible religious, moral, social, cultural, political, and other non-cognitive influences in its quest for empirical and explanatory knowledge about religions and religion. The third approach to the study of religion in the academy is that of the postmodernists who reject modern science as simply another ideology, and therefore seek understanding through "thick descriptions" of religions (and religion) in place of explanatory and theoretical accounts of religion. This not only involves a rejection of the modern scientific study of religion but also appears, at least at first blush, to differ from the premodern form of inquiry. Nevertheless, like the premodern faith-imbued science, the postmodern study of religion is, therefore, a modern form of Gnosticism in search of a "knowledge" of religion that lies beyond the bounds of science. Each of these approaches to the study of religion is represented in our colleges and universities, and although they are partially overlapping, they are nevertheless also, ultimately, mutually exclusive.

In my judgment, however, only the strictly scientific approach to the study of religion is appropriate in the context of the modern research university, although I am quite aware that the modern research university still retains a shadow of the pluralism of purpose that characterized the premodern university and continues to concern itself with liberal education and the preparation of students for public service in addition to pure research. Nevertheless, insofar as the modern research university is primarily committed to the creation and dissemination of knowledge and to the promotion and development of the skills necessary for acquiring new knowledge, then it is only the modern, strictly scientific, study of religion that functions legitimately within the university and is an appropriate part of its curriculum, for it alone, so to speak, has transformed "religion" from a supernatural reality into an object of science; "religion," that is, came to function as a taxonomic indicator used to designate a specific range of human behavior involving, to put it succinctly, belief in the supernatural which was now open to natural explanation. In this sense, then, the scientific study of religion is comparable to economics, political science, sociology, and psychology, among other disciplines, in that, like them, it simply tries to account for a specific range of human behavior in non-religious and non-theological terms. Jonathan Z. Smith captures this reality precisely when he writes: "'Religion' is not a native term; it is a term created by scholars for their intellectual purposes and therefore is theirs to define. It is a second-order, generic concept that plays ... [an important] role in establishing a disciplinary horizon. .... There can be no disciplined study of religion without such a horizon" (Smith 1982: xi; see also Smith 1998: 269) For Smith, therefore, religious studies is a science, although not a full-fledged science. On Stephen Toulmin's understanding of science (1972), claims Smith, religious studies would not constitute a full-blown discipline because it lacks certain methodological and institutional structures that make the natural sciences, in Toulmin's vocabulary, "compact disciplines." In compact disciplines, that is, there is consensus over intellectual goals, and strategies exist for improving the repertory of concepts and procedures that allow for the rational development of those disciplines and these are not present in the field of religious studies. In his article "'Religion' and 'Religious Studies': No Difference at All," Smith confesses that he doubts that religious studies constitutes a "coherent disciplinary matrix in and of itself" (1988: 235). He is not much bothered by this, however, since he recognizes that, on Toulmin's analysis, the same conclusion must be drawn with respect to the "other humanistic and social scientific fields." Religious studies, therefore, like the other fields of research interest are, in Toumin's terminology, either "diffuse" or "would-be" disciplines.

I find myself in essential agreement with Smith in this analysis, although unlike him I do not see religious studies as a would-be discipline but rather think it more accurate to speak of it as a scientific "enterprise," a distinction I shall spell out in just a moment or two. Nevertheless, there is no fundamental difference between Smith's position and mine given that "religious studies" in my account—using Robert McCaughey's terms—is a scientific "enterprise" within the framework of the modern research university but with many of the "deficiencies" Toulmin ascribes to "diffuse disciplines." However, Richard Miller (1996), professor of ethics at the University of Chicago Divinity School—who also adopts Toulmin's account of the nature of university "disciplines"— maintains that my view of religious studies is still that of a full-fledged science. But Miller's interpretation of Toulmin's views about what counts as science, I will show, is misleading and inappropriately applied to my view of the nature of the religious studies enterprise.

In his analysis of the notion of discipline, Toulmin distinguishes what he calls compact disciplines from diffuse disciplines and those intellectual exercises that strive to become compact disciplines. And, according to Miller, I hold a view of the academic study of religion as a compact discipline when in fact, according to Miller, it is both a diffuse discipline and, therefore, unscientific. But this is wrong on all counts. Miller seems not to realize, for example, that, for Toulmin, "diffuse" and "would-be" disciplines rightly aim at "compact science" status and that what makes disciplines scientific does not depend upon their "compactness" or "diffuseness" but rather on whether their goal is an explanatory one or not. As Toulmin puts it: "Where [the] common goal is an explanatory one, the discipline is a scientific one" (1972: 364). Furthermore, he fails to recognize that I acknowledge the "diffuse" character of the academic study of religion as it is currently carried out in our colleges and universities *and* that I see this as a condition to be overcome. Consequently, there is Toulminian justification, so to speak, for my view of religious studies as a scientific undertaking given that Toulmin himself sees the social sciences as diffuse disciplines—because "the preconditions [necessary to their development] do not yet apparently exist"—but not on that account as unscientific or forever incapable of achieving "compact science" status. "I am not claiming any absolute or permanent contrast between the social and the physical sciences," writes Toulmin; "On the contrary: I have merely been trying to diagnose certain special difficulties which face the theoretical sciences of human behaviour at the present time" (1972: 386).

Despite the difficulties faced in "disciplining" the academic study of religion, then, it is clear that an explanatory, and therefore scientific, approach to the field is possible, and I hope scholars and researchers in the field will recognize themselves as members of an "enterprise" that strives for such disciplinary stature. Adoption of Miller's alternative, non-disciplinable, poetic approach to the study of religion in the modern university, which is based neither on experiment nor argument, but rather merely on *conversation* that will guarantee a moral and religious literacy that will contribute meaning to human existence, is to make of "religion" a cultural idiom rather than an object of investigation. And in doing so, it seems to me that humanistically oriented religious studies scholars buy into either a premodern or postmodern conception of the religious studies enterprise which—even if it has (had) a coherent rationale—is not one appropriate in the context of the modern research university.

In conclusion allow me to emphasize that "the academic study of religion"—that study of religion appropriate in the context of a modern research university—is a new kind of intellectual inquiry into religious phenomena that is not subject to the traditional structures of knowledge and authority that governed the premodern university. Rather, it possesses a normative structure consistent with the notion of reason as a nonmoral instrument of inquiry that is operative in both the natural and social sciences. And within that framework the notion of "religion" refers merely to a range of human behaviors inspired by myths or metaphysical constructions of transcendent beings, powers, or states. For the scientific student of religion that concept does not refer to transcendent realities that lie beyond the methods of inquiry applicable to the study of quotidian, everyday-ordinary realities and events but only to culturally postulated "transcendent" realities that are intersubjectively available for scientific analysis and explanation. On the one hand, then, the academic study of religion is, as I have already noted, comparable to economics, political science, sociology, and psychology, among other disciplines in that, like them, it simply tries to account for a specific range of human behavior in non-religious, non-theological, and non-metaphysical terms. On the other hand, religious studies differs from them in its multidisciplinary and polymethodic character and is better described as an "academic enterprise" because it is essentially an organized group of scholars and scientists from a diverse range of disciplines who have gained this "academic identity" by virtue of their common interest in religious thought and behavior. And it is essentially a scientific enterprise because it is chiefly characterized by an epistemic intention and takes for granted that the natural and social sciences are the only legitimate models for the objective study of religion appropriate in the modern university. Although the multidisciplinary and polymethodic character of this scientific enterprise constitutes a centrifugal force that threatens its coherence and identity, the commitment to finding a theory of religion that will provide a causal explanatory account of religious phenomena creates a counterbalancing centripetal force, making religious studies more than a miscellaneous agglomeration of humanistic and social-scientific disciplines. The modern student of religion, therefore—whether working at the level of the "naturalist" in the collection, description, and classification of data, or at the level of analysis and interpretation of the meanings which the data have for the devotee, or at the level of comparative analysis of religious systems of thought and practice that might provide useful generalizations about religion(s), or at the level of theory that might provide a causal explanation of the data is essentially concerned to find an account of religion in terms of warrantable (testable) claims and therefore contributes to a cumulative body of knowledge about a specific type of human behavior.

These, then, are the constraints within which I think any and all discussion about religion and religions in the academy ought to be framed. It is not the task of the modern research university to provide a forum for "conversation" about religion that will guarantee a moral and religious literacy that in turn will contribute meaning to human existence. That would make of students of religion a new clerisy rather than scientists and scholars.

13

Modernism and the Study of Religion

"Modernism" is a general term in cultural history which has come to be attached to an extraordinarily broad range of cultural developments, including architecture, art, literature, and religion. So broad has been its application that for some it is doubtful whether it denotes a unitary human phenomenon, however overwhelmingly complex; its polysemic character suggesting a multiplicity of phenomena and a diversity of modernisms. Nevertheless, I will argue here that the term is appropriately applied to significant developments in seventeenth- and eighteenth-century Europe, and that its proper understanding is essential to comprehending the role of the academic study of religion in the contemporary university. That study of religion is clearly differentiable, I shall argue, from an earlier religious and theological study of religions and it is so because it is a product of what is reasonably called the modern mind. And it is to a proper understanding of the *modern* study of religion to which I shall pay attention here because I believe that, as John F. Wilson has put it, the relatively recent emergence of university programs in the study of religion "may be the single most significant development associated with modernity that affects religion in new ways in our time" (1987: 17). "Those of us whose professional lives are so defined," he continues, "should be the first to recognize this interface between modernity and religion [because] it is possibly the one decisively new factor in the situation we are working to understand" (1987: 17).

Wilson, unfortunately, did not elaborate on this aspect of the relation of religion to modernity; he chose rather to examine the ways in which modernity—defined simply as "a period of intense social and hence cultural change" (1987: 17)—influences religious behavior and belief. The results of that analysis, however, are rather meager and shed no light on the issue of modernism and the study of religion: "I conclude," he writes, "that modern times or the modern era has proven to effect religion heterogeneously" (1987: 16).

In attempting to understand the influence of modernity on religion Wilson advises the scholar that "our task is to understand the modern, not to either embrace or excoriate it" (1987: 13). This is advice I intend to follow here although I recognize it is not altogether free of paradox in that it may itself well be a product of the modern mind-set. In following the advice, therefore, it could be argued that I am at least implicitly involved in making out a case for a modern as opposed to a traditional study of religion. There is some justification in such a charge, although, as will become clear later in this chapter, I will provide explicit argument to this effect. I believe it essential, however, to keep such explicit argument distinct from an account of the nature of modernism as it emerged in the West. If this chapter is to be of value to the reader in understanding modernism, that is, it must be more than simply an expression of the author's point of view.

At least two essays in the past fifteen years have given explicit attention to the relation of modernism to the study of religion: Martin E. Marty's 1985 public lecture at Arizona State University, "What is Modern About the Modern Study of Religion" and Catherine Bell's recent review essay entitled "Modernism and Postmodernism in the Study of Religion" (1996). Marty recognizes as modern the fact that the study of religion today finds itself located primarily in the university setting rather than in the ecclesia (religious community). He also recognizes that such programs of study are, or at least claim to be, neutral, reductionistic, and focused on a concern for knowledge rather than meaning, yet he insists that in answering the question of what is modern in the study of religion today, one must recognize the involvement of at least two additional "publics," the ecclesia and the republic (society at large). However, in his insistence that all three publics must be involved in answering the question posed in the title of his address, Marty fails to understand the essential role played in the emergence of modern society and culture by science, or of the essentially detached character of the scientific enterprise itself. For Marty there can be no clear line of demarcation between objectivity and engagement and, therefore, no absolute differentiation between the academy and the ecclesia (1985: 8). "Teaching about religion instead of teaching religion," he insists therefore, although without the benefit of argument, "is its own kind of quasi-creedal commitment" (1985: 8). What is peculiarly modern in the modern study of religion for Marty, then, is not its scientific character but rather the recognition that "the republic of modern religious studies" involves—for Marty, ought to involve—a multiplicity of voices and, therefore, a multiplex consciousness (1985: 10). The modern study of religion for Marty, therefore, is one given over to political and religious concerns in addition to the epistemic objective, as is clear from the following declaration, proclaimed in order to warn the student of religion about the evils of too narrow a view of the enterprise: "To yield all to the academics might be to obscure commitment to religion. To yield all to the religionists might be to produce a clerisy or theocracy. The interaction profits all" (1985: 9). Marty's essay, unfortunately, provides the reader only an implicit critique of modernism rather than with an account of modernity and its implications for the study of religion. Indeed, Marty outlines here the structure of an alternative to a modern study of religion that might more appropriately be labelled as either premodern or postmodern.

Although as critical of modernity as Marty, Catherine Bell has a clearer understanding of modernism and its significance for the study of religion. Bell maintains that a modern study of religion is wholly characterized by the assumption that science is a system of thought which can and has escaped the determinations of culture in contrast to religion which is a system of thought "completely entangled in culture" (1996: 183), and that the application of scientific method in the study of religion is, therefore, epistemically superior to the study of religion undertaken within a theological or confessional framework. In a critique of J. Samuel Preus's *Explaining Religion: Criticism and Theory from Bodin to Freud* (1987) and Tom Lawson's and Robert McCauley's *Rethinking Religion: Connecting the Cognitive and the Cultural* (1990) she maintains that the modern study of religion is naive in its claim that there was a "smooth process of rational and progressively scientific thinking that yielded a 'coherent research tradition' with which to replace the reigning theological paradigm" (1996: 180), and that the trust in science to provide us with objective knowledge of religion is simply not justified. According to Bell, that is, the moderns too easily dismiss the nonrational influences upon the development of science itself and its attendant consequences (which, unfortunately, she does not spell out) and the nonrational influences that even now continue to undermine science and support a continued use of the theological framework for the study of religious phenomena (1996: 183). She maintains, moreover, that theology itself is a product of the Enlightenment and that it is, therefore, every bit as much a modernist enterprise as science. Consequently, the absolute contrast between religion and the study of religion insisted upon by modernists, she concludes, is not only groundless but also problematic for the study of religion. Postmodernists have shown, Bell argues, that neither religion nor science are exempt from significant cultural determination. Insisting that "all concepts and terms are embedded in particular experiences and 'conventional perspectives,'" she maintains that there is "little possibility of a shared, cross-cultural terminology that affords systematic methods of analyzing commonalities and differences in the practices we speak of as religion" (1996: 185), which in turn shows that all knowing—including so-called modern scientific knowing—is inevitably political (1996: 186).

In coming to this conclusion, however, Bell, strangely, does not insist that all our attempts to know "are politically, epistemologically, and morally suspect" (1996: 187), and she does not, therefore, completely reject the modern notion that religion can be studied neutrally (1996: 185). Nevertheless she is convinced, it appears, that the modernist debate that created the concern over "outsider" versus "insider" (that is, neutral as opposed to confessional) approaches to the study of religion is exhausted—despite what she refers to as "the nearly paranoid degree of anti-theology polemic of the last decade" (1996: 187)—and that no resolution of that fundamental tension is possible within either a modernist or postmodernist framework. What is needed, she insists, is a view of science that does not simply repeat the ideology of science but rather allows for a study of religion "that is not universal or hegemonic" (1996: 188). And such a view of science, she insists—without elaboration, however—can be found in Bruno Latour's analysis of the nature of modern science. That Latour's work provides a fruitful alternative to the scientific study of religion proposed by Preus, Lawson, McCauley, and others, which is not itself confessional is, I think, doubtful. Indeed, there is good reason to question whether Latour's critique of modern science is coherent and consistent; whether it can actually ground a framework of analysis that, as Bell suggests, can transcend current theological and scientific approaches to the study of religion is similarly in question. I shall respond to Bell's suggestion in this regard, however, only after engaging more fully the debate about modernism and modernity.

In a broad sense "modernism" is used to name a complex series of developments in the economic, social, and political life of Western European societies that radically transformed them from relatively simple, homogeneous to complex and highly differentiated communities. "Modernism," therefore, is intimately connected with such notions as capitalism, industrialization, urbanization, development, and modernization. The radical transformation of the social structures of society was associated not simply with material changes brought about by technology but also with changes in consciousness involving the rejection of traditional religious structures of authority which led to the emergence of a new, secular, social order in Europe. Ernest Gellner summarizes this development in terms of a shift from traditional martial to commercial values in which change rather than stability becomes the norm for society. As he puts it, "Perpetual improvement under the name of Progress becomes the key notion of a new vision, and the basis of a new morality. . . . Riches are worth seeking when they are protected, and constitute the path to power, rather than the other way around" (1997: 11; see also his 1988). Central to this transition in cultural styles, Gellner insists, was the emergence of science—what Gellner appropriately calls an effective form of cognition. The birth of the modern, then, involved a new way of thinking not only about the natural world but also about the human condition—about humanity and society. For modern intellectuals, that is, scientific detachment was combined with a reformist involvement that included a critique of tradition and the demise of traditional social hierarchies which in turn created a need for moral sciences such as political economy, history, sociology, and psychology, which would promote progress and human emancipation. In addition to scientific cosmology, therefore, modern thinkers, as Peter Gay points out, "called for a social and political order that would be secular, reasonable, humane, pacific, open, and free" (1969: 397), and a critical social science that would "unmask pleasing dreams for the sake of realistic programs [and] fictions for the sake of reality" (1969: 335).

Modernism in this sense, as the discussion of Wilson above has already indicated, is of immense importance to students of religion because of the impact such changes in structures of society, and consciousness to which it refers, have had upon religious beliefs and practices. Given the centrality of science to modernism so understood, however, it is appropriate also to refer to the intellectual developments leading to the ascendancy of science as modernism, because these developments constitute a fundamental change of mentality that differentiate the culture it effects from all previous traditional cultures, archaic, ancient or medieval. There is a real sense in which the new structures of thought that emerged in seventeenth- and eighteenth-century Europe opposed established traditions and authority in matters of knowledge and action in a fashion which pitted them against the "ancients" as "moderns." As Peter Gay puts it, the project of the Enlightenment was the pursuit of modernity in that it moved beyond the fatalism characteristic of the ancient and medieval worlds. "The ancients," he writes, "had felt helpless before the forces of nature and man's irrationality, and the philosophers of antiquity had rationalized this impotence in systems pervaded by a profound pessimism" (1969: 84), and the moderns, he argues, developed a new style of thinking which involved the search for wholly naturalistic explanations of phenomena and rejected the infusion of theological, metaphysical, and aesthetic concerns characteristic of ancient modes of thought. It is not that the moderns wholly rejected classicism but rather that they kept "their respect for their ancestors within proper bounds" (1969: 125) and placed greater emphasis upon reason and the growth of knowledge which provided them with "an expansive sense of power over nature and themselves" (1969: 3). The world was being emptied of mystery by the advance of knowledge. And it is this development that is of greater significance in our understanding of religion and the study of religion than the material changes wrought by the Industrial Revolution associated with this change in mentality—that is, with the rise of science.

I will attempt to provide an understanding of modernism in this restricted sense by means of an analysis of and commentary on the accounts of the phenomenon provided by Timothy Reiss in his *Discourse of Modernism* (1982) and Hans Blumenberg's *Legitimation of the Modern Age* (1987). Although Reiss and Blumenberg disagree in their evaluations of modernity, their accounts of its substance and character are remarkably convergent and, consequently, can provide a reasonable entry point into a discussion of the implications of modernism for the study of religion.

Modern discourse, Reiss argues, is analytico-referential and emerged in the West by overcoming what he calls a theocratico-theological discourse that had dominated thought in the Middle Ages.

By "discourse" Reiss means "the visible and describable praxis of what is called 'thinking'" (1982: 9); for him the term parallels Foucault's notion of "episteme" in that a discourse provides the conceptual tools "that control the analysis and understanding of the majority of human practices" (58). For Reiss, as for Foucault, there can only be one dominant discourse in effect in any period of history, although there usually are other subordinated and dominated discourses contemporaneous with it. Such alternative discourses, however, cannot hold meaning for society, he insists, because they cannot be expressed within the framework of the dominant discourse.

According to Reiss, analytico-referential discourse is most clearly exemplified by science (30), and the telescope, he claims, appropriately symbolizes the emergence of this new mode of conceptualization—the emergence of the ordering of the world by the mind wherein the linguistic sign came "to be defined as an arbitrarily selected transparent instrument placed between concept and object" (26). Such a discourse he writes,

> assumes that the world as it can be and is to be known, represents a fixed object of analysis quite separate from the forms of discourse by which men speak of it and by which they represent their thought. . . . Equally basic is the assumption that the proper *use* of language will not only *give* us this object in a gradual accumulation of detail (referentiality), but will also *analyze* it in the very form of its syntactic organization. . . . The assumption of this coincidence of universal reason and general grammar was essential. (42, emphasis in original)

This way of conceptualizing the world, then, suggests Reiss, "marks a total distancing of the mind from the world and the imposition of a system which belongs to the realm of discourse" (140). As he puts it: "Scientific discourse sought first of all to grasp an exterior, coming to view itself as a simple translation of the world of objects into a conceptual order. It claimed there was an adequately explicable correspondence between a referent supposed to be in nature and a sign which was assumed to mediate the other entirely passively" (141).

This "discourse of modernism," Reiss claims, arose out of an earlier dominant discourse which he refers to as "a discourse of patterning" (46) which depends upon an entirely different process of conceptualizing or ordering the world—one which uses words "as though they are in some way essential and inherent in the object" (41). Such a discourse constitutes "a system of transformations organizing a comprehension of society and the individual, of nature and culture, of the 'natural' and the 'supernatural.'" (49). Such a form of thought is mythical rather than narrative and linear, and, unlike the latter, refuses to draw a distinction between the ontological and the epistemological realms and "assumes that discourse is a part of the 'world' and not distinct from it [granting privilege neither] to the enunciator of discourse [n]or to the act of enunciation" (30). In such a system of thought knowledge involves subordination of the human mind "to an order of concrete events exterior to the mind" (141). Thus, knowledge is constituted by a discursive exchange "within the world" in the patterning mode of thought whereas in the analytico-referential discourse the expression of knowledge is "a reasoning practice upon the world" (30). Reiss argues, therefore, that the patterning mode of thought is conjunctive and totalizing rather than disjunctive, as in the analytico-referential mode of thought; and the conjunctive mode of thought involves a form of union with the divine in regard to cognition while the modern mode of thought is disjunctive in that it accentuates human responsibility for one's being in its understanding of the act of knowing (72, 106). Thus, Reiss insists that in the patterning mode of thought the "concepts of *use, arbitrariness, will, intention, individual, person,* and *self* are all quite different [and that they] cannot but provide an utterly dissimilar practice of discourse" (95). Reiss consequently insists that in tracing the role of will as an aspect of self-identity and the significance of self-identity as a center of knowing will reveal what is central to an understanding of the moderns (59) and show why the modern age was incomprehensible to the age it succeeded. The emergence of this new disjunctive mode of discourse from within the frame of a conjunctive mode of discourse is clearly captured, Reiss suggests, in Kepler's *Somnium* (1634). "I suggest," he writes, "that Kepler's *Somnium* manifests a moment when two different classes of discourse function with equivalent power—a moment of transition which must obviously be brief, for the one is being produced from the other. And it may be possible to generalize here and suggest that a whole type of literary discourse is being undermined as well" (148–49).

The text of the *Somnium*, claims Reiss, does not operate in an analytical fashion but an analysis of the notes, he points out, permits "what is *contained* in the dream to become a part of an analytical knowledge," and in the process of doing so, changes "the very structure of discourse" (149). Thus, we see here a disappearance of a class of discursive activity, "a passage from what one might call discursive *exchange within* the world to the expression of knowledge as a reasoning *practice upon* the world" (30). And what is seen only hesitantly in Kepler becomes in Francis Bacon a new and dominant discourse: "*The New Organon* (1620) will view a particular class of writing and the specific organization of discourse it necessitates as the fundamental requirement of all 'right' knowing" (198). Reiss continues:

> Bacon's is not . . . an idea of science limited to a relatively brief moment at the beginning of the seventeenth century. It remains our own. It remains indeed by and large the underlying premise behind all our discourses of truth and, therefore,

behind all the forms of what we term "knowledge." For Baconian experimentalism is not *simply*, as is often claimed, the active manipulation and forcing of natural phenomena. Such manipulation is dependent, as it is, for Galileo, on prior theory. (226–27, emphasis in original)

It is true that later scientific research was often affected by theological beliefs, but this does not mean that such research was not governed by the new analytico-referential discourse. As Reiss notes, although scientific theory was not left untouched by religious belief, "being 'touched' and being organized by are two different things" (221).

Determining *when* the modern emerges in Europe is not without significance to the issue of the character of modern thought. Reiss maintains that the analytico-referential mode of thought arose in the seventeenth century even though he concedes that there is some continuity with thought patterns in the twelfth century and acknowledges "that there is no question but that some kind of analogous split did occur between the sixth and fourth century B. C." (58; see Wiebe 1991). He argues, however, that the conceptual break between antiquity and the Middle Ages did not simply lead on to the emergence of modernity. He also insists that the ancient Greek development does not "permit us to assume that it resulted in the rule of discourse identical to that which may have been dominant in the Middle Ages or to one which became dominant from the European Renaissance on" (58).

Blumenberg's treatment of modern European thought also recognizes it to be significantly different from both that of antiquity and the Middle Ages which is especially evident in its concern with human self-assertion and its unwillingness to rely on divine providence. The moderns, Blumenberg insists, adopt a rational approach to the resolution of human problems rather than passively accepting a promise of salvation; they relate, therefore, to a natural, rather than a supernatural, world which is open to scientific understanding. And it is to this break with traditional thought to which Blumenberg devotes his attention in *The Legitimation of the Modern Age*. Whereas in *The Genesis of the Copernican World* (1987) Blumenberg looks at the emergence of a new mode of thought with the Copernican revolution in astronomy and cosmology, in *The Legitimation of the Modern Age* he devotes himself to refutation of the claims of the romantics and other critics of modernity who deny its rupture with the traditional mode of existence in the Middle Ages, and he pays special attention to those who would deny the legitimacy of the modern age on the ground that it really is little more than the secularization of Christian ideas. Thus he writes:

The occasion for talk of the legitimacy of the modern age does not lie in the fact that this age conceives of itself as conforming to reason and as realizing this conformity in the Enlightenment but rather in the syndrome of the assertions that this epochal conformity to reason is nothing but an aggression (which fails to understand itself as such) against theology, from which in fact it has in a hidden manner derived everything that belongs to it. (97)

In contrast to such claims Blumenberg argues that modernity constitutes a break with the dominant theme of divine omnipotence in the Middle Ages and that it is an affirmation of the contingency of the world which involves a critical commitment to rationality both in knowing the world and in living in it. Blumenberg does not deny that the modern age has some connection with the Middle Ages in that it accepted, as he puts it, "a mortgage of prescribed [residual] questions . . . as its own obligation" (65) but insists, nevertheless, that it is not a continuation of it. "What mainly occurred in the process that is interpreted as secularization," he writes, "should be described not as the *transposition* of authentically theological questions . . . into secularized alienation from their origin but rather as the *reoccupation* of answer positions that had become vacant and whose corresponding questions could not be eliminated" (65). The Enlightenment, that is, took over the explanatory functions of Christianity in the same way Christianity had taken over the explanatory functions from antiquity (69). This is characteristic, Blumenberg argues, of all epochal thresholds during "the phases of more or less rapid change in the basic rules for the procurement of very general explanations" (66).

According to Blumenberg, then, even though the moderns recognized the value of the legacy of antiquity, they nevertheless rejected the "fundamental Renaissance thesis of the unsurpassability of ancient literature" (125) and he, therefore, insists "that the modern age is neither a renewal of the ancient world nor its continuation by other means" (126). Nor is the modern age for Blumenberg merely a continuation of Christianity; it emerges, rather, as a response to the crises experienced by Christianity by providing a comprehensive understanding of human life through reason and theory arising from a transition from a naive to a self-conscious curiosity about the world (237). This last transition gave rise to an unrestricted cognitive drive, argues Blumenberg, whereas the Middle Ages had tied knowledge to happiness. Thus, according to Blumenberg:

> From a central affect of consciousness there arises in the modern age an indissoluble link between man's historical self-understanding and the realization of scientific knowledge as the confirmation of the claim to unrestricted theoretical curiosity. The "theoretical attitude" may be a constant in European history since the awakening of the Ionian interest in nature; but this attitude could take on the explicitness of insistence on the will and right to intellectual curiosity only after it had been confronted with opposition and had had to compete with other norms of attitude and fulfilment in life. (232–33)

The success of this "theoretical curiosity," and the search for knowledge free of all restriction in respect to other "human existential interest posited as absolute" (233), is therefore a chief characteristic of the modern age. And "when, as in the modern age," writes Blumenberg, "a form of life first begins to depend on science for the conditions of its possibility does the problem of knowledge as such become so elementally acute for it that the problem of the possibility of life poses itself even before that of happiness in life" (271). Truth, that is, "has become the result of a renunciation for the modern age . . . a renunciation that lies in the separation between cognitive achievement and the production of happiness" (404).

What the analyses of Reiss and Blumenberg bring into clear relief, it seems to me, is that the modern age arises with the ascendancy of scientific thought and that science itself is essentially due, as Michael Roberts in *The Modern Mind* (1937) argues, to a restriction of the notion of reason in seventeenth- and eighteenth-century thought (1937: 123). As Robert Hoopes puts it in his detailed analysis of the issue in *Right Reason in the English Renaissance* (1962):

> The intellectual history of the seventeenth century is marked by the gradual dissociation of knowledge and virtue as accepted and indivisible elements in the ideal structure of human reason, a shift from the tradition of right reason to the new tradition of scientific reasoning. (161)

The point Hoopes makes is that "right reason" is not merely reason in our current sense of the term; it has a much broader meaning that the single word "reason" no longer possesses (4). In earlier times, Hoopes points out, the notion of right reason referred to a mode of knowing, a way of doing, and a condition of being. "Right reason," he writes,

> may thus be thought of as a faculty which fuses in dynamic interactivity the function of knowing and being, which stands finally as something more than a proximate means of rational discovery or "a nonmoral" instrument of inquiry, and which affirms that what a man knows depends upon what, as a moral being, he chooses to make himself. (5)

Consequently, for right reason truth is a matter not only of the intellect but also of virtue and involves the discovery of truth and the doing of the good. And insofar as such a notion presupposes a belief in absolute and eternal values, right reason "refers not only to logical activity or discourse, but to the highest faculty and function of man" (21–22).

The notion of right reason, as Hoopes informs us, finds its origins in classical Greek and Roman thought. But he also goes on to show that right reason eventually colonized Christian thought, even though the Christian notion of original sin undermines it by rendering persons intellectually incapable of achieving knowledge without assistance and morally unable to achieve the good. Hoopes writes:

> Although classical humanistic idealism hesitated on the threshold of the Christian world, it entered with ease the moment Christian thinkers succeeded in their effort to soften and minimize the paralysing consequences of Adam's sin. With that entrance we see the birth of the set of attitudes we now call Christian humanism, and which is at once like and unlike the humanism of the Greek and Roman worlds. (54–55)

Right reason for Christian humanists, therefore, became possible through a gift of grace which allowed persons to overcome their human limitations. Right reason in this context, that is, involved "the fusion of—and not the choice between—reason and faith, of the works of man in alliance with the grace of God" (97). We see clearly here the continuity between the world of antiquity and the medieval world.

There is not, however, a corresponding continuity between the medieval and the modern worlds for, as Hoopes has shown, the seventeenth-century thinkers like

Francis Bacon, René Descartes, and Thomas Hobbes had developed a notion of reason distinct from right reason by severing cognition from virtue. And with such a new form of reason a scientific knowledge of both the natural and the social worlds became a distinct possibility. Science, that is, became possible by refusing to subordinate the desire to know to the achievement of a non-cognitive goal such as salvation and the virtuous life; no longer is intellection restrained by moral and religious ideals. "Discursive reason, as the epic repeatedly makes clear," writes Hoopes, "denotes induction or disinterested science, which discovers truths but not the Truth for Man" (198).

With this transformation of "reason," then, we have the ascendancy of science as an objective, neutral, universalistic discourse about the world, both natural and social. Exactly how it achieved ascendancy has not been delineated here, nor can it be in any great detail. It is important, however, to point out that essential to this development was the creation of what Toby Huff refers to as "neutral spaces" in society which could sustain the role of the scientist by freeing the scientist from social and political concerns. The breakthrough to science, Huff writes in his *The Rise of Early Modern Science*, "was a breakthrough that destroyed the received worldview and established a new and legally protected institutional location within which intellectual inquiries of the most far-reaching cultural and intellectual consequences could be carried out without hindrance" (1993: 203). Although Huff recognizes that modern science emerged in seventeenth-century Europe (19), he nevertheless maintains that some of the foundations for that development were already laid down in the twelfth-century renaissance in Europe (106), which were supported by peculiar legal developments with respect to the autonomous corporate character of European universities (161). He writes: "If the scientific worldview is to prevail, its elements of universalism, communalism, organized scepticism, and disinterestedness must be given paradigmatic expression in the dominant structures of a society" (213). And according to Huff, the universities had already established such "neutral zones" which could politically legitimate "a disinterested agenda of naturalistic inquiry" (336) by the end of the thirteenth century. "From our point of view," he then writes,

> the modern scientific revolution was a social and intellectual revolution that at once reorganized the scheme of natural knowledge and validated a new set of conceptions of man and his cognitive capacities . . . [which] found an institutional home in the cultural and legal structures of medieval society. Together they laid the foundations validating the existence of neutral institutional spaces within which intellects could pursue their guiding lights and ask the most probing questions. The religious, legal, and philosophical presuppositions built into medieval state and society created the foundations of modernity that have continued to spread around the world. (362)

The emergence of a scientific study of religion wholly dissociated from and neutral with respect to religion and theology in the nineteenth century ought not to come as a surprise. The *modern* university had continued to develop "neutral intellectual spaces," as Huff describes them, within which anything and everything in the natural and social worlds could be subjected to scientific analysis and explanation.

Julie Reuben's *The Making of the Modern University: Intellectual Transformation and the Marginalization of Morality* (1996) leaves no room for doubt about that assessment, and especially so with respect to matters religious and moral. Despite Catherine Bell's concerns noted above, therefore, the modern study of religion represented in the work of scholars like Preus, Lawson, and McCauley, which clearly demarcate scientific from religious modes of thought, is wholly consistent with the cognitive agenda of the modern research university. Their goal of disinterested knowledge as opposed to self-involving research is naive, as Bell charges, only if the rationale of the modern university itself is naive, and this, as I have noted, has not been established by Bell. Nor is this simply to reject out of hand Bell's claim that moderns too easily dismiss the nonrational influences upon the development of science. It is rather a recognition that despite the fact that very specific local conditions affect the development of science, there is a radical difference of character between scientific inquiry and other non-universalizing modes of thought. And contrary to Bell's suggestion, I do not believe Bruno Latour's understanding of modernity and science provides an adequate alternative framework for that task. In looking at this claim, however, I shall restrict my comments on Latour here to his *We Have Never Been Modern* (1993).

According to Latour, science is not a peculiarly modern phenomenon that distinguishes modern from traditional societies (primitive, ancient, or medieval). Distinguishing the science of the modern West from the ethno-science of archaic cultures, he claims, is unwarranted; we must not, according to Latour, "create a divide between pre-logical and logical cultures" (112) and assume that knowledge of nature and society has only been achieved by moderns by virtue of their capacity "to distinguish between the laws of external nature and the conventions of society" (130), and thereby avoid the confusion created by archaic cultures who mix "the constraints of rationality with the needs of their societies" (130). Indeed, our culture, he maintains, must be studied in the same way archaic cultures are studied—anthropologically— because there is no radical difference between ancients and moderns (10). Modern Western culture, that is, has not rationalized and disenchanted the world and there is, therefore, no clear epistemological or rational asymmetry between the West and other cultures. There is, consequently, no need to be "defending the purity of science and rationality from the polluting influence of passions and interests; defending the unique values and rights of human subjects against the domination of scientific and technical objectivity" (124) as antimodernists are wont to do.

According to Latour, then, we have never been modern. He admits, however, that there exists a "modern Constitution" which "invents a separation between the scientific power charged with representing things, and the political power charged with representing subjects" (29), which, by means of a process he calls purification, guarantees the existence of the universal laws of things and the inalienable rights of human persons (50). According to that constitution, he writes, "the obscurity of the olden days, which illegitimately blended together social needs and natural reality, meanings and mechanisms, signs and things, gave way to a luminous dawn that clearly separated material causality from human fantasy" (35). But the modern world, he insists, has never been able to function according to the rules of its constitution because, in addition to populating the world with natural and cultural phenomena (via the process of purification), it has created a whole new realm of entities which are neither, yet are mixtures of both the natural and the human—"things" like the ozone hole, global warming, deforestation, etc. So-called modern cultures, therefore, have never really abandoned the old anthropological matrix, characteristic of archaic and ancient cultures, that blends fact and value in knowledge and makes knowledge contextual and local rather than decontextualized and global. As Latour puts it:

> The modern Constitution as a whole had already declared that there is no common measure between the world of subjects and the world of objects, but that same Constitution at once cancelled out the distance by practising the contrary, by measuring humans and things alike with the same yardsticks, by multiplying mediators in the guise of intermediaries. (59)

Latour therefore insists that "if we link together in one simple picture the work of purification and the work of mediation that gives it meaning we discover, retrospectively, that we have never truly been modern" (91); that we have never thoroughly held nature and society to be wholly distinct realities. Our so-called modern science, therefore, is bound to the social world in the same way as are the ethno-sciences which the "modern" science of anthropology presumes to study objectively. The claim that the modern age has radically distinguished humans from nonhumans while archaic and ancient cultures have failed to distinguish epistemic from social concerns, he maintains, simply does not describe either "modern" or archaic reality. Such a description merely defines "the particular way Westerners had of establishing their relations with others as long as they felt modern" (103). Hence the following description:

> We are the only ones who differentiate absolutely between Nature and Culture, between Science and Society, whereas in our eyes all others—whether they are Chinese or Amerindian, Azande or Barouya—cannot really separate what is knowledge from what is Society, what is Sign from what is thing, what comes from Nature as it is from what their cultures require. Whatever they do, however adapted, regulated and functional they may be, they will always remain blinded by this confusion; they are prisoners of the social and language alike. Whatever we do, however criminal, however imperialistic we may be, we escape from the prison of the social or of language to gain access to things themselves through a providential exit gate, that of scientific knowledge. (99)

According to Latour, then, the conceptual difficulties inherent in the modern constitution can only be resolved by means of an "intellectual retooling" (101) that does not require the postulation of a "great divide" between nature and culture. We must, that is, see that there are only "nature-cultures" and that they are all similar "in that they simultaneously construct humans, divinities, and nonhumans" (106). In such a framework "modern knowledge and power are different not in that they would escape at last the tyranny of the social, but in that *they add more hybrids in order to recompose the social link and extend its scale*" (109, emphasis in original).

Having argued that we are not modern, and never have been (47) he also admits, problematically, that we may have been modern but are no longer entirely so (127); moreover, he is clear that we are not premodern (127). He writes: "Moderns do differ from premoderns by this single trait: they refuse to conceptualize quasi-objects [hybrids] as such" (112). More importantly, Latour is certain not only that we are not premodern but also that we do not want to become premodern in overcoming what he sees as the shortcomings of modernity. Significantly, becoming premodern would, it appears, cripple science. "The non-separability of natures and cultures," he admits,

> had the disadvantage of making experimentation on a large scale impossible, since every transformation of nature had to be in harmony with a social transformation, term for term, and vice versa. Now we seek to keep the moderns' major innovation: the separability of a nature that no one has constructed—transcendence—and the freedom of manoeuvre of a society that is of our making—immanence. (140)

Thus, he acknowledges that "there is indeed a nature that we have not made, and a society that we are free to change; there are indeed indisputable scientific facts and free citizens" (140). And he consequently admits that the moderns' "nature-convention" distinction is not mistaken although he, nevertheless, still insists that its emergence does not require "an absolute distinction between the two terms and the continual repression of the work of mediation" (140). Thus, he concludes: "We have been modern. Very well. We can no longer be modern in the same way" because the "asymmetrical rationality [of the Enlightenment] is just not broad enough for us" (142).

The problems with Latour's analysis of modernity and modern science here are significant. In addition to the difficulties created by his alternating rejections and affirmations of modernity, his understanding of the nature and role of scientific thought in the modern age is ambiguous at best and appears at times simply to recapitulate the standard interpretation against which he rails. Furthermore, Latour's talk of modernity is not nuanced with respect to twentieth-century developments; he fails, that is, to recognize that doubt rather than certitude is a pervasive feature of modern science and modern critical reason. Even though modern science is post-traditional, it does not simply replace ancient sureties with absolute scientific knowledge. This reflexive awareness in contemporary scientific thought does in some sense confound Enlightenment expectations, but it is still, nevertheless, a product of Enlightenment thought. The lack of certitude in scientific knowledge, that is, does not permit the conclusion that therefore science is indistinguishable from premodern modes of thought. Nor does the fact that Latour's hybrid realities are more difficult to treat scientifically than objects of nature justify Latour's claim that moderns treat these realities as did the ancients. Given these difficulties with Latour's analysis of modern science, it is unclear just what Bell thinks Latour provides the student of religion for the construction of an alternative framework for the study of religion that is neither modern nor postmodern. Indeed, Bell's own critique of the science of religion exhibits similar problems of inconsistency in that the framework for the study of religion she seeks must acknowledge that all knowing is inevitably political without rejecting the modern notion that religion can be studied neutrally.

Rejection of Latour's and Bell's arguments is not to deny that since the last third of the nineteenth century, as Reiss points out, scientific discourse has come under increasing attack and is being put into serious question (1982: 382). Reiss, obviously, is not alone in making such a claim. Many have criticized modernism as having fostered a purely instrumental relationship to nature and in doing so, excluding issues of moral and existential import. Nevertheless, Reiss claims that we are at the "nether end" of its development even though he also admits that he is not sure that it will be displaced. In his judgment, however, any attempt to displace it would be of benefit because he believes it would make possible the recognition of the essentially perspectival nature of the human mind and so relativize science, which in turn would make possible the creation of new meaning (382). A "processive communicational network" discourse, he suggests tentatively, may provide such an alternative "where fixity, discrete, denotated objects of knowledge, analytical knowledge itself, discursive transparency, objective grasp, [and] absence of the 'subject' would all be strangers" (382). He admits the danger that such a science-transcending discourse could simply become a new form of mysticism, although he does not consider that risk too high to take (382n44). Others, however, do, for it could well entail a return to traditional, overarching, normative structures of thought and life and a failure to make use of scientific knowledge about social life in the service of transforming society.

Neither Latour nor Reiss, it seems, have fully realized how uniquely successful has been the culture-transcending science which characterizes the modern world. In matters of cognition, that is, the intellectual style of modern science—whereby knowledge is gained by freeing the thinker from social, political, and cultural constraints—as Gellner puts it, is sovereign, and a refusal to recognize "the universal diffusion, authority, and applicability of [this] particular cognitive style" is at least misguided if not simply fraudulent (1998: 185). Gellner also recognizes that there are spheres of life in which science is obviously an inadequate tool for the resolution of problems—for example, for providing a sense of belonging, or a basis for obligation and cooperation in society, or for consoling persons who have experienced tragedy in their lives, and so on. And he readily admits that science's "defectiveness in these respects is as distinctive and conspicuous as is its superiority in the spheres of cognition and production" (184). Gellner, moreover, acknowledges that this new cognitive style has not been able to extend itself with much success into "the sphere of social and human phenomena" (191). Whether or not this is an inherently impossible task for science, however, Gellner leaves open to debate, but this does not, he insists, justify refusal to deal with both the successes and defects of science; nor do the defects of science to which he refers provide grounds for an epistemology in which knowledge is gained by means of immersion in the "wisdom" of a cultural system or "form of life" which transcend the individual.

In *Can Modernity Survive?* (1990) Agnes Heller makes some interesting suggestions about how we might go about providing the linkage Gellner insists must be found between our values and life-style, on the one hand, with our modern way of knowing the world, on the other. Unlike Gellner, Heller is much less pessimistic about the extension of the new cognitive style into the sphere of the social. For her, recognition of the legitimacy of science even in the social sphere does not involve assuming science to be the only value for human society. Modernity is not, she argues, a "totality" nor does it attempt to provide a "single model of a supreme way of life" (9). Modernity is characterized by core values but it involves neither commitment to everything that is modern nor does it reject everything that is not (9). And science as the search for true knowledge as distinct from a search for truth (meaning, value) is one of those core values. "Truth and true knowledge are simply different in kind" (14), she writes, even though the two may be intimately connected. True (scientific) knowledge, however, "cannot become Truth [meaning/value] simply by presenting itself as true knowledge" (14), she argues along Weberian lines, and scientists must not seek insight into the meaning of life in their scientific pursuits. The "cultural sphere" of science (over against other cultural spheres such as the political, legal, aesthetic, economic, or religious) stands on its own with norms and rules intrinsic to itself (13): "[It] must be chosen as a vocation and not as a path leading to Truth. To offer insight into Truth through the pursuit of true knowledge is to make a false promise, one that the social sciences have no authority to keep" (15). For Heller, then, science is "core knowledge" compared to what she calls "ring knowledge" which is gained by virtue of a person's particular personal and/or cultural interests and experience and is concerned with existential matters of meaning and value. Heller argues that these two kinds of knowledge can be combined in what might be called *Gesamtwissenschaft* or a "science of the whole" that connects knowledge and existential concerns. She warns, however, that if the "ring knowledge" is too thick the project will be more a work of fiction or of ideology, and if it is too thin, the core knowledge will be informative but probably not of any great significance to anyone (20). Thus, she reiterates her main concern with respect to scientific knowledge and claims that "as long as a genre remains social science, to the extent that it does so, the constitution or the 'unconcealment' of Truth cannot be either intended or pretended by it . . . . The quest for true knowledge has a different ambition" (21). *Gesamtwissenschaft*, therefore, cannot transform the character of the science which contributes to it; reason in science, that is, is never "right reason."

It is in this sense, I think, that one must consider the modern scientific study of religion as radically different from theology and religion; it is concerned with knowledge *about* religion and even though it may have relevance to issues of meaning in religion, it is not itself a religious quest. Bell is simply wrong, that is, to claim that the modernist debate over the "outsider" versus "insider" approaches to the study of religion is exhausted. Indeed, her own critique of science itself continues that debate. Unless we are to return to a premodern form of the study of religion—to a form of *Glaubenswissenschaft*—therefore, it is clear that the social sciences provide us the only acceptable model for the study of religion in the modern university setting.

Rejecting a "Science-Lite" Study of Religion in the Modern University

I will argue in this chapter that if "religious studies," by which moniker the scholarly study of religion is most widely known today, is to retain any respectability in the modern university, it will have to recognize that it must seriously incorporate the search for a scientific explanation of religious thought and practice—that is, to the search for empirically testable knowledge about religions. I will show here (1) that this epistemic ideal first emerged in what we might reasonably bill as an old *Methodenstreit* or conflict of methods between the pre-Socratic cosmologists and the Platonists in ancient Greece and (2) that the emergence of this new cultural value of knowledge for the sake of knowledge alone (a) "motivated" the scientific revolution in sixteenth-century Europe and (b) became the raison d'être of the modern research university.

I begin with some general comments about the sciences, natural and social, and the humanities, drawing first on physicist Steven Weinberg's comments from his recent book, *To Explain the World*, on the connection between modern natural science and the thought of the ancient Greeks. With a few bright Greek exceptions, writes Weinberg,

> science before the sixteenth century seems to me very different from what I experience in my own work, or what I see in the work of my colleagues. Before the scientific revolution science was suffused with religion and what we now call philosophy, and had not worked out its relation to mathematics. In physics and astronomy after the seventeenth century I feel at home. I recognize something very like the science of my own times: the search for mathematically expressed impersonal laws that allow precise predictions of a wide range of phenomena, laws validated by comparison of these predictions with observation and experiment. There was a scientific revolution. (Weinberg 2015: 146)

Not to put too fine a point on Weinberg's comment here about the Greek-inspired scientific style of thought that emerged in the West, it is clear that it ultimately created the possibility of gaining a "culture-transcending knowledge" about the purely material aspects of the universe. This revolutionary style of thought, as anthropologist and philosopher Ernest Gellner puts it, has allowed us to a very large extent to escape "from the conditions of socially inhibited production of cognition [knowledge]" (Gellner 1997: 10). As he describes it:

> What distinguishes the scientific style of thought from prescientific ones is notably the fact that instead of satisfying many criteria—including social cohesion,

authority-maintenance, morality, etc.—it sheds all but one aim, that is, explanatory power and congruence with the facts. (Gellner 1981: 55)

As Gellner argued in an earlier essay, scientific knowledge claims, therefore, possess a kind of epistemic "diplomatic immunity" from other sociocultural and moral values, and from what he calls the "political obligations" and "decencies" of society (Gellner 1973). In response to the anti-scientific backlash of postmodernism, Gellner writes: "I am not so sure whether indeed we possess morality beyond culture, but I am absolutely certain that we do indeed possess knowledge beyond both culture and morality" (Gellner 1992: 54)—that is, a knowledge that is best described as "knowledge for the sake of knowledge alone."

Gellner is well aware that even though we have "effective knowledge of nature," there is as yet "*no* effective knowledge of man and society" (Gellner 1997: 9). Recognizing that this is so, it is often argued that no clear distinction can be drawn between the social sciences and the humanities, and that the social sciences, therefore, are no more worthy of inclusion in the modern research university curriculum than the humanities. Such an argument, however, fails to recognize that "the larger conception of knowledge" espoused by humanists in their effort to "make sense" of the world, and our existence in it, amounts to conflating the descriptive and explanatory with the evaluative and status-conferring role of language characteristic of archaic and traditional societies in which all epistemic claims must be in harmony with the social and moral order of one's society. However, the social sciences, even if they do not presently match the spectacular results of the natural sciences in the production of "effective knowledge" about social reality, nevertheless remain committed to seeking the same kind of culture-transcending (scientific) knowledge about individual and collective human behavior that the natural sciences provide us of the material world; consequently, they appear rightfully to occupy a curricular niche in the modern research university.

Although there are many ways of knowing, not all are of central concern in this context. That fact, however, as anthropologist Marvin Harris points out, justifies neither the claim that scientific knowing amounts to mere "ethnocentric puffery" (1979: 27–28) nor the claim that science is only one among many equally credible epistemic subcultures that have a rightful place in the modern research university as Peter Worsley maintains (1997: 13).

The old *Methodenstreit* and the emergence of a new cultural value

It is clear that if organisms are to survive and to pass on their genes to the next generation they must have a solid knowledge of the environments in which they live. Biologist Lewis Wolpert points out, that the brains—and hence the behavior—of *Homo sapiens* "have . . . been selected for dealing with the immediate world around us. We are very good at certain types of thinking, [he writes], particularly that which leads to both simple and quite complex technology and control of our immediate environment"

(Wolpert 1993: 11). In this regard there is no doubt that there is continuity between our thought and that of our evolutionary forebears. There is no surprise, therefore that, as archaeologist Stephen Mithen argues, the cognitive foundations for scientific thought came about in a "piecemeal [fashion] over at least five million years" (Mithen 2002; 40). But continuity does not mean identity. There are important discontinuities in thought patterns at various stages of human evolution from our primate forebears to us, and between archaic humans and anatomically and behaviorally modern humans. Thus, even though some of our ancestors "were perhaps reliant on key elements of [later] scientific thinking for their survival" (Mithen 2002: 24), their thinking did not amount to being scientific as some scholars seem to suggest (Dunbar 1995). Learning was essential to our ancestors, but reflective critical or theoretical learning was not, as is obvious from the fact that it was not necessary for dealing with their immediate environment. Moreover, as historian of science H. Floris Cohen points out,

> In traditional society, the investigation of natural phenomena is [only] one among many activities that may be undertaken to fulfill the need of human beings to make sense of the world around them. . . . [Therefore], if pursued at all, [such knowledge] is pursued, as a rule, in the framework of a larger conception of how things in the universe cohere. (Cohen 1994: 506)

That "larger conception" of how things in the universe cohere, moreover, results from the emergence of what Michael Tomasello, co-director of the Max Planck Institute for Evolutionary Anthropology, calls a "species-specific" mode of thought in *Homo sapiens* (Tomasello 1999; 2014) but which amounted to what might best be called a mythopoetic rather than a "science-like" mode of thought. As Mithen correctly points out, "The emergence of science as a discrete domain of behaviour is likely to have required a suite of social, historic and economic circumstances that had not . . . [previously] arisen in human history" (Mithen 2002: 40).

There is broad agreement in the scholarly community that ancient Greek society of the sixth century BCE provided such a unique suite of social, historic and economic circumstances that anticipated the emergence of science as we understand it today (Gay 1967; Nisbet 1971; Wolpert 1993; Wiebe 1991). It is also widely recognized that many of the pre-Socratic cosmologists—from the Milesians in the sixth century BCE to the Atomists in the fourth century BCE—were interested in a new kind of question about the cosmos and its contents, unconnected either to a larger, that is, mythic conception of the *meaning* of the universe and human existence in it or to the practical economic and political concerns of daily life. They simply sought to understand the cosmos in terms of the ultimate character of the substance or substances of which it was made and the principles of transformation of that substance or substances into the myriad of things and events in the world. Their intellectual pursuits in this regard had no intrinsic ethical, moral, or religious content or intent; their goal was simply to obtain knowledge about the world. In restricting their interests in this way, the ancient Greek cosmologists (unintentionally) created both a new cultural value of "knowledge for the sake of knowledge alone," and reason as a new, nonmoral instrument of inquiry. Historian of philosophy Richard McKirahan described this development of Greek thought as a decisive step "of abandoning mythological ways of thought and rejecting traditional ways of looking at the world" (McKirahan 1994: 19). And sociologist Robert Nisbet summarizes this development as follows:

> Twenty-five hundred years ago a dogma[1] was born among the Greek rationalist philosophers. The dogma said: "knowledge is good." Not necessarily knowledge in service to self-survival, nor to power, nor to affluence, nor to religious piety; but knowledge in its own service. The kind of knowledge that springs from the itch of curiosity, from dispassionate, disinterested desire to obtain objective knowledge of nature, society, and man. (Nisbet 1971: 238)

This is the beginning of what Gellner calls the "modern Western epistemic tradition" (Gellner 1992: 85) which is best exemplified in the European scientific revolution and becomes institutionalized in the modern research university.

The fragility of the scientific revolution

The "modern Western epistemic tradition," Nisbet points out, "proved to be a fragile one." "It has been almost constantly assaulted," he writes,

> by those unable or unwilling to comprehend why knowledge should be its own end, why knowledge should ever serve ends other than of physical survival, political power, or revolution, religious doctrine, economic influence, and the whole broad spectrum of needs, desires, and passions of day-to-day living. (Nisbet 1971; 238)

Socrates and Plato, for example, rejected the materialist drift of thought among their predecessors, as classicist Francis M. Cornford puts the matter, because they did not covet a "detailed picture of *how* [events] came about but . . . [rather] *why* [they] came about" (Cornford 1932: 2). Despite the dominance of Platonism in the antique Mediterranean world, however, the Hellenistic period was not devoid of interest in obtaining knowledge of the natural and social worlds for its own sake, including physical studies, medicine, mathematics, and philological and literary studies, inspired largely by the work of Aristotle (Lucio Russo 1996).

With the rediscovery of Aristotle's works in the eleventh and twelfth centuries, there was a renewed interest in knowledge of the natural world and a reliance on the autonomy of reason in achieving it. Although this did not amount to the emergence of modern science, it was instrumental in bringing about the scientific revolution in Europe that most historian see as arriving with the works of Nicholas Copernicus and Galileo Galilei (Michael Hobart 2018). From this point on, the quest for knowledge of the natural world for its own sake was vastly extended by a range of new intellectual tools. And even though it is acknowledged that the newly emerging sciences were not the only avenues for gaining knowledge, they were seen as "epistemologically distinguished," as philosopher of science Susan Haack puts it, because they vastly extended the tools available to the pre-Socratic forebears in a way that made possible the cumulative growth of knowledge. These include

> systematic effort to isolate one variable at a time; systematic commitment to criticism; experimental contrivance of every kind; instruments of observation from the microscope to the questionnaire; all the complex apparatus of statistical evaluation and mathematical modeling; and the engagement, cooperative and competitive, of many persons within and across generations . . . . [This mode of thought and inquiry] has by all means listed, enormously deepened and extended the range of experience and the sophistication of reasoning of which it avails itself. (Haack 1998: 96–97)

This is why Cohen, among others, maintains that the notion of "revolution" most accurately describes the origin of this cascade of epistemic developments because it "denotes that unique moment in history when the West succeeded in acquiring an intellectual and operative mastery of nature" (Cohen 1994: 501). And this search for knowledge of nature for its own sake was taken up and supported by the eighteenth-century philosophes who, as historian Peter Gay points out, created a "culture of criticism," that called for an end to myth and the disenchantment of the universe. This critical posture, Gay insists, was a general method of looking at the world, both physical and social, as a natural rather than a created reality, and explicable in terms of causal laws with no admixture of religious, mythopoetic, political, or any other way of thinking (Gay 1967: 145–46).

The "Dogma" of the modern research university

Although Nisbet is aware that there are "countless peoples, including some of the most creative and intellectually advanced in history, [who] have met the problem of knowledge in ways other than institutionalized in the university" (Nisbet 1971: 17), he also shows that the university is an extraordinary institution in that it is entirely committed to the new cultural value created and nurtured by the ancient Greek philosophers. As Nisbet puts it, the university is built on the assumption that knowledge for its own sake is important—"Just that," he writes: "Not 'relevant' knowledge; not 'practical' knowledge,' not the kind of knowledge that enables one to wield power, achieve success, or influence others. [*Just*] *Knowledge!*" (Nisbet 1971: 24). And although the modern research university was wholly committed to this epistemic goal, it did not reach its prominence until the early nineteenth century (William Clark 2006; Thomas Howard 2006; Brad Gregory 2012). However, as sociologist Toby Huff points out, from the earliest formation of the university in Europe it had created what he calls "neutral zones" "within which men could entertain all sorts of questions about the constitution of the world" (Huff 1993: 338). And these neutral zones, as Huff puts it, allowed scholars to "pursue their genius free from the censure of political and religious authorities" (Huff 1993: 212), relatively free from constraint by "reverence for traditional knowledge passed down through the centuries" (Huff 1993: 166). Nisbet, I think, rightly judges the university's commitment to such a search for knowledge for its own sake as its majesty:

> There is no inherent, self-sustaining majesty in the university; only the majesty that is conferred upon the university by a social order that, for whatever reason, has come to believe that there is something distinctive, something precious, something profoundly important in the university that is to be found nowhere else in society—not in a factory, not in foundation, not in government agency, not in media, not in church, not in mental health clinic, not anywhere else. And when this belief is allowed to erode, majesty erodes with it. (Nisbet 1971: 235)

In Nisbet's judgment, therefore, as also in mine, it is neither honest nor coherent to try to harness the dispassionate rational attempt to gain and distribute knowledge about physical or sociocultural phenomena with non-epistemic enterprises (Nisbet 1971: xiv, 8). This does not mean that the university is not concerned with service to society, but rather that, as in the past, it is of service in an indirect fashion based on the possession of knowledge about the world it serves (Nisbet 1971: 127–28). As Stanley Fish puts it, if scholars or scientists wish to do more than pass on knowledge and confer skills on their students—to become activists or revolutionaries, public intellectuals, therapist, or sages—they should seek another place of employment (Fish 1995; 2008; see also Dreger 2015 and Weber 1946 [1919]).

On not taking religion "Seriously": The new *Methodenstreit*

In one sense, there is no problem with a scientific study of religions and religion because religion, like other social institutions, is a purely human, and therefore, a natural phenomenon subject to critical analysis and scientific explanation like any other natural phenomenon. And its study as a purely human phenomenon emerged as early as the eighteenth century with David Hume's *The Natural History of Religion* (Hume 1956 [1777]). In the last quarter of the nineteenth century the ideal of seeking knowledge about religion for the sake of that knowledge alone was being promoted in England by Friedrich Max Müller and in Holland by C. P. Tiele, both regarded as founders of the modern scientific study of religion (Sharpe 1986a; Wiebe 1998). That ideal was also adopted by the scholars who organized the international history of religions congress in Paris in 1900 which was the first of a series of such congresses that eventually led to the creation of the IAHR, which took over the responsibility not only for organizing subsequent international congresses but also for promoting the scientific study of religions in universities, first in Europe and, ultimately, worldwide (Sharpe 1986).

Although some universities in the late nineteenth and early twentieth centuries created departments in which the metaphysical claims of religions could be treated simply as culturally postulated realities, for the most part this approach to the study of religions was, and still is, criticized, especially by postmodernists, for "not taking religion seriously"—that is, not treating religion as another source of knowledge. The naturalism underlying the scientific approach to the study of religions, it is then argued, simply substitutes a materialist metaphysics for an agentic religious one, and in doing so the scientific study of religion fails to explain why religious devotees think the way they do. It is, therefore, claimed that even though religious traditions may be legitimate objects of scientific research and analysis, science cannot provide a full account of these phenomena. Only a humanistic approach to the study of religion that sympathetically *understands* the devotee, it is claimed, can bring to light the moral import and meaning of religion. These claims, among others similar to them, have generated a new *methodenstreit,* but they are without force because they are based on a failure to understand both the methodological character of the naturalism that underlies the sciences, and what Nisbet calls the "dogma" of the university. As cultural anthropologist Marvin Harris points out, naturalism (materialism) in the study of cultural phenomena involves more than an emic understanding of why people think the way they do. Satisfaction with such an emic understanding, he shows, is settling for what we might call a science-lite study of cultural reality. "It is imperative," he writes, "that we reserve the right not to believe [the] explanation" offered by believers and "to seek alternative accounts of their behaviour" (Harris 1979: 340; see also Burkert 1983: xxi). Failing that, we are left floundering in epistemic relativism. Harris is aware "that discrepancies between science as an ideal and science as it is practiced substantially reduces the difference between science, religion, and other modes of looking for the truth. But, [he also points out that], it is precisely as an ideal that the uniqueness of science deserves to be defended" (Harris 1979: 28).

Religious studies today

In my judgment that ideal of science for the study of religion is not defended by the majority of scholars in the field of "religious studies" today and is certainly not adopted by many departments for the study of religion in our modern research universities. The IAHR, on the other hand, has from time to time vigorously defended this scientific ideal since its founding and beyond. Historian of religions, R. J. Zwi Werblowsky, a formidable figure in the history of the association and its secretary-general from 1970 to 1985, records, for example, that the IAHR's attempt "to enlarge the scope of its activities [beyond Europe and North America] whilst preserving strictly scientific standards" actually resulted in lowering the scholarly level of contributions to the ninth (first Tokyo) IAHR international congress (Werblowsky 1958: 235). This lowering of scholarly standards recurred again at the tenth (Marburg) international congress which, according to Werblowsky, was attended by dilettantes and scholars with religiously inspired aims and goals (Weblowsky 1960). Many scholars at each of these congresses, moreover, complained "that the Western [strictly scientific] approach to religion was too strictly disinterested, analytical, and hence 'scientifically irreligious'" (Werblowsky 1960: 219). Werblowsky was aware that continued defense of the scientific approach was going to "involve some long-range up-hill work" (Werblowsky 1958: 235) and he took steps to ground such a defense of the scientific study of religion by creating some "Basic Minimum Presuppositions" to be followed by scholars attending IAHR international congresses (Schimmel 1960: 236–37). In his closing comments on the tenth international congress Werblowsky wrote: "The coming years will determine whether the IAHR is up to carrying out this [scientific] mandate" (Werblowsky 1960: 220). I think the record will show that most successive executive committees of the IAHR have continued to defend the ideal of the scientific study of religion, but there is a good deal of evidence to show that the IAHR's stance on this matter has had little to no effect on its national member associations or on the departments of "religious studies" those national associations represent. I do not claim that departments of "religious studies" in our universities are simply stocked with dilettantes and religiously inspired scholars but rather only that many, if not most, contemporary university departments are not committed to working within the scientific framework of the "modern Western epistemic tradition" which undermines our intellectual and academic credibility within the modern research university.

Conclusion: Need Religious Studies Remain "Conspicuously Unscientific"?

Some students of religion might wish to dispute the reasonableness of the question I raise here. It commits the logical fallacy of complex question, they could rightly claim, like asking whether or not one has given up gambling when in fact one has never gambled her whole life long. In this case, however, I am not simply assuming that what is called "religious studies" in our modern universities is conspicuously unscientific, because I believe I have shown in earlier studies that this so-called academic discipline is not primarily concerned with explaining religious thought and behavior; in other words, it is not interested in simply gaining objective knowledge, either empirical or theoretical, about religion in the way that the natural and social sciences, for example, are concerned with obtaining such knowledge about the natural and social worlds in which we live. Professor Luther Martin and I have pointed out in a recent article published in the journal *Religio* in Europe and the *Journal of the American Academy of Religion* in America that "the historical record . . . shows that no undergraduate departments of religious studies have fully implemented a scientific program of study and research since such an approach was first advocated in the later nineteenth century" (Martin and Wiebe 2016: 221). When first formed, new departments for the study of religion in our academic institutions were almost always connected with preexisting departments of theology where the enterprise flourished as a liberalized form of *Glaubenswissenschaft* or "faith-imbued science," and where, even today, the teaching of religious studies most often takes the form of offering religion appreciation courses that might contribute to the formation of students as fully rounded persons.

"Religious studies": The academic naturalization of a confessional enterprise

When I entered the field of religious studies forty years ago as a graduate student, the enterprise was an "academic" undertaking clearly differentiated from confessional theological concerns—that is, from what I have called a "capital-c" confessional agenda of disseminating some particular denominational set of religious beliefs or a more broadly liberal religious or theistic set of intellectual commitments (Wiebe 1984). But the study of religion in these new departments was "scholarly" rather than scientific.

The scholarship involved, moreover, was not simply concerned with philological and historical matters but rather, in an Emersonian manner, with the discernment of *meaning* and the *formation* of students. That is, it was engaged in the pursuit of "truth" relevant to what some have called "Life Realities" or "Life Questions" rather than simply with seeking objective knowledge of the natural determinants of human religious behaviors. The so-called scholarly study of religion, therefore, was, in effect, what I have called a "small-c" confessional theology in that it assumed the existence of some vaguely defined ultimate reality that undergirds the otherwise ephemeral character of human existence with meaning and sets out to ascertain that meaning by way of hermeneutical and phenomenological "analyses." And the influence of such research on "teaching religion" in the university, it was hoped, would create a moral and religious literacy that would have a positive effect on individuals and society.

Whether all scholarly approaches in the field of religious studies that maintain science is incapable of providing an exhaustive account of human behavior wholly within a materialist framework are necessarily crypto-theological (i.e., engaged in "small-c" confessional accounts of religion), it must be admitted, is open to question. I don't, however, think that this in itself justifies a claim, such as we find in Clifford Geertz's work (1983), that we can have a wholly exhaustive hermeneutical account of religion or any other cultural phenomenon. According to Geertz, for example, seeking "thick descriptions" of cultural phenomena can provide us with "more" than can be found in reductionist scientific accounts of systems of human behavior without assuming "the more" to be of a transcendent character. Nevertheless, "the more" that interests Geertz, and others in the field, it is still supposed, is not reducible to the material substrate with which it coexists, and in that sense makes of culture a kind of sui generis reality, *explicable/understandable* only by way of what he calls "thick description" of all its elements. This, however, is to conflate description with explanation, and makes of the understanding sought, a kind of interior *gnostic* capacity to *discern/intuit* the hidden *essence* of cultural phenomena. This, of course, makes the cultural reality *discerned* a mystery in that it can only be *understood*, not *explained*. But without explanation and theory we have mere discourse—not science (Wiebe 1975, 1983, 2005).

I should note here that I entered the field of religious studies as a philosopher with a quasi-religious agenda—first at McMaster University in Canada and then under the supervision of Professor Ninian Smart at the University of Lancaster, England. My discomfort with the dominant phenomenological ethos in the field emerged only gradually and, to some degree, in concert with new winds of change that were, so to speak, blowing through the discipline since about 1970. In 1973 I had been asked by Smart to teach an undergraduate course on theory of religion which woke me up to the rather chaotic (not, as Smart would have it, a positively valenced polymethodological) state of affairs in the field. It also brought to my attention the existence and mission of the IAHR—which was clearly an institutional structure providing support for non-theological study of religions even if largely limited to philological and historical analyses of religious texts and institutions—and its concern with the apparently unruly nature of the field which moved them to sponsor the first self-conscious conference on methods and methodology in the field (Honko 1979). Hans Penner and Edward Yonan's paper entitled "Is a Science of Religion Possible?" had come out in 1972 and pushed the boundaries of the field's self-understanding in looking for theoretical developments not yet championed by the IAHR. In 1975 I raised a similar set of questions in an early paper on explanation in the study of religion and in my first international paper presented to the twelfth international congress of the IAHR in Lancaster, England (Wiebe 1975, 1978). And by 1984 it seemed to me that a sufficiently radical change had taken place in the self-understanding of the field itself, and not just my perception of it, that I felt comfortable in writing about the "failure of nerve" on the part of many who claimed religious studies as their discipline but feared following through on those epistemic and methodological commitments. And with the formation of the NAASR in 1985 (Martin and Wiebe 2004), which gave structural and institutional support for moving the field beyond merely descriptive, comparative, phenomenological, and hermeneutical studies of religions, it seemed to me that one could reasonably talk about the field as having achieved, *notionally, and to a limited extent, institutionally,* the status of a genuinely scientific discipline and that it need not, therefore, remain "conspicuously unscientific." And it still seems to me to be so now, although one might complain that I have the obligation of providing a generally acceptable understanding of the nature of science and the sciences, and of showing how the religious studies of which I have been speaking conforms to that picture. That is what I shall attempt now to do.

On the study of religion as a purely scientific enterprise

In chapter eight of his *Casuistry and Modern Ethics* (1996)—"On Not Keeping Religious Studies Pure"—Richard B. Miller, professor of ethics in the University of Chicago Divinity School, draws on Stephen Toulmin's conception of a scientific discipline (Toulmin 1972) to argue that religious studies is "conspicuously unscientific," and is therefore best understood as "a series of overlapping and mutually reinforcing conversations that constitute the fibres of the enterprise" (Miller 1996: 204, 207). In arguing this claim Miller is critical not only of my position on this matter but also of similar positions espoused by Hans Penner and Edward Yonan (1972), and J. Samuel Preus (1987), among others. But to see just what force his argument has, it will be helpful to review briefly Toulmin's take on scientific disciplines even though his account of them is not altogether coherent or perspicuous.

To begin with, Toulmin contrasts fully disciplined enterprises like physics with what he calls non-disciplinable fields like literary studies, ethics, fine arts, and philosophy. In such "quasi-disciplines," as he also calls these non-disciplined (and apparently non-disciplinable) enterprises, intellectual activities cannot be separated from other values; in everyday life, that is, "actions and choices are meshed together" which requires a form of reasoning much broader than that required in the disciplines (Toulmin 1972: 402). The scientist, on the other hand, "pursues the goals of her or his discipline in isolation from extra-professional goals" (Toulmin 1972: 402). Within the disciplinable fields he distinguishes *compact disciplines* (with physics as the best model here) from what he calls *diffuse disciplines* (for which, unfortunately, he provides no examples) and *would-be disciplines* (with the behavioral sciences being his chief exemplars).

A compact discipline for Toulmin is one that, despite showing some striking changes of direction in its historical development, has achieved "agreed goals and strategies around which the cumulative development of a well-structured science can proceed" (Toulmin 1972: 382, 384). Such disciplines will also have a common set of assumptions and presuppositions, as well as overlapping sets of concepts, methods, and techniques of research. Moreover, they will also have structural and institutional supports including university recognition, professional forums, associations, and societies, formal methods of disseminating the results of their research, and so on.

To all intents and purposes Toulmin lumps the categories of "diffuse" and "would-be" disciplines together. As Miller points out, one problem with these kinds of sciences is that they appear not to have "a sufficiently agreed-upon goal in terms of which common problems can be identified and tackled" (Miller 1996: 204). One reason for that, according to Toulmin, may be that such sciences are "immature," and they may remain immature because they do not have adequate institutional support. But that, according to Toulmin, need have no lasting negative import with respect to the character of such sciences. As he notes:

> If I have argued here that, at the level of general theory, psychology and sociology remain today "would-be disciplines," I am not claiming any absolute or permanent contrast between the social and the physical sciences. On the contrary: I have merely been trying to diagnose certain special difficulties which face the theoretical sciences of human behaviour at the present time. In earlier centuries, physical theory too had the same inconclusive character; indeed, many of the methodological difficulties afflicting sociology and psychology today had counterparts in earlier physical sciences. (Toulmin 1972: 386)

And further on in this discussion he notes that we "*have discovered that it is both functionally possible and humanly desirable to isolate certain classes of issues, and make them the concern of specialized bodies of enquiries; while with issues of other kinds this turns out to be either impossible or undesirable, or both at once*" (Toulmin 405; emphasis added).

In an earlier criticism of Miller's critique of those who champion a science of religion (Wiebe 1999a) I did not point out clearly enough that the study of religions and religion as carried on (and taught) in many, if not most, of our university departments, in the past and now, is diffuse in character largely because the scholars involved refuse to countenance the possibility of the study of religion as a single-valued pursuit and to distinguish and isolate these intellectual concerns from activities of other kinds. Miller simply fails to see not only that it is possible but also that some scholars have actually been able to separate the search for "knowledge *about*" religion as a human phenomenon from the hope of producing an "understanding of" religion that will transform students into religiously literate persons committed to structuring a meaningful and socially responsible existence in light of some transcendent ultimate reality or other (Wiebe 2002b).

Now it is true that the University of Berlin, established in 1810, was the earliest model for the modern research university, and that it actually harbored an Emersonian conception of scholarship that involved a great deal more than a search for knowledge or the creation of tools and techniques for obtaining new knowledge. Brad S. Gregory rightly points out that at its inception the University of Berlin actually constituted what he calls "the Romantic research university" in that it was as much concerned with the formation of students as it was with producing knowledge; that is, that it was as consciously engaged in *Bildung* as it was concerned with *Wissenschaft*. As he puts it: "The modern university was originally hatched from a Romantic vision of research as an adjunct to student self-realization" (Gregory 2012: 349). However, Gregory also rightly points out that Protestantism's influence on the sciences over the past two centuries has effected a "secularization of knowledge in research universities" that extends to "the consideration of religious traditions strictly as objects of study rather than as potential sources of knowledge" or avenues of transformation or self-realization (Gregory 2012: 359; see also Howard 2006 and Reuben 1996). What happened to the study of religion in the modern research university of the later nineteenth and early twentieth century then, to use Toulmin's language, is that that enterprise became single-valued in a way that made it possible for scholar-scientists to engage in them in isolation from other everyday and religious activities. In other words, the academic study of religion was moving toward becoming a "compact discipline."

A brief description of religious studies as an emerging scientific discipline here may be helpful in determining the constant issues in keeping it scientific. First and foremost, of course, is that the scientific study of religion operates with the same understanding of the secularization of knowledge that Brad Gregory correctly notes characterizes the modern Western research university. This means that the "mission" (i.e., purpose) of religious studies must be the same as that of any and all other scientific disciplines in the university, namely, that its primary task is to provide a soundly based knowledge of religion as a human phenomenon—that is, of human behavior influenced, to whatever extent, by beliefs in the supernatural. And the knowledge sought must not be merely descriptive: that is, providing empirical data, phenomenological portraits, critical comparative analyses of religious traditions, accounts of their historical development, and the like. These, clearly, are important aspects of religious studies, but to be fully scientific it must move on to a search for explanations of religious behavior, religious institutions and traditions, and theoretical accounts of human behavior that give depth to those explanations. To put it bluntly, students of religion must aim at providing intersubjectively testable propositional and theoretical claims about religiously determined states of affairs in the world. And this means, contra Miller, that (scientific) purity for the student of religion sets the parameters of her/his academic and pedagogical responsibilities. It is especially important here to emphasize the significance of the limits of science for this enterprise given the fact that what one might call "methodological slippage" is more likely to occur in the study of human social and cultural (that is, intentional) phenomena than in, say, the study of physics. The point that needs making is that the "scientific purity" Miller rightly claims is sought by me and others in the field is not a search for some comprehensive alternative secular framework within which one might understand one's broader social responsibilities or within which one might make sense of life in some holistic fashion. And it is a matter of the utmost importance, therefore, that the scientific student of religion refrain from taking up positions that might be so interpreted because this can only embroil the study of religion in social, political, and metaphysical debates that are outside its mandate. The only social obligation the scientific student *qua* scientist has, that is, is to make the knowledge about religion gained available to the public and to those who have taken on the responsibility for the management of the affairs of society. Those who wish to do more than this should, as Stanley Fish (2008) advises colleagues in his field of literary studies, give serious consideration to a change of profession—a matter to which I give further attention below.

Miller, and others, quite correctly point out that departments for the study of religion in most of our research universities do not operate in this fashion; that they do not limit themselves to what can be said about religion within such strict boundaries. He, therefore, suggests this indicates that the field is, at best, a "diffuse discipline," and more likely a "would-be discipline," and he, consequently, proposes a "poetic" rather than a "theoretical" approach to this field of study (Miller 1996: 200). I suggest, however, that given the significant number of scholars in the field today—both within and without the context of the academy—whose sole purpose is to understand and explain religion in the spirit I have just outlined is a clear indication, contra Miller, that religious studies as a compact scientific discipline is actually emerging, even if at the moment it holds only a "minority position" within university and college departments for the study of religions, and could possibly (although not likely) become the dominant position in the future. That there are many university-trained scientists and scholars—some even within the academic setting although not likely in departments of biology—who believe in scientific creationism or intelligent design theory and on that basis incorporate sociopolitical and religious agendas into their work, does not undermine the claim that evolutionary biology is a genuine science; nor would it do so even if they (the intelligent design types) were to gain positions within university and college biology departments.

Although neither the dominant paradigm for the study of religion in most, if not all, university and college departments for the study of religion, nor finding much, if any support, for this paradigm in that setting, it is nevertheless the case that there is considerable structural and institutional support for this approach in the broader academic world. There are now, in a number of universities, special institutes, centers, and other units given over to the scientific study of religion. There is, for example, the Institute for Cognition and Culture at Queen's University, Belfast, that has for some time been engaged in the scientific study of religion; the more recent establishment of the Centre for Anthropology and Mind at Oxford University and its sponsorship of the Explaining Religion Project; the Religion, Cognition and Culture research unit in the Department for the Study of Religion at Aarhus University; the Cultural Evolution of Religion Research Consortium at the University of British Columbia and Simon Fraser University; and the Center for Mind, Brain, and Culture at Emory University is another special unit that strongly supports the scientific approach to the study of religious phenomena. In addition to the involvement of such university- and college-based institutions there are also a number of independent associations, societies, and institutes whose primary objective is to support the scientific study of religion. The IAHR is the oldest of these institutions and its mission statement not only includes its support "for the critical, analytical and cross-cultural study of religion, past and present" but also clearly states that the IAHR "is not a forum for confessional, apologetical, or other similar concerns."[1] More recently those who are interested in the import of the cognitive and neurosciences for the study of religion formed the International Association for the Cognitive Science of Religion, and a group of independent scholars in Toronto formed the Institute for the Advanced Study of Religion committed to advancing a general scientific understanding of religion through organizing research and educational activities to that end.[2] Finally, there are a number of journals and other publishing ventures that are committed to the support of a science of religion, journals such as *Numen*, the highly regarded journal of the IAHR; *Method and Theory in the Study of Religion* which accepts articles from a variety of naturalistic/scientific perspectives; the *Journal of Cognition and Culture* which is a primary venue for research in the cognitive sciences and other evolutionary psychological perspectives; and, more recently the *Journal for the Cognitive Science of Religion* and the *Journal for Cognitive Historiography*. Given these buttresses to the scientific study of religion lends considerable support to my argument above about the nature of the academic study of religion being, or becoming, a compact science.

On keeping "religious studies" scientific

Few will dispute that the natural sciences have been incredibly successful in explaining aspects of the physical universe in which we live. Nor are there many who will claim that the scientific explanations we have of our biological and social world are bogus knowledge claims. Despite that success, however, scientific thought in a number of ways is also quite fragile. Evolutionary psychologists, for example, point out that science is not a natural mode of thought but rather emerged as a cultural phenomenon in recent history and could not exist without strong institutional support for the sustained critical reflective thought it requires (McCauley 2000; 2011). And this suggests that without care, and in periods of cultural crisis, it is not impossible that the sciences could be seriously curtailed or lost altogether (McCauley 2011: 286). Further, philosophers, with some justification, suggest or claim that modern science is without a solid philosophical grounding and that scientists' commitments to their disciplines, therefore, involve "a leap of science" (Gellner 1974), and that this leaves them open to criticism from several vantage points. The fact that the sciences operate on the basis of a "methodological atheism," moreover, and are ultimately reductionistic in their search for "mechanistic" explanatory accounts of all aspects of our universe, including human behavior, means that they disenchant the universe (Weber 1946 [1919]). And such disenchantment, of course, challenges past and present "certainties" by which people have guided their lives. Consequently, reductionist science is often seen as morally offensive. This, needless to say, constitutes something of a threat to the social and political stability of science and negatively effects funding for the sciences (Sorell 1991; Midgley 1992)—and the scientific study of religion in particular. Finally, the fact that science, as a culture-transcending mode of thought, and the fact that it cannot replace the moral certainties it undermines with better alternatives, has spawned what can only be called an anti-science backlash that threatens to undermine the very purpose of the modern research universities committed to producing reliable objective knowledge about our natural and social worlds (Wiebe 1997b).

Given the fragility of science, and the attack on science by postmodernists in the university itself, it seems to me that an important aspect in keeping religious studies scientific is that we become actively engaged in criticism of radically postmodern attempts to paint the scientific study of religion as a regime of epistemic violence (King 1999; Chidester 1996). This, in my judgment, requires both an intellectual and a political component if it is to be successful (Wiebe 1997b, 1999b, and 2002c).

It is not possible, unfortunately, on the intellectual end of things, to structure a rational argument that will undermine postmodernism since that would require the postmodern critics to buy into the very "hegemony of reason" they believe themselves to have undermined. Equally, the scientist cannot without self-contradiction attempt such a critique from a postmodern perspective, although one might think the claim—not argument—that deconstructivism is itself simply a social construction and therefore without force of rational argument might do the trick. What one can do, however, is provide a careful history of the origin and development of science and the sciences to show that science is a new, and in some important senses, peculiar value, namely, the quest for "knowledge for the sake of knowledge alone" (Weber 1946 [1919]). Whether the truth of that "mantra" could ever be established need not be debated here since it expresses an idea and ideal that can be thought and sought, even if not attained. On establishing this historical claim one can then elaborate the obvious, namely, that the concerns of the sciences are wholly epistemic—concerned only with the formulation and testing of empirical and theoretical propositional claims about states of affairs in the world, and leaving matters of truth, value, and meaning to other "conversations." There is also a clear awareness that the reason of the scientist is not pragmatic, and a recognition that science is of little, if any, help in establishing a basis of obligation and cooperation in society, or for providing consolation for the afflicted (Gellner 1974, 1992). Nor is there here a hegemonic conception of reason which would argue that all spheres of culture—morality, art, religion, and science—can be molded by reason into a harmonious framework for meaningful existence. Nor is the reason of science spoken of here that of the "philosopher as comprehensive sage" but rather simply that of a nonmoral instrument of inquiry that allows one (1) to cut short special pleading; (2) to seek out and neutralize as best one can hidden ideological influences; and (3) to formulate all knowledge claims in propositional form and submit them to rational analysis and empirical test. It is for precisely this sort of project that the modern research university was brought into existence.

The political component of the task in protecting science and the scientific study of religion is strictly limited to the academic realm. It seems to me that we need to become more deeply involved in pressing for changes in the curriculum of the departments in which we work that will, at the very least, balance the overwhelming number of what we might call religious appreciation courses with courses that involve the student in critical and theoretical reflection on religion as a social and cultural reality. We ought also to press both our chairs and our deans to review the overall complement of courses in our departments to ensure that there is a purpose for and coherence in the curriculum that takes it beyond simply "serving a multicultural demographic" in our cities, provinces, and states. Finally, we need to be alert to the fact that departments of religious studies are often appropriated by others in the university community who are religious, as an avenue through which a religious agenda can be re-established in the university curriculum, and work together with deans and provosts to ensure this does not happen, even if it means, at times, taking up a "crusading" spirit (Wiebe 1998, 2001).

I think a final comment or two on the vulnerability of the sciences and the modern research university as an important cultural institution deliberately created to foster this peculiar and fragile mode of thought may buttress the critique of postmodernists in the field of religious studies. Scientific students of religion may be unaware of the fact that science was not discovered but have no need to try to hide the fact that it is the creation of the human spirit. But what the postmodern critic of the scientific study of religion fails to recognize is that science emerged for a very limited purpose—producing and accumulating propositional knowledge about the world and states of affairs in the world. However, the desire for such knowledge, as everyone knows, is but one cultural value among many. As Weber noted nearly a hundred years ago: "Whether . . . science is a worth while 'vocation' for somebody, and whether science itself has an objectively valuable 'vocation' are again value judgments about which nothing can be said in the lecture-room. To affirm the value of science is a presupposition for teaching [in the university classroom]" (Weber 1946 [1919]: 152). Nevertheless, this new cultural value stands apart from other cultural values for, as Ernest Gellner puts it, it can only function properly as a knowledge-seeking enterprise by claiming "diplomatic immunity" from all other cultural values (Gellner 1973). And it is in virtue of its "diplomatic immunity" from other values—not being constrained by other cultural value, moral, political, or religious commitments—that the method by which knowledge is obtained stands as a unique mode of thought and produces what can be reasonably described as culture-transcending knowledge. And, to repeat myself, it is for the promotion of this scientific method that the modern research university came into being (Weber 1946 [1919]).

There is no mandate, law, or revelation that requires a person to espouse the value of "knowledge for the sake of knowledge alone" in the study of religion or in any other discipline. However, if one does espouse that value, or is a member of an institution that has espoused it, one is then committed to the special epistemic morality linked to the sciences; to a set of intellectual presuppositions and social obligations without which science cannot function. And one is then simultaneously committed to upholding that "morality" in the modern research university. If one wishes rather to search for the meaning of life and the universe, or to find a way of creating a set of conditions necessary for social harmony, or discover principles to console the ills and sorrows of one's family, friends, or neighbors, one ought not turn to the research university for support. As Weber pointed out, the university is neither a social agency nor a dispenser of wisdom: "Science is a 'vocation' organized in special disciplines in the service of self-clarification and knowledge of interrelated facts. It is not the gift of grace of seers and prophets dispensing sacred values and revelations, nor does it partake of the contemplation of sages and philosophers about the meaning of the universe" (Weber 1946 [1919]: 152).

Other obstacles to keeping "religious studies" scientific

So much then for those who would criticize science and the university as oppressive cultural and social institutions and structures. Before bringing this argument to completion, however, I wish briefly to identify a few other issues that may create obstacles to keeping religious studies scientific. The first is the resurgence of religion around the world. On the one hand, governments having to deal with a new set of religious problems are putting pressure on scholars of religion to be "socially relevant" and are beginning to influence, if not politically determine, research agendas in the university (Alles 2007). Whereas financial support for basic research is thin, support for research tailored for political agendas seem likely to be approved (Wiebe 2009). On the other hand, this resurgence of religion has encouraged a number of scholars in the field, as well as departments as a whole, to become engaged in the political issues generated. The opportunity to get involved in matters on the national and international stage is just too tempting for some scholar/researchers to ignore. Russell McCutcheon, for example, thinks we should be very much engaged in public affairs because otherwise we leave the public realm and its concerns with law, justice, social welfare, and the like open only to the influence of the religious communities (McCutcheon 1997: 444). Consequently, he argues vigorously, that the student of religion should be a public intellectual (McCutcheon 1997: 444). But this, clearly, is to draw students of religion away from their basic responsibilities as scientists—the "vocation," as Weber has it, for which they are being paid (Weber 1946 [1919]). But if it is the national or international stage on which one wishes to make her or his mark, then Stanley Fish's observation about his colleagues in literary studies who illegitimately "employ the academy's machinery and resources in the service of those other purposes" (Fish 2008: 81) also applies to scholars of religion. And if they wish to save the world, Fish correctly points out, they should do it on their own dime and time. (This "syndrome" is only exacerbated, I would argue, by an increasing number of natural scientists who, in addition to their work in the natural or social sciences, wish to draw on that work in order to fill what I would call "the meaning vacuum" they think is left in the wake of a strictly scientific account of the world [see, for example, Owen Flanagan 2007 or Stuart A. Kauffman 2008]).

The flipside of this problem is what we might call the "New Atheism Problem." Many of our colleagues seem overjoyed with the publicity the New Atheists have brought to the field of religious studies. There seems to be some justification for the claim that the interest shown by Richard Dawkins and Daniel Dennett in atheism has brought some much needed public attention to what we do in religious studies. This, however, needs to be rethought. First, it is clear that the New Atheists have become hopelessly engaged in religio-theological argumentation that can make no positive contribution to our work. Secondly, the New Atheists function not as students of religion but as public intellectuals concerned for the welfare not only of their academic communities but also of their countries and of the whole world. But these tasks do not belong to the scientific study of religion. The only atheism that is of interest and benefit to the student of religion is "methodological atheism," and to cozy up to the New Atheists and their metaphysical and political concerns can only damage the image of religious studies. As Joseph Ben-David points out, any association with the New Atheists and the work of other ideologists is problematic for science. As he puts it: "If science is perceived as partial to some social interests, and scientists are seen in an invidious light, then people start doubting the moral value of seeking scientific truth for its own sake and apply it for the purpose of changing the world. This may spell the end of scientific culture" (Ben-David 1971: 180).

Finally, a serious concern for students of religion, especially since the advent of experimental studies and the growth of collaborative research projects in our field, is the lack of sufficient "no-strings-attached-funding." This should not be altogether surprising for a field in which most of the university departments involved have been largely engaged in programs dedicated to student self-realization and moral and political formation, or to programs of "religious appreciation courses" that are designed to contribute to peaceful relations in pluralistic cultures, or to programs that are designed to show the complementarity of science and religion in order to highlight how the sciences confirm religious truths. The problem, of course, is that since *bona fide* science funding agencies will be suspicious of such "religious studies projects," funding remains meager at best. This in turn "pushes" scholars in our field to seek other sources for their projects and many of these have been religious in character. Whether funding from those sources has actually skewed the writing of research grant proposals in order to insure favorable attention or not is difficult to tell. Nevertheless, funds from such organization for research in religious studies will likely only further generate suspicion in many scientific circles about the quality of the religious studies research being carried out. Serious attention needs to be given to the avenues open to us to gain access to more reputable sources of financial support for our work (Wiebe 2009).

To sum up: I maintain that the idea and ideal of an empirically testable scientific study of religion is rationally sound. It is also beyond question that there were many scholars in the field of religious studies in the past who sought and gained a degree of recognition for this field in their universities and beyond. Furthermore, I think we can all agree that there are more such scholars in the field today than there were in the past. And the field has seen some very important developments which suggest that a scientific study of religion may actually come to dominate the field in the future because of the serious research into the deep (evolutionary) history of religious behavior; by taking seriously the fact that the natural and social sciences have set important boundary conditions for the research on religion and that theories in religion really do need to cohere with theories in other disciplines; and because of the exponential increase in experimental work that the cognitive science of religion, among other sciences, has brought to the field. And these developments may at some point provide the kind of centripetal force that will bring into a coherent pattern what today remains as scattered studies of individual scholars in religious studies who are committed to providing a scientific explanation for religious belief and behavior. But as of now, this model does not characterize the field of religious studies either in our university departments or, unfortunately, in many of the societies and associations that support "religious studies." Moreover, as I have pointed out, it is also still true that the financial and institutional supports for these more recent developments in the field are themselves scattered in, with, and among institutions, societies, and associations still committed to religiously imbued agendas and therefore remain, so to speak, under threat. Nevertheless, as Robert McCauley notes, it took more than two hundred years for Antonie van Leeuwenhoek's discovery of microorganisms to eventually triumph in the germ theory of disease and we might leave open the possibility that the "triumph" of the scientific study of religion in our university departments of "religious studies" may be a similar, but shorter, "scientific revolution in slow motion" (McCauley 2011: 108) that will ultimately result in the dominance of a scientific study of religion in our university departments of religious studies.

Epilogue: Tending to Werblowsky's Concerns

The IAHR was created in 1950 to oversee periodic international congresses committed to a scientific understanding and explanation of religious phenomena. However, the IAHR had been colonized and co-opted by religious and theological forces from the first decade of its existence. In 1960, R. J. Zwi Werblowsky, secretary-general of the IAHR from 1975 to 1985, advised the executive committee and general membership of the IAHR to reaffirm its basic minimum academic/scientific presuppositions as essential to its mission and to be the required guidelines for national association members of the IAHR and scholars participating in the IAHR's international congresses (Werblowsky 1960). Nevertheless, Werblowsky remained doubtful, that "the IAHR [would be] up to carrying out this [scientific] mandate" (Weblowsky 1960: 220; see Chapter 14 in this volume).

The criticisms of the religious and theological nature of most study of religious thought and practice carried on in colleges and universities around the world today, and the arguments in support of a scientific study of religion in our colleges and universities that I have put forward in this volume, clearly suggest that Werblowsky's minimal academic standards for the study of religion are not generally accepted by "religious studies" departments nor are they rigorously applied to the national associations and societies that are member associations in the IAHR. As I made clear in my assessment of the IAHR international congresses for the volume on *The Academic Study of Religion and the IAHR: Past, Present, and Future* (2015b), it appears that the IAHR is not up to the task of requiring scholars who attend the IAHR international congresses to abide by the minimal academic standards laid out by Werblowsky. In 2005 the Japanese society for the study of religion, for example, quite deliberately ignored those minimal standards in favor of supporting a "religious studies" which, in their view, would become "an important bearer of a new kind of common knowledge" that would benefit international consensus "in solving practical problems" and creating "mutual understanding" (276). The IAHR world congress in South Africa in 2000 similarly focused attention on sociopolitical dilemmas rather than on issues of understanding and explaining "religion" and religious phenomena.

Given this drift away from the IAHR mandate, I had hoped that I could convince a younger scientifically oriented scholar in Canada to invite the twentieth IAHR world congress to Canada. I had directed an international IAHR congress in Winnipeg in 1980 and did not think I had the energy thirty years on to do it again. Unsuccessful in enticing others to undertake the task, and fearful that a third world congress focused on social, political, or theological and crypto-theological questions could be the ruin of the IAHR, I, reluctantly, agreed to submit a bid to the IAHR executive committee to organize the twentieth world congress in Toronto in order to ensure, as far as possible, that its program would adhere to the IAHR mission statement. Those of us engaged in this task wanted to use this occasion to put into practice, so to speak, the arguments we had made orally and in print for so many years as to what the academic study of religion ought to be. There were "murmurs" of concern on the part of some participants that the congress was too scientific. Other attending scholars and would-be participants were offended when their submissions, which did not adhere to the IAHR standards, were rejected because they were focused on religious or religo-political issues, or were requested to "revise" and resubmit their proposals in keeping with the IAHR mission statement. Despite the few complaints that reached us, the follow-up survey of the congress by Rosalind Hackett—then president of the IAHR—indicated that "79% of participants recorded satisfaction with the overall academic program of the Congress" (Wiebe 2011: 119). As I noted in my report in the published proceedings of the congress, we received "many letters and comments . . . regarding various aspects of the program. Virtually all communications were appreciative, of the academic program of the Congress" (Wiebe 2011: 123).

Despite the success of the Toronto congress, we were aware that some scholars in the field, and some in the leadership of the IAHR, saw the Toronto congress as involving too drastic a change with its strict adherence to the IAHR standards for congress participation. Consequently, the Institute for the Advanced Study of Religion (IASR: Toronto), which had been responsible for organizing the Toronto IAHR Congress, sponsored a "consultation" with the intent of providing the executive committee of the IAHR with an independent perspective on whether, as Werblowsky put it, the IAHR is fulfilling the obligations of its own mandate. Those invited to the consultation— essentially scholars with long experience in the institutional operations of the IAHR— were asked to come prepared with ideas about steps the IAHR must take to ensure that its scientific mandate will not be diluted by religious, theological, or sociopolitical and cultural agendas.

The consultation was held in Aarhus, Denmark, in July 2012. Membership in the consultation included four honorary life members of the IAHR, one of the co-directors of the XXI IAHR international congress, and two colleagues "at large." The fundamental issues, among other more practical and technical questions that were raised, included the following: (1) Does the IAHR need to make clearer to its national and regional member associations and affiliates that the IAHR is not a forum for confessional or political concerns? (2) Are there ways in which the IAHR can make a strong and attractive case for the scientific study of religion? (3) Would a change of name of the association to more clearly reflect its scientific objectives make a difference in this regard? (4) Given the present resources of the IAHR, can it realistically presume to assist and support national and regional associations around the world? and (5) Does the IAHR's connection to UNESCO still benefit the IAHR or does it impose obligations that the IAHR cannot properly discharge?

Clear recommendations were made in the consultation's report to the IAHR executive committee with respect to the first three questions. They included asking the executive committee to take forward a recommendation for a change of name of the IAHR to the international committee and the general assembly at the 2015 Quinquennial Congress: first, to the "International Association for the Scientific

Study of Religion," and, after much discussion, to "International Association for the Historical and Scientific Study of Religion," (Wiebe and Martin 2016). The members of the IASR consultation also recommended that the IAHR revise its webpage and remove religious images and terminology that does not clearly express its scientific objective. Furthermore, it recommended that the IAHR find ways of keeping its national member associations well informed about and committed to the primary purpose of the IAHR as an organization committed to supporting the scientific study of religion. The consultation questioned the IAHR's association with UNESCO concerning the possible interference of UNESCO's political agenda with the association's commitment to an exclusively scientific agenda.

Members of the consultation soon learned that the executive committee of the IAHR was not pleased with this IASR event, seeing it as unwarranted interference in its work. Although there is little indication that the executive committee took the IASR's report seriously, it did at least remove religious imagery from the IAHR website and took up the recommendation for a change of name of the IAHR (Wiebe and Martin 2016) which it brought to the attention of the international committee of the IAHR at the twenty-first Congress in Erfurt. The motion for a change of name, brought with no support from the executive committee, was soundly defeated by the international committee. The executive committee's displeasure with the well-intended "interference" of the IASR's consultation on the future of the IAHR, and defeat of the motion for a change of name that would clearly indicate the IAHR's commitment to the scientific study of religion, seems to indicate that the IAHR, as Werblowsky feared, is simply not up to the task of carrying out its own scientific mandate.

Notes

Chapter 5

1 I will focus attention in this chapter primarily on the career of religious studies in English-speaking Canada. However, a brief comment on developments in the field in Quebec can be found in my treatment of the "state-of-the-art" reviews in Chapter 1 and in note 9.

2 I think the word *Glaubenswissenschaft* is the appropriate term to designate the systematic intellectual exploration of a faith-tradition from within the perspective of the faith-tradition. Consequently I render it here as "faith-imbued science." In the past I have also used "theology" as a shorthand way of talking about a method that involves a confessional, rather than a religiously neutral, orientation in the study of religion. In this chapter I also distinguish "capital-c" confessionalism from "small-c" confessionalism: the former refers to religious commitment/belief defined by a specific historical religious tradition and the latter refers to a general, usually vaguely articulated, acceptance of the existence of a transcendent something or other as presupposition to study and analysis of religious phenomena.

3 It might be argued by some that I unjustifiably assume that science is neutral and value-free and that I am obligated to make a case for such a claim before proceeding. Unfortunately there is not sufficient space here to undertake that task but I suggest that the objective of the sciences is simply to obtain "public knowledge of public facts." By "public knowledge" I mean non-idiosyncratic knowledge mediated through intersubjectively tested sets of statements, and by "public facts" I mean "states of affairs in the world." Scientific students of religion, therefore, seek "neutral" knowledge of religious phenomena expressed in statements that transcend "self-involving" language, just as physicists, chemists, biologists, and social scientists express their knowledge of states of affairs in the world in as neutral a fashion as possible. Students of religion, like their scientific colleagues, then, must work to free themselves from religio-theological, moral, political, and humanistic agendas when engaged in their respective research projects.

4 Some might wish to argue that "scientific" and "academic" legitimation are not the same thing. By using the terms interchangeably here I am pointing to what I think ought to be the case for religious studies. Radically different and conflicting agendas characterize departments of religious studies in different universities and all of them are "academically" legitimated by virtue of their inclusion in one or other university curriculum. Within the modern research university, however, it is a discipline's epistemic/cognitive character—its scientific contribution (as defined in note 3 above)—that justifies extending to its academic legitimation. I treat this matter at greater length in Wiebe (2005a).

5 I am aware that *Studies in Religion* is the official journal for several constituent societies of the Canadian Corporation for Studies in Religion. They include the Canadian Society of Biblical Studies, the Canadian Society of Church History, the

Canadian Society of Patristic Studies, the Canadian Theological Society, and the Société Québecoise pour l'Étude de la Religion. Given this fact, some might not think it at all odd that the contents of *Studies in Religion* reveal a decidedly "theological" bias. Nevertheless, it will become clear that the majority of the scholars who publish in the journal, regardless of their society affiliation, exhibit at least a "small-c" kind of confessionalism in their work. As Randi R. Warne points out in her presidential address to the 2002 meeting of the Canadian Society for the Study of Religion (an unpublished document brought to my attention by an SR reader), letters in the CSSR archive indicate that professors Sheila McDonough and Kathleen Going were heavily engaged in those activities.

6 At this time McMaster, McGill, and Concordia universities were the dominant players in the field of religious studies, and scholars in those institutions wielded the greatest influence. The scholars from those institutions to whom I pay attention here are those who have published views on the nature of the discipline they see being supported by the proposed society. However, they are not necessarily those who were most involved in the ground level organizational work required for this enterprise to get off the ground.

7 The SR reader who brought to my attention Randi R. Warne's presidential address refers to it "as an objective history" of the society, "albeit a brief one," and suggested that this contradicts my claim that no such objective history exists. In my judgment, however, the Warne paper is far too brief (and virtually without foundation for significant claims about the state of the society after the 1990s) to constitute a sound history of the society. While her address provides some information gleaned from correspondence that fills out the view I present of the early years of the society in note 6, she provides no serious data relevant to the issues I focus on in this section of the chapter, and certainly none to undermine the thesis argued here. Issues of funding, student participation in the society, bilingualism, sexist language and gender issues receive considerably more attention than the question of the scientific character—or lack of it—of the society, and particularly so in the last two decades of its existence. Warne claims that the 1990s reveal "interesting developments," including the addition of the study of non-Christian religious traditions and the replacement, so to speak, of philosophy of religion, phenomenology, and systematic theology with such topics as science and religion, art and religion, and feminism and the study of religion. The claim, however, is based entirely on a reading of a draft program book for the 1990 meeting of the society. Moreover, without close analysis of the papers listed, there is no way of telling whether the "interesting developments" were such as to move the society away from its earlier traditional religious, moral, and social concerns. The limited evidence I provide below for the contrary thesis (namely, that no significant change of direction in ethos or program can be seen in the history of the society from its inception until now) is more substantial than that provided by Warne. I acknowledge once again, however, that further close study will have to be carried out to provide my provisional assessment here with a wholly secure foundation. Interestingly, Warne's own recommendations for the direction the society should follow in the future would, as she admits, bring it back to its earliest raison d'être; she recommends that the society become engaged in the critique of worldviews (and the powers that underlie them) and in advocacy of better ways of life—a secularized version of the emancipatory/redemptive agendas of a religiously orientated enterprise rather than the cognitive/scientific agenda that I am arguing should be the objective of the study of religion to be included in the curriculum of a modern research university.

8 *The Oxford English Dictionary* notes that Coleridge used the term in a new fashion to refer to "learned men as a body, scholars" which does not preclude women scholars, and *The Oxford American Dictionary* spells out the more modern or contemporary meaning of the term as "a distinct class of learned or literary people." The original association of the term with "clergy" provides overtones of the "natural" or "appropriate" leadership it was generally assumed such persons ought to have in society at large.

9 www.wlu.ca.

10 www.wlu.ca.

11 As my colleague Professor Marsha Hewitt and an SR reader have brought to my attention, the "corporatization" of the university over the past decade or so has put considerable pressure on disciplines in the humanities, including religious studies, to be relevant to broader community needs and that my argument, therefore, does not sufficiently recognize how those demands have shaped, or misshaped, humanities scholarship. They suggest, that is, that having to make humanities scholarship accessible to society at large in a practical way may well be the cause, or at least a cause, for the present state of affairs in religious studies in Canada. I have no doubt that this is, at least to some extent, true of the humanities as a whole. However, I believe that claims to this effect for the individual disciplines must provide evidence in their support. A further comment on this matter, it seems to me is in order: if my argument above is anywhere near the mark, then many practitioners of religious studies in Canada would/will actually see such demands as wholly appropriate and applaud external government pressures to ensure that the study of religion will benefit society and its diverse religious communities in some direct way; if that is not the case, one should be able to find evidence of resistance of the discipline to such interference but no such evidence, as far as I am aware, has yet come to light.

12 See Philip Kitcher (1993) and John H. Zammito (2004).

Chapter 8

1 https:vimeo.com/194880435.

2 It can be recovered at https:soundcloud.com/rsn-aar-2017-aar-presidential-address-eddie-glaude-religion-and-the-most-vulnerable.

3 See http://bulletin.equinoxpub.com/2016/12/revolutionary-love-scholars-respond-to-the-aars-2016-conference-theme-david-gushee/.

Chapter 9

1 My concern in this paper is with religious studies as an "academically enclosed enterprise" in the sense of that notion used by Robert A. McCaughey, namely, as an "organized undertaking of sufficient magnitude and duration to permit its participants to derive a measure of identity from it" (1984: xiii). This does not preclude pursuit of the study of religion under conditions other than those that exist in the modern research university but recognizes that such an intellectual exercise may be a significantly different one.

2 Science as a nonmoral instrument of inquiry may, nevertheless, be characterized in another sense as "moral"; as having a moral structure peculiar to itself (Wiebe 1973, 1977).

3 It is obvious that social, political, and cultural constraints impinge upon all thought, but recognizing this is not tantamount to the claim that all thought is fundamentally ideological in character. Scientific thought is characterized by its self-conscious, critical attempt to free itself from such constraints so as to obtain—as far as it is possible—knowledge of the world that is free from personal, social, and cultural idiosyncrasy.

4 That edification or spiritual enrichment may be a by-product of this activity for some people is not being denied; the claim is simply that this is not the intention of the scientific study of religion. Although there is no necessary connection between the scientific study of religion and edification, it is clear that the results of scientific research in this field can be applied to other concerns; scientific knowledge about religion, that is, may become the raw material for philosophical and theological speculation, but those undertakings are clearly distinct from that of the scientific enterprise itself.

5 It is obvious that for many people, post-secondary educational institutions in the United States are concerned with a good deal more than the creation and dissemination of knowledge, the making of scientists, or even preparation for a career. Martha Nussbaum, for example, argues that colleges and universities must also be concerned with preparing student for citizenship and, more generally, with "cultivating humanity" by helping students to reason well about the urgent questions of life (Nussbaum 1997: 294). The good citizen, according to Nussbaum, involves more than the "learning of a lot of facts and mastering techniques of reasoning"; "it means learning how to be a human being capable of love and imagination . . . who can function with sensitivity and alertness as a citizen of the whole world" (Nussbaum 1997: 14, 8). And religion, for Nussbaum, plays a significant role in that task as a "guide" to reason and she castigates the modern research university for failing to engage religion even, so she maintains, in religious studies departments (Nussbaum 1997: 264). For Nussbaum, it is possible for a university to be both a religious institution and truly a university (Nussbaum 1997: 265), but she acknowledges that in the case of Brigham Young University and the University of Notre Dame, students are provided with two different directions for citizenship (Nussbaum 1997: 290) apparently unaware that there could be as many such models for citizenship as there are religions and philosophies. It is hard to conceive how teaching in such a global situation could be distinguished from indoctrination. For a case for inclusion of religion in the academic vocation in American colleges and Universities, see Mark R. Schwehn (1993).

6 See here R. J. Zwi Werblowsky's response to the "encroachment" of religious and theological concerns on the academic program of the Xth International Congress of the History of Religions sponsored by the IAHR (1960) in which he reflects on the nature of the IAHR. The IAHR, he insists, came into being as an institutional support for *Religionswissenschaft* "as a discipline well-defined and scientific enough to make it worthwhile for scholars to maintain a special organization for its promotion" (1960: 216). See also Annemaire Schimmel (1960) for a summary of the discussion of Werblowsky's paper, and Donald Wiebe (1994) for a subsequent reflection on the same theme at the 1990 Rome International Congress sponsored by the IAHR.

7 On the medieval origin of this notion, see Peter Harrison's analysis of the re-conception of the study of nature as a theological enterprise (1998). Harrison shows how knowing nature was equivalent to knowing the mind of God and that knowing God brings to unity one's knowledge of nature.

8 I find myself in disagreement with Wasserstrom's claim that this paradigm is not a central factor in the academy today (Wasserstrom 1999: 238–39). Insofar as Eliade's "illuminist sense of scholarship" made of the history of religions "a kind of Christian Kabbalah," I think it would be safe to say that the paradigm was never dominant in the field. But I would argue that Eliade's approach in muted form did become pervasive (Wasserstrom 1999: 24, 49). Eliade's understanding of the study of religion as both intellectually sound and religious, that is, appealed to many as the only way to "make sense" of religion on its own terms, and was seen as a viable option to the reductionistic sciences in the academic study of religion. Just how pervasive such an anti-reductionist study of religion has become is clearly evident, I think, in the new Macmillan *Encyclopedia of Religion* (1987) edited by Eliade (see Wiebe 1988). Interestingly, Wasserstrom himself maintains that contemporary students of religion must try to recover from Eliade—and others of his type—"something of what we need to teach the next generation of students of religion," which for him includes teaching "ways to engage the perennial mystery of religion" (Wasserstrom 1999: 246, 247). (The idea of the science of religion as itself a religious enterprise, as Erwin R. Goodenough maintained in his address at the founding of the American Society for the Study of Religion (1959), has characterized not only that society but through it also much of the American scene.)

9 This is not to deny that there are also scientific students of religion to be found in departments of religious studies in the United States or among the members of the AAR who, nevertheless, continue their work with a minimum of structural support from their departments or national professional associations.

10 As Sam Gill points out, "The American Academy of Religion is for many a rambling organ that hosts annual meetings for a large variety of specific religious study groups. The bulk of the productivity of the academic study of religion goes on through these small and often highly rigorous groups. The overwhelming majority of work in the Academy is the business of specific studies within the Christian tradition. . . . Too few of these contribute to or benefit from the concerns that ought to be the main business of the academic study of religion" (Gill 1994: 974–75). (Malcolm David Eckel (1994), Douglas R. Brooks (1994), and Charles Prebish (1994) provide clear evidence that other religions receive a similar hearing in the Academy). The point Gill is making is that "the academic study of religion is no more than a cumbersome rubric that makes possible what to them is the actual study of religion, *their specific area of study conducted commonly as a religious study*" (Gill 1994: 974; emphasis added.) According to Gill, such eclecticism is seen by members of the AAR as an antidote to narrow-mindedness and intolerance but in effect is nothing more than a refusal to draw boundaries by way of clear distinctions which prevents the creation of a sound academic tradition in the study of religious phenomena.

11 Although contemporary students of religion do not seem to believe a religious appropriation of science is possible, it is clear that there is considerable interest among philosophers and theologians in the religious benefits of the dialogue between science and religion. But unlike the university reformers, today's philosophers and theologians do not have the same interest in scientific religion or study of religion.

12 For Thomas J. J. Altizer that concern over values is the responsibility of the student
    of religion and the academic institutions that support the study of religion. Altizer
    calls upon the student of religion to take up a "sacred role" in bringing humankind
    to ultimacy and urges academic institutions to take up "a priestly role of sanctioning
    our society, and sanctioning it in its own deepest ground" (Altizer 1994: 1014). And
    for Altizer, the AAR has a special task in this regard: "One would think that of all our
    academic societies the American Academy of Religion would be most prepared to
    exercise such a role, and while thus far it has received little public support or response,
    it would seem to have enormous potentialities for the future, potentialities which are
    now perhaps becoming actualities, and surely so if this academy is at last becoming
    united to our world" (Altizer 1994: 1014). I am arguing in this chapter that the AAR
    is in fact fulfilling this role, although this is sometimes obscured by its persistent
    management of its image as a scholarly and academic enterprise. That is also an
    important task for the AAR, however, for without the prestige that comes by virtue
    of its legitimation by the university, it could not fulfil the very role Altizer wishes it to
    take on with more vigor.
13 Rosalind Hackett has informed me that the timing of the SBL/AAR Congress was
    negotiated with the AAR so that participants in that congress might also attend the
    IAHR Quinquennial Congress. The AAR also publicized the IAHR Congress and
    linked that congress to its own website. Hackett believes these and other "courtesies"
    indicate that greater cooperation between the two organizations is possible in the
    future. In my judgment, however, this is wholly unlikely given the thirty-five years of
    tension between the two since the eleventh international congress held in Claremont,
    California (Sharpe 1986a: 284; Bleeker 1968: 4–5), and the fact that virtually no
    evidence of a change of heart exists, beyond some publicity and negotiation of the
    date of the Cape Town SBL/AAR Congress.
14 In 2016 Professor Luther Martin and I came to the unhappy conclusion that the
    idea of a fully scientific study of religion is unlikely ever to emerge in undergraduate
    departments of religious studies. We expressed our disappointment in reaching
    that conclusion in an essay entitled "Religious Studies as a Scientific Discipline: The
    Persistence of a Delusion" (Martin and Wiebe 2016a).

Chapter 10

1 One ought perhaps to keep in mind in our current discussion of the Cold War
   Bothwell's comment that "hindsight, in the case of the Cold War, is not very old. As
   history goes, the Cold War is very recent, and much remains secret in the hands of
   governments that have an interest in obscuring or protecting past errors" (1998: 108).
   Although I am not dealing with primary documents in this discussion, authors to
   whom I refer have no doubt suffered from such interests. Jessica Wang (1999), for
   example, points out that the FBI records she consulted are so heavily censored that she
   had to fill in the gaps with "informed speculation" (59). Moreover, there may be many
   writing about the Cold War today with scores to settle or ideological commitments,
   past or present, seeking confirmation or justification, which also may contribute
   to obscuring the past. As Wang warns, "The contemporary passions involved in
   understanding the Cold War will make the problem of interpretation a complicated
   and contentious undertaking" (290).

2 The argument here regarding the impact of the Cold War on religious studies in the United States is, with but slight modification, applicable to religious studies in Canada. For lack of space I shall confine my analysis and comments to the American situation.

3 This was not the greatest threat to scholars of the period, however, since, as Lewontin points out, "there was never a coherent state security policy" (1997: 18) to enforce comprehensive compliance. The greater danger to the individual scholar, he insists, was the cowardice shown by administrators in defending the principle of academic freedom in the university.

4 This is the essence of Jessica Wang's argument in her *American Science in an Age of Anxiety: Scientists, Anticommunism and the Cold War* (1999). According to Wang, there was a serious "narrowing of American political discourse" (250) between 1945 and 1950. Before that period, she maintains, it was still possible "to argue publicly for the political legitimacy of the American Left" (250) but that by the end of the decade that tolerance was lost. The negative effects of the removal of scientists as an alternative source of political influence, she maintains, are still in force: "America's current crisis of political faith has strong roots in the intellectual poverty of the Cold War political consensus" (290).

5 This kind of failure to distinguish the aims of history as an academic undertaking from other broader aims and goals is clearly evident, for example, in William H. McNeill's *Mythistory and Other Essays* (1986). The historian, McNeill argues, must not focus simply on matters of fact but rather must fill the role of global mythmaker (91) because human society is based upon myths which, from time to time, are in need of care and repair. Whether McNeill is right or not about the human need for myth, it should be clear that in taking on the task not only of the care and repair of myths but also of their manufacture, history as an autonomous discipline will be undermined. This kind of work is ideologically driven and cannot, therefore, pass for science.

6 Jessica Wang (1999) provides a similar study of the effects of the Cold War on American scientists and shows that they were afraid of criticizing Cold War politics because of the possible loss of influence, if not their jobs. Although she insists that their silence on political issues helped shape the Cold War consensus, she does not argue that such political repression in any sense constituted an ideological subversion of the sciences.

7 Because "economic wars" might substitute for the Cold War in its organizing capacity, Lewontin believes that even though the wars, hot and cold, have ended "the socialization of intellectual work is here to stay" (1997: 33). Daniel Kevles (1998) agrees and insists that there is nothing to be feared in this development (224). And he argues optimistically that science and the scientists should have "a vision of the larger purposes that science can and should serve, of the kind of good society that it can and could help create both at home and abroad" (232), for "history suggests that the quest for basic knowledge can flourish amid ultimate utilitarian commitments" (233). On this point, see also Roger Geiger (1993: 309).

8 A close study of the role of foundations in relation to religion and the study of religion might well provide evidence of a greater impact of Cold War values than I have been able to trace here. It is common knowledge that foundations have not refrained from political activity (Cunninggim 1972) and particularly of the conservative and hyper-conservative variety (Colwell 1993). Even though conservatism dominates the philosophy of most foundations (Curti and Nash 1965) little direct evidence has been produced of what could be called Cold War funding of religious projects or

institutions concerned with the study of religion. Further study of the influence of foundations on the emergence, establishment, and development of the academic study of religion, however, will have to await another occasion.

9 This list of founders for the reinvented discipline is a curious one; it has been more plausibly argued that scholars like Joachim Wach and Mircea Eliade in fact carried out the founding in North America, but I will not pursue this matter further here.

10 I can add to this testimonial evidence a conversation with Professor Edward Conze in the early 1970s. While a graduate student at the University of Lancaster, I had been asked to "look after" Professor Conze while visiting lecturer there. On a number of occasions Professor Conze would complain to me about the treatment he received from the government while teaching in the United States because of his former communist associations. He also told me, however, and with a degree of pride as I recall it, that in the late 1970s the Pentagon was very much interested in his knowledge of Buddhism in South East Asia. He did not elaborate on the nature of his cooperation with any government agencies.

11 The Center for International Relations at MIT is often pointed to as an institution created to meet the needs of the federal government, with the implication that its work is intellectually suspect. Roger Geiger (1993), however, points out that such centers were founded to enlarge academic knowledge of world affairs, and that members of such research units became defensive about the academic character of their work. Although such units may have been intended to meet the knowledge-requirements of the government, as Geiger puts it, they, ironically, also underwent "academic enclosure" that protected them from political distortion. See also Robert A. McCaughey's *International Studies and Academic Enterprise: A Chapter in the Enclosure of American Learning* (1984).

Chapter 11

1 Mark C. Taylor, in the introduction to *Critical Terms for Religious Studies* (1998), makes a similar claim. Although he acknowledges the profound influence of the Enlightenment on the development of the study of religion and argues that its distinctive contours have been shaped by the Second World War, it is the Civil Rights and anti-war movements, rather than the Cold War, that he sees as having been significant for the contemporary academic study of religion. "In order to understand the significance of recent discussions of religion," he writes, "it is necessary to appreciate the institutional contexts in which they have unfolded . . . [and it is these movements] that gave rise to multicultural sensibilities, which are still socially significant and politically influential" (10 & 11). He concludes:

> Though the contemporary study of religion is the product of developments dating back to the Enlightenment, its distinctive multidisciplinary orientation and multicultural focus reflect a world that is undeniably postmodern. (15)

2 Stoll's work is, as one might expect, controversial but, as Hal Cohen (1999) points out, it has not only provoked criticism but also earned support from a broad range of scholars.

Chapter 14

1   By "dogma" Nisbet means "a system of principles or ideals widely believed to be not merely true or right but also beyond the necessity of the more or less constant verification we feel obliged to give to so many other aspects of our lives," although not necessarily incapable of being provided (22–23).

Conclusion

1   Homepage, http://www.iahr.dk/.
2   Homepage, http://www.trinity.utoronto.ca/iasr/.

References

Allan, Charlotte. (1996). Is Nothing Sacred? Casting Out the Gods from Religious Studies. *Lingua Franka*, 6 (7): 30–40.

Alles, Gregory D. (2007/2008). *Religious Studies: A Global View*. London: Routledge.

Altizer, Thomas J. J. (1994). The Challenge of Nihilism. *Journal of the American Academy of Religion*, 62: 1013–22.

Anderson, Charles P. (1972). *Guide to Religious Studies in Canada*. Toronto: Corporation for the Publication of Academic Studies in Canada.

Baderstscher, John M., Gordon Harland, and Roland E. Miller. (1993). *Religious Studies in Manitoba and Saskatechewan: A State-of-the-Art Review*. Waterloo: Wilfred Laurier Press.

Barrett, Justin. (2004). *Why Would Anyone Believe in God?* Walnut Creek: AltaMira Press.

Barrett, Justin. (2008). Small Grant Competition. http://www.cam.ox.ac.uk/research/co gnition-religion-and-theology/research-funding/small-grant-competition/

Bell, Catherine. (1996). Modernism and Postmodernism in the Study of Religion. *Religious Studies Review*, 22: 179–90.

Ben-David, Joseph. (1984 [1971]). *The Scientists' Role in Society: A Comparative Study*. Chicago: University of Chicago Press.

Benson, Thomas L. (1987). Religious Studies as an Academic Discipline. In Mircea Eliade (ed.), *Encyclopedia of Religion (Vol. 14)* (88–92). New York: Macmillan Press.

Bischoff, Guntrum G. (1975). The Pedagogy of Religiology. In Anne Carr and Nicholas Piediscalzi (eds.), *Public Schools Religious Studies* (127–35). Missoula: American Academy of Religion.

Bjerke, Svein. (1979). Ecology of Religion, Evolutionism and Comparative Religion. In Lauri Honko (ed.), *Science of Religion: Studies in Methodology* (237–48). The Hague: Mouton Publishers.

Blumenberg, Hans. (1983). *The Legitimation of the Modern Age* (Trans. Robert M. Wallace). Cambridge: MIT Press.

Blumenberg, Hans. (1987). *The Genesis of the Copernican World* (Trans. Robert M. Wallace). Cambridge: MIT Press.

Bothwell, Robert. (1998). *The Big Chill: Canada and the Cold War*. Toronto: Irwin Publishing.

Bourdieu, Pierre. (2004). *Science of Science and Reflexivity*. Chicago: University of Chicago Press.

Bowlby, Paul W. R. (2001). *Religious Studies in Atlantic Canada*. Waterloo: Wilfred Laurier Press.

Boyer, Pascal. (1994). *The Naturalness of Religious Ideas: A Cognitive Theory of Religion*. Los Angeles: University of California Press.

Braybrooke, Marcus. (1990). Religious Studies and Interfaith Development. In Ursula King (ed.), *Turning Points in Religious Studies* (132–41). Edinburgh: T & T Clark.

Brooks, Douglas R. (1994). The Thousand-Headed Person: The Mystery of Hinduism and the Study of Religion. *Journal of the American Academy of Religion*, 62: 1111–26.

Brown, James Robert. (2001). *Who Rules in Science*. Cambridge: Harvard University Press.

Burkert, Walter. (1983). *Homo Necans: The Anthropology of Ancient Greek Sacrificial Ritual and Myth*. Los Angeles: University of California Press.

Cahill, Joseph. (1982). *Mended Speech: The Crisis of Religious Studies and Theology*. New York: Crossroad.

Cain, Seymour. (1987). History of Study. In Mircea Eliade (ed.), *The Encyclopedia of Religion Vol. 14* (64–83). New York: Macmillan Press.

Capps, Walter H. (1995). *Religious Studies: The Making of a Discipline*. Minneapolis: Fortress Press.

Caputo, John D. (2008). Open Theology – Or What Comes After Secularism? *Bulletin of the Council of Societies for the Study of Religion*, 37 (2): 45–49.

Chalmers, Alan. (1990). *Science and Its Fabrication*. Minneapolis: University of Minnesota Press.

Cherry, Conrad. (1992). The Study of Religion and the Rise of the American University. In Joseph M. Kitagawa (ed.), *Religious Studies, Theological Studies, and the University Divinity School* (137–50). Atlanta: Scholars Press.

Cherry, Conrad. (1995). *Hurrying Toward Zion: Universities, Divinity Schools, and American Protestantism*. Bloomington: Indian University Press.

Cherry, Conrad, Betty DeBerg, and Amanda Porterfield. (2001). *Religion on Campus*. Chapel Hill: University of North Carolina Press.

Chidester, David. (1996). *Savage Systems: Colonialism and Comparative Religion in Southern Africa*. Charlottesville: University Press of Virginia.

Clark, William. (2006). *Academic Charisma and the Origin of the Research University*. Chicago: University of Chicago Press.

Clarke, Justice. (1964). 'Obiter dicta': Supreme Court Report. *West Publishing Com.*, 83A: 1573.

Clebsch, William A. (1981). Apples, Oranges, and Mana: Comparative Religion Revisited. *Journal of the American Academy of Religion*, 49: 3–22.

Clifford, N. Keith. (1991). Church History, Religious History, or the History of Religions? In Klaus K. Klostermaier and Larry W. Hurtado (eds.), *Religious Studies: Issues, Prospects and Proposals* (171–81). University of Manitoba Studies in Religion, 2. Atlanta: Scholars Press.

Cohen, Hal. (1999). The Unmaking of Rigoberta Menchu. *Lingua Franka*, 9 (5): 48–55.

Cohen, H. Floris. (1994). *The Scientific Revolution: An Historical Inquiry*. Chicago: University of Chicago Press.

Cole, W. Owen. (1990). The New Educational Reform Act and Worship in County Schools of England and Wales. In Ursula King (ed.), *Turning Points in Religious Studies* (117–31). Edinburgh: T & T Clark.

Colwell, Mary Anna Culleton. (1993). *Private Foundations and Public Policy: The Political Role of Philanthropy*. New York: Garland Publishing.

Combs, Eugene. (1977). Learned and Learning: CSSR/SCER, 1965–1975. *Studies in Religion/Sciences Religieuses*, 6 (4): 57–63.

Cornford, Francis M. (1932). *Before and After Socrates*. Cambridge: Cambridge University Press.

Coward, Harold. (1991). The Contribution of Religious Studies to Secular Universities in Canada. In Klaus K. Klostermaier and Larry W. Hurtado (eds.), *Religious Studies: Issues, Prospects and Proposals* (18–37). University of Manitoba Studies in Religion, 2. Atlanta: Scholars Press.

Coward, Harold. (2014). *Fifty Years of Religious Studies in Canada: A Personal Retrospective*. Waterloo: Wilfrid Laurier University Press.

Crites, Stephen et al. (1990). *Liberal Learning and the Religious Major (an AAR Task Force on the Study in Depth of Religion)*. Syracuse: American Academy of Religion.

Crockett, Clayton. (2008). Secular Theology and the Academic Study of Religion. *Bulletin of the Council of Societies for the Study of Religion*, 37 (2): 37–40.

Cunninggim, Merrimon. (1947). *The College Seeks Religion*. New Haven: Yale University Press.

Cunninggim, Merrimon. (1972). *Private Money and Public Service: The Role of Foundations in American Society*. New York: McGraw-Hill Book Company.

Cunningham, Adrian. (1990). Religious Studies in the Universities: England. In Ursula King (ed.), *Turning Points in Religious Studies* (21–31). Edinburgh: T & T Clark.

Curti, Merle, and Roderick Nash. (1965). *Philanthropy in the Shaping of American Higher Education*. New Bruswick: Rutgers University Press.

Davis, Charles. (1974). The Reconvergence of Theology and Religious Studies. *Studies in Religion/Sciences Religieuses*, 4 (3): 205–21.

de Concini, Barbara with Catherine L. Albenese, Judith Berling, Delwin Brown, Warren G. Frisinia, William Scott Green, Robert C. Monk, Robert C. Neville, Susan Brooks Thistlewaite, Raymond Williams, and Edith Wyschogrod. (1993). AAR Self-Study Committee Findings [Part II]. *Religious Studies News*, 8 (4): 10 and 14.

DiCenso, James. (2004). *Department and Centre for the Study of Religion, University of Toronto: Academic Plan, 2004–2010*. Toronto: Department and Centre for the Study of Religion, 10pp.

Doniger, Wendy. (1980). *Women, Androgynes, and Other Mythical Beasts*. Chicago: University of Chicago Press.

Doniger, Wendy. (1984). *Dreams, Illusion and Other Realities*. Chicago: University of Chicago Press.

Dreger, Alice. (2015). *Galileo's Middle Finger: Heretics, Activists, and the Search for Justice in Science*. New York: Penguin Press.

Drijvers, H. J. W. (1973). Theory Formation in Science and Religion and the Study of the History of Religions. In Th. P. Van Baaren and H. J. W. Drijvers (eds.), *Religion in Culture and Methodology* (57–77). The Hague: Mouton Publishers.

Dunbar, Robin. (1995). *The Trouble with Science*. Cambridge: Harvard University Press.

Eck, Diana. (2007). Prospects for Pluralism: Voice and Vision in the Study of Religion. *Journal of the American Academy of Religion*, 75 (4): 743–76.

Eckel, Malcolm David. (1994). The Ghost at the Table: On the Study of Buddhism and the Study of Religion. *Journal of the American Academy of Religion*, 62: 1085–110.

Eliade, Mircea. (1989). *Journal II, 1957–1969* (Trans. Teresa Lavender Fagan). Chicago: University of Chicago Press.

Ellis, John M. (1997). *Literature Lost: Social Agendas and the Corruption of the Humanities*. New Haven: Yale University Press.

Ellwood, Robert L. (1999). *The Politics of Myth: A Study of C. G. Jung, Mircea Eliade, and Joseph Campbell*. New York: SUNY Press.

Esposito, John L. (2014). Islam in the Public Square. *Journal of the American Academy of Religion*, 82 (2): 291–306.

Feyerabend, Paul. (1975). *Against Method*. London: NLB.

Feyerabend, Paul. (1995). *Killing Time: The Autobiography of Paul Feyerabend*. Chicago: Chicago University Press.

Fish, Stanley. (1995). *Professional Correctness: Literary Studies and Political Change*. New York: Oxford University Press.

Fish, Stanley. (2008). *Save the World on Your Own Time*. New York: Oxford University Press.

Flanagan, Kieran. (1996). *The Enchantment of Sociology: A Study of Theology and Culture*. Basingstoke: Macmillan.

Flanagan, Owen. (2007). *The Really Hard Problem: Meaning in a Material World*. Cambridge: MIT Press.

Ford, David. (1999). *Theology: A Very Short Introduction*. Oxford: Oxford University Press.

Ford, David F., Ben Quash, and Janet Martin Soskice, eds. (2005). *Fields of Faith: Theology and Religious Studies for the Twenty-first Century*. Cambridge: Cambridge University Press.

Fraser, Brian J. (1995). *The Study of Religion in British Columbia: A State-of-the-Art Review*. Waterloo: Wilfred Laurier University Press.

Frisinia, Warren. (1993). Barbara De concini on the AAR's Self-Study [An Interview]. *Religious Studies News*, 8: 1–2.

Gardaz, Michel. (2003). Call for Papers: Religious Studies in Canada: Past, Present and Future, May 7–9th 2005, University of Ottawa. *Studies in Religion/Sciences Religieuses*, 32 (3): 353.

Gay, Peter. (1967). *The Enlightenment: An Interpretation, Vol 1. The Rise of Modern Paganism*. New York: Knopf.

Gay, Peter. (1969). *The Enlightenment: An Interpretation, Vol. 2. The Science of Freedom*. New York: Knopf.

Geertz, Clifford. (1983). *Local Knowledge: Further Essays in Interpretive Anthropology*. New York: Basic Books.

Geertz, Armin W., and Russell T. McCutcheon. (2000). The Role of Method and Theory in the IAHR. *Method and Theory in the Study of Religion,* 12 (1–2): 3–37.

Geiger, Rober L. (1993). *Research and Relevant Knowledge: American Research Universities Since World War II*. New York: Oxford University Press.

Gellner, Ernest. (1973). The Savage and the Modern Mind. In Robin Horton and Ruth Finnegan (eds.), *Modes of Thought* (162–81). London: Faber and Faber.

Gellner, Ernest. (1974). *Legitimation of Belief*. Cambridge: Cambridge University Press.

Gellner, Ernest. (1981). Pragmatism and the Importance of Being Ernest. In I. C. Jarvie and J. Agassi (eds.), *Spectacles and Predicaments: Essays in Social Theory* (241–62). Cambridge: Cambridge University Press.

Gellner, Ernest. (1988). *Plow, Sword and Book: The Structure of Human History*. London: Collins Harvill.

Gellner, Ernest. (1992). *Postmodernism, Reason, and Religion*. London: Routledge.

Gellner, Ernest. (1997). Knowledge of Nature and Society. In Ikulas Teich, Roy Porter, and Bo Gustafson (eds.), *Nature and Society in Historical Context* (9–17). Cambridge: Cambridge University Press.

Gellner, Ernest. (1998). *Language and Solitude: Wittgenstein, Malinowski, and the Habsburg Dilemma*. Cambridge: Cambridge University Press.

Gill, Sam. (1994). "The Academic Study of Religion". *Journal of the American Academy of Religion*, 62/4: 965–75.

Glaude, Eddie. (2017). Religion and the Most Vulnerable. Available on audio at https:soundcloud.com/rsn-aar-2017-aar-presidential-address-eddie-glaude-religion-and-the-most-vulnerable (accessed February 2019).

Goodenough, E. R. (1959). Religionswissenschaft. *Numen*, 6: 77–95.

Grant, George. (1968). The Academic Study of Religion in Canada. In R. H. Hubbard (ed.), *Scholarship in Canada 1967: Achievement and Outlook*, Symposium presented to Section II of the Royal Society of Canada. University of Toronto Press, 1965.

Gregory, Brad. (2012). *The Unintended Reformation: How a Religious Revolution Secularized Society*. Cambridge: Harvard University Press.

Griffiths, Paul J. (1999). *Religious Reading: The Place of Reading in the Practice of Religion*. New York: Oxford University Press.

Gross, Paul R. and Norman Levitt. (1994). *Higher Superstition: The Academic Left and Its Quarrels with Science* (2nd ed). Baltimore: Johns Hopkins University Press.

Gushee, David. (2016). Revolutionary Love. *Bulletin for the Study of Religion*. Religion Bulletin: The Blogging Portal of the Bulletin for the Study of Religion, December 22, 2016. http://bulletin.equinoxpub.com/2016/12/revolutionary-love-scholars-respond-to-the-aars-2016-conference-theme-david-gushee/ (accessed February 2019).

Gushee, David. (2018). In the Ruins of White Evangelicalism: Interpreting a Compromised White Christian Tradition through the Witness of African-American Literature. *Journal of the American Academy of Religion*, 87 (1): 1–17. Typscript.

Guthrie, Stewart. (1993). *Faces in the Clouds: A New Theory of Religion*. New York: Oxford University Press.

Haack, Susan. (1998). Puzzling Out Science. In Susan Haack (ed.), *Manifesto of a Passionate Moderate* (90–103). Chicago: Chicago University Press.

Haack, Susan. (2003). *Defending Science Within Reason*. New York: Prometheus Press.

Harland, Gordon. (1991). Religious Studies in a Time of Change and Conflict. In Klaus K. Klostermaier and Larry W. Hurtado (eds.), *Religious Studies: Issues, Prospects and Proposals* (1–14). University of Manitoba Studies in Religion, 2. Atlanta: Scholars Press.

Harris, Marvin. (1979). *Cultural Materialism: The Struggle for a Science of Culture*. New York: Random House.

Harrison, Jan Ellen. (1909). The Influence of Darwinism on the Study of Religion. In A. C. Seard (ed.), *Darwin an Modern Science: Essays in Commemoration of the Centenary of the Birth of Charles Darwin and of the Fiftieth Anniversary of the Publication of the Origin of Species* (494–511). Cambridge: Cambridge University Press.

Harrison, Peter. (1998). *The Bible, Protestantism and the Rise of Natural Science*. Cambridge: Cambridge University Press.

Hart, D. G. (1992). American Learning and the Problem of Religious Studies. In G. M. Marsden and B. J. Longfield (eds.), *The Secularization of the Academy* (195–233). Oxford: Oxford University Press.

Hart, D. G. (1999). *The University Gets Religion: Religious Studies in American Higher Education*. Baltimore: Johns Hopkins University Press.

Hart, Ray L. (1985). To Be and Not to Be: *Sit Autem sermo (Logos) Vester Est, Est' Non, Non*. *JAAR*, 53 (1): 5–22.

Hart, Ray L. (1991). Religious and Theological Studies in American Higher Education. *Journal of the American Academy of Religion*, 69: 715–827.

Heller, Agnes. (1990). *Can Modernity Survive?* Berkeley: University of California Press.

Henaut, Barry. (1992). *The Really Hard Problem: Meaning in a Material World*. Cambridge: MIT Press.

Hillerbrand, Hans J. (2006). On Book Burnings and Book Burners: Reflections on the Power (and Powerlessness) of Ideas. *Journal of the American Academy of Religion*, 74 (3): 593–614.

Hobart, Michael E. (2018). *The Great Rift: Literacy, Numeracy, and the Religion-Science Divide*. Cambridge: Harvard University Press.

Holley, R. (1978). *Religious Education and Religious Understanding*. London: Routledge Kegan Paul.

Honko, Lauri. (1979). *Science of Religion: Studies in Methodology*. The Hague: Mouton Publishers.

Hoopes, Robert. (1962). *Right Reason in the English Renaissance*. Cambridge: Harvard University Press.

Howard, Thomas Albert. (2006). *Protestant Theology and the Making of the Modern German University*. Oxford: Oxford University Press.

Huff, Toby E. (1993). *The Rise of Early Modern Science: Islam, China and the West*. Cambridge: Cambridge University Press.

Hull, John. (1984). Religious Education in a Pluralistic Society. In John Hull (ed.), *Studies in Religion and Education* (45–55). London: The Falmer Press.

Hume, David. (1956 [1777]). *The Natural History of Religion*. Stanford: Stanford University Press.

Jackson, Robert. (1990). Religious Studies and Development in Religious Education. In Ursula King (ed.), *Turning Points in Religious Studies* (102–16). Edinburgh: T & T Clark.

Jones, Serene. (2016). Revolutionary Love. Available on video at https:vimeo.com/194880435.

Jouco Bleeker, C. (1968). Opening Address. In *Proceedings of the XIth International Congress of the IAHR, Vol. 1 The Impact of Modern Culture on Traditional Religions* (3–12). Leiden: E. J. Brill.

Juergensmeyer, Mark. (1993). *The New Cold War? Religious Nationalism Confronts the Secular State*. Boulder: NetLibrary, Inc.

Juergensmeyer, Mark. (2010). Beyond Words and War: The Global Future of Religion. *Journal of the American Academy of Religion*, 78 (4): 882–95.

Kaufmann, Stuart A. (2008). *Reinventing the Sacred: A New View of Science, Reason, and Religion*. New York: Basic Books.

Kemeny, P. C. (1998). *Princeton in the Nation's Service: Religious Ideals, Educational Practice*. New York: Oxford University Press.

Kevles, Daniel J. (1998). A Time for Audacity: What the Past Has to Teach the Present About Science and the Federal Government. In W. G. Bowen and H. T. Shapiro (eds.), *Universities and Their Leadership* (199–240). Princeton: Princeton University Press.

King, Richard. (1999). *Orientalism and Religion: Postcolonial Theory, India and the Mystic East*. London: Routledge

King, Ursula. (2002). Is There a Future for Religious Studies as We Know It? Some Postmodern, Feminist, and Spiritual Challenges. *Journal of the American Academy of Religion*, 70 (2): 365–88.

Kippenberg, Hans. (2002). *Discovering Religious History in the Modern Age*. Princeton: Princeton University Press.

Kitagawa, Joseph M. (1959): The History of Religions in America. In Mircea Eliade and Joseph Kitagawa (eds.), *The History of Religions: Essays in Methodology* (1–30). Chicago: University of Chicago Press.

Kitagawa. (1975). Theology and the Science of Religion. *Anglican Theological Review*, 29: 33–52.

Kitagawa, Joseph. (1983). Humanistic and Theological History of Religion with Special Reference to the North American Scene. In Peter Slater and Donald Wiebe (eds.), *Traditions in Contact and Change: Selected Proceedings of the XIVth Congress of the International Association for the History of Religions* (553–63). Waterloo: Wilfrid Laurier University Press.

Kitcher, Philip. (1993). *The Advancement of Science: Science Without Legend, Objectivity Without Illusions*. Oxford: Oxford University Press.

Klostermaier, Klaus K., and Larry W. Hurtado. (1991). Editors' Preface. In Klaus K. Klostermaier and Larry W. Hurtado (eds.), *Religious Studies: Issues, Prospects and Proposals* (viii–xi). University of Manitoba Studies in Religion, 2. Atlanta: Scholars Press.

Lacy, Michael J. (1989). Introduction: The Academic Revolution and American Religious Thought. In Michael J. Lacey (ed.), *Religion and Twentieth Century American Intellectual Life* (1–11). Cambridge: Cambridge University Press.

Laperrière, Guy, and William Westfall. (1990). Religious Studies. In Alan F. J. Artibise (ed.), *Interdisciplinary Approaches to Canadian Society: A Guide to the Literature* (39–76). Montreal: McGill-Queen's University Press.

Laporte, Jean-Marc. (1993). Review of Harold Remus, et al. (eds.), *Religious Studies in Ontario: A State-of-the-Art Review. Toronto Journal of Theology*, 9 (2): 249.

Latour, Bruno. (1993). *We have Never Been Modern* (Trans. Catherine Porter). Cambridge: Cambridge University Press.

Lawson, E. Thomas, and Robert N. McCauley. (1990). *Rethinking Religion: Connecting the Cognitive and the Cultural*. Cambridge: Cambridge University Press.

Lefkowitz, Mary. (2008). *History Lesson: A Race Odyssey*. New Haven: Yale University Press.

Lewis, Lionel. (1998). *Cold War on Campus: A Study of the Politics of Organizational Control*. New York: Transaction Books.

Lewis-Williams. (1981). *Believing and Seeing: Symbolic Meanings in Southern San Rock Paintings*. London: Academic Press.

Lewontin, Richard C. (1997). The Cold War and the Transformation of the Academy. In A. Schiffrin (ed.), *The Cold War and the University: Toward an Intellectual History of the Postwar Years* (1–34). New York: The New Press.

Maduro, Otto. (2013). Migrants' Religions Under Imperial Duress: Reflections on Epistemology, Ethics, and Politics in the Study of the Religious 'Stranger.' *Journal of the American Academy of Religion*, 80 (1): 35–46.

Marsden, George. (1994). *The Soul of the American University: From Protestant Establishment to Established Nonbelief*. New York: Oxford University Press.

Martin, Craig. (2008). Editorial. *Bulletin of the Council of Societies for the Study of Religion*, 37 (2): 30–31.

Martin, Luther H., and Donald Wiebe. (2004). Establishing a Beachhead: NAASR, Twenty Years Later, available at www.naasr.com/Establishingabeachhead.pdf and reprinted. In Luther H. Martin and Donald Wiebe (eds.), *Conversations and Controversies in the Scientific Study of Religion* (36–41). Leiden: E. J. Brill.

Martin, Luther H. and Donald Wiebe. (2016a). Religious Studies as a Scientific Discipline: The Persistence of a Delusion. In Luther H. Martin and Donald Wiebe (eds.), *Conversations and Controversies in the Scientific Study of Religion* (221–30). Leiden: E. J. Brill.

Martin, Luther H. and Donald Wiebe. (2016b). On Declaring WAR: A Critical Comment. In Luther H. Martin and Donald Wiebe (eds.), *Conversations and Controversies in the Scientific Study of Religion* (17–23). Leiden: E. J. Brill.

Marty, Martin E. (1983). Seminary/Academy: Beyond the Tensions. *The Christian Century*, 100: 83–84.

Marty, Martin. (1985). What is Modern about the Modern Study of Religion? *The University Lecture in Religious Studies at Arizona State University*. Tempe: Department of Religious Studies, Arizona State University.

Masuzawa, Tomoko. (1998). Culture. In Mark C. Taylor (ed.), *Critical Terms for Religious Studies* (70–93). Chicago: University of Chicago Press.

Masuzawa, Tomoko. (2004). An Interview with Tomoko Masuzawa. *Religious Studies News*, 19 (4): 20 and 22.

McAuliffe, Jane Dammen. (2005). Reading the Qur'ān with Fidelity and Freedom. *Journal of the American Academy of Religion*, 73 (3): 615–35.

McCaughey, Robert A. (1984). *International Studies and Academic Enterprises: A Chapter in the Enclosure of American Learning*. New York: Columbia University Press.

McCauley, Robert N. (2000). The Naturalness of Religion and the Unnaturalness of Science. In F. Keil and R. Wilson (eds.), *Explanation and Cognition* (61–85). Cambridge: MIT Press.

McCauley, Robert N. (2011); *Why Religion Is Natural and Science Is Not*. New York: Oxford University Press.

McCutcheon, Russell T. (1997). A Default of Critical Intelligence? The Scholar of Religion as Public Intellectual. *Journal of the American Academy of Religion*, 65 (2): 443–68.

McCutcheon, Russell T. (1997). *Manufacturing Religion: The Discourse on* Sui Generis *Religion*. New York: Oxford University Press.

McIntire, Thomas C. (2007). How Religious Studies Misunderstands Religion. *Academic Matters: Journal of Higher Education*, December Issue, 9–13.

McKirahan, Richard D. (1994). *Philosophy Before Socrates: An Introduction with Texts and Commentary*. Indianapolis/Cambridge: Hackett Publishing Company, Inc.

McLelland, Joseph C. (1972). The Teacher of Religion: Professor or Guru? *Studies in Religion/Sciences Religieuses*, 2 (3): 226–34.

McNeill, William H. (1986). *Mythistory and Other Essays*. Chicago: University of Chicago Press.

Menchu, Rigoberta. (1984). *I Rigoberta Menchu: And Indian Woman in Guatemala*. (Edited and Introduced by Elisabeth Buro-Dbray, Trans. Ann Wright). London: Verso.

Michaelson, Robert S. (1973). The Engaged Observer: Portrait of a Professor of Religion. *Journal of the American Academy of Religion*, 40: 419–24.

Midgley, Mary. (1992). *Science as Salvation: A Modern Myth and Its Meaning*. London: Routledge.

Miller, Richard B. (1996). *Casuistry and Modern Ethics: A Poetics of Practical Reasoning*. Chicago: University of Chicago Press.

Mithen, Steven. (2002). Human Evolution and the Cognitive Base of Science. In Peter Carruthers, Stephen Stitch, and Michael Segal (eds.), *The Cognitive Basis of Science* (23–40). Cambridge: Cambridge University Press.

Montgomery, David. (1997). Introduction: Prosperity Under the Shadow of the Bomb. In Andrè Schiffrin (ed.), *The Cold War and the University: Toward an Intellectual History of the Postwar Years* (xi–xxxvii). New York: The New Press.

Murphy, Murray G. (1989). On the Scientific Study of Religion in the United States, 1870–1980. In M. J. Lacy (ed.), *Religion in Twentieth-Century American Intellectual Life*. Cambridge: Cambridge University Press.

Myscofski, Carol and Richard Pilgrim et al. (1993). Religious Studies and the Redefining Scholarship Project: A Report of the AAR Committee on "Defining Scholarly Work." *Religious Studies News*, 8 (3): 7–8.

Needell, Allen A. (1998). Project Troy and the Cold War Annexation of the Social Sciences. In Christopher Simpson (ed.), *Universities and Empire: Money and Politics in the Social Science During the Cold War* (3–38). New York: The New Press.

Nesbitt, Eleanor. (1990). Sikhism. In Ursula King (ed.), *Turning Points in Religious Studies* (168–79). Edinburgh: T & T Clark.

Neufeldt, Ronald W. (1983). *Religious Studies in Alberta: A State-of-the-Art Review*. Waterloo: Wilfrid Laurier University Press.

Neusner, Jacob and Noam Neusner. (1995). *The Price of Excellence: Universities in Conflict During the Cold War*. New York: Continuum.

Newton, Roger G. (1997). *The Truth of Science: Physical Theories and Reality*. Cambridge: Harvard University Press.

Nicholls, William. (1971). Editorial: A New Journal and Its Predecessor. *Studies in Religion/Sciences Religieuses*, 1 (1): 1–3.

Nicholson, Eric, ed. (2003). *A Century of Theological and Religious Studies in Britain*. Oxford: Oxford University Press.

Nisbet, Robert. (1971). *The Degradation of the Academic Dogma: The University in America, 1945–1970*. London: Heinemann.

Novak, Michael. (1971). *Ascent of the Mountain, Flight of the Dove: An Introduction to Religious Studies*. New York: Harper and Row.

Nussbaum, Martha C. (1997). *Cultivating Humanity: A Classical Defense of Reform in Liberal Education*. Cambridge: Harvard University Press.

Ogden, Shubert M. (1986 [1975]). Theology in the University. In Shubert M. Ogden (ed.), *On Theology* (121–33). San Francisco: Harper and Row.

Olson, Alan M. (1990a). Religious Studies. In Iris V. Cully and Kendig Brubaker Cully (eds.), *Encyclopedia of Religious Education* (549–51). San Francisco: Harper and Row.

Olson, Alan M. (1990b). University. In Iris V. Cully and Kendig Brubaker Cully (eds.), *Encyclopedia of Religious Education* (673–74). San Francisco: Harper and Row.

Orsi, Robert. (2004). A New Beginning Again. *Journal of the American Academy of Religion*, 72 (3): 587–602.

Passmore, John. (1978). *Science and Its Critics*. London: Duckworth.

Penner, Hans and Edward Yonan. (1972). Is a Science of Religion Possible? *The Journal of Religion*, 52: 107–33.

Popper, Karl R. (1963). *Conjectures and Refutations*. New York: Harper and Row.

Popper, Karl R. (1967). *The Open Society and Its Enemies* (2 Vols). New York: Harper and Row.

Porterfield, Amanda. (2001). *The Transformation of American Religion: The Story of a Late Twentieth-Century Awakening*. New York: Oxford University Press.

Porthero, Stephen. (2007). *Religious Literacy: What Every American Needs to Know, but Doesn't*. San Francisco: Harper.

Prebish, Charles S. (1994). The Academic Study of Buddhism in the United States: A Current Analysis. *Religion*, 24: 271–78.

Preus, J. Samuel. (1987). *Explaining Religion: Criticism and Theory from Bodin to Freud*. New Haven: Yale University Press.

Prozesky, Martin. (1990). Africa's Contribution to Religious Studies. *Journal of Southern Africa*, 70, 0–20.

Pui-Lan, Kwok. (2012). Empire and the Study of Religion. *Journal of the American Academy of Religion*, 80 (2): 285–303.

Pye, Michael. (1991). Religious Studies in Europe: Structures and Desiderate. In Klaus K. Klostermaier and Larry Hurtado (eds.), *Religious Studies: Issues, Prospects and Proposals* (51–75). Winnipeg: University of Manitoba Press.

Pye, Michael. (1994). Religion: Shape and Shadow? *Numen*, 41: 51–75.

Pye, Michael. (1999). Methodological Integration in the Study of Religions. In Tore Ahlbäck (ed.), *Approaching Religion (Vol. 1)* (189–205). Åbo: Åbo University Press.

Pyysiäinen, Ilkka. (2001). *How Religion Works: Towards a New Cognitive Science of Religion*. Leiden: E. J. Brill.

Ramsey, Frank. (1965 [1925]). The Foundation of Mathematics. In R. B. Braithwaite (ed.), *The Foundation of Mathematics* (238). London: Routledge & Kegan Paul.

Redner, Henry. (1987). *The Ends of Science: An Essay in Scientific Authority*. Boulder: Westview Press.

Reiss, Timothy J. (1982). *Discourse of Modernism*. Ithaca: Cornell University Press.

Remus, Harold E. (1988). Religion as an Academic Discipline (Part I: Origins, Nature and Changing Understandings). In Charles H. Lippy and Peter M. Williams (eds.), *Encyclopedia of the American Religious Experience, Vol. 3* (1653–65). New York: Charles Scribners Sons.

Remus, Harold E., William Clossan James, and Daniel Fraikin. (1992). *Religious Studies in Ontario: A State-of-the-Art Review*. Waterloo: Wilfrid Laurier University Press.

Rescher, Nicholas. (1984). *The Limits of Science*. Los Angeles: University of California Press.

Reuben, Julie. (1996). *The Making of the Modern University: Intellectual Transformation and the Marginalization of Morality*. Chicago: Chicago University Press.

Reynolds, Frank E. (1990). Reconstructing Liberal Education: A Religious Studies Perspective. In Freank E. Reynolds and Sheryl L. Burkhalter (eds.), *Beyond the Classics? Essays in Religious Studies and Liberal Education* (3–18). Atlanta: Scholars Press.

Riley, Philip Boo. (1984). Theology and/or Religious Studies: A Case Study of *Studies in Religion/Sciences Religieuses* 1971–1981. *Studies in Religion/Sciences Religieuses*, 13 (4): 423–44.

Robbins, Jeffrey W. (2008), Theses on Secular Theology. *Bulletin of the Council of Societies for the Study of Religion*, 37 (2): 31–36.

Roberts, Michael. (1937). *The Modern Mind*. London: Faber & Faber.

Rousseau, Louis, and Michel Despland. (1988). *Les sciences religieuses au Quèbec depuis 1972*. Waterloo: Wilfrid Laurier University Press.

Russo, Lucio. (1996). *The Forgotten Revolution: How Science Was Born in 300 BC and Why It Had to be Reborn*. Berlin: Springer.

Saunders, Ernest W. (1982). *Searching the Scriptures: A History of the Society of Biblical Literature, 1880–1990*. Atlanta: Scholars Press.

Schiffrin, Andrè. (1997). *The Cold War and the University: Toward an Intellectual History*. New York: The Free Press.

Schimmel, Annemarie. (1960). Summary of the Discussion. *Numen*, 7: 235–39.

Schneider, Mark A. (1993). *Culture and Disenchantment*. Chicago: University of Chicago Press.

Schrecker, Ellen W. (1986). *No Ivory Tower: McCarthyism and the Universities*. New York: Free Press.

Schüssler Fiorenza, Francis. (1993). Theology in the University. *Bulletin of the Council of Societies for the Study of Religion*, 22: 34–39.

Schwehn, Mark R. (1993). *Exiles from Eden: Religion and the Academic Vocation in America*. New York: Oxford University Press.

Sharpe, Eric J. (1986a [1975]). *Comparative Religion: A History* (2nd edn). London: Duckworth.

Sharpe, Eric J. (1986b). From Paris 1900 to Sydney 1985 (An Essay in Retrospect and Prospect). In Victor C. Hayes (ed.), *Identity Issues and World Religions: Selected Proceedings of the Fifteenth Congress of the International Association for the History of Religions* (245–52). Redford Park: Flinders University Press.

Sharpe, Eric J. (1987). Methodological Issues. In Mircea Eliade (ed.), *Encyclopedia of Religion Vol. 14* (84–88). New York: Macmillan Press.

Shepard, Robert S. (1991). *God's People in the Ivory Tower: Religion in the Early American University*. New York: Carlson Publishing Inc.

Simpson, Christopher. (1998). *Universities and Empire: Money and the Universities*. New York: Free Press.

Smart, Ninian. (1973). *The Science of Religion and the Sociology of Knowledge*. Princeton: Princeton University Press.

Smart, Ninian. (1990). Concluding Reflections: Religious Studies in Global Perspective. In Ursula King (ed.), *Turning Points in Religious Studies* (299–306). Edinburgh: T & T Clark.

Smart, Ninian. (1995). Religious Studies in Higher Education. In John R. Hinnells (ed.), *The New Penguin Dictionary of Religions* (420–21). London: Penguin.

Smart, Ninian. (1996). Some Thoughts on the Science of Religion. In Arvind Sharma (ed.), *The Sum of Our Choices: Essays in Honor of Eric J. Sharpe* (15–25). Atlanta: Scholars Press.

Smith, Jonathan Z. (1982). *Imagining Religion: From Babylon to Jamestown*. Chicago: University of Chicago Press.

Smith, Jonathan Z. (1988). 'Religion' and 'Religious Studies': No Difference at All. *Soundings*, 71 (2–3): 231–44.

Smith, Jonathan Z. (1998). Religion, Religions, Religious. In Mark C. Taylor (ed.), *Critical Terms for Religious Studies* (269–84). Chicago: University of Chicago Press.

Smith, Richard Norton. (1986). *The Harvard Century: The Making of a University Into a Nation*. Cambridge: Harvard University Press.

Smith, Wilfred Cantwell. (1950). The Comparative Study of Religion: Reflections on the Possibility and Purpose of a Religious Science. Inaugural Lecture, Institute for Islamic Studies, McGill University.

Smith, Wilfred Cantwell. (1962). *The Meaning and End of Religion*. New York: The MacMillan Company.

Smith, Wilfred Cantwell. (Unpublished). The Dilemma of the Professor of Religion: Communication of Objective Data and Personal Experience. Paper presented to the 1967 meeting of the Canadian Society for the Study of Religion.

Sokal, Alan. (2008). *Beyond the Hoax: Science, Philosophy and Culture*. Oxford: Oxford University Press.

Sokal, Alan, and Jean Bricmont. (1998). *Fashionable Nonsense: Postmodern Intellectuals' Abuse of Science*. New York: Picador.

Solomon, Julie Robin. (1998). *Objectivity in the Making: Francis Bacon and the Politics of Inquiry*. Baltimore: Johns Hopkins University Press.

Sorell, Tom. (1991). *Scientism: Philosophy and the Infatuation of Science*. London: Routledge.

Stark, Rodney. (2003). *For the Glory of God: How Monotheism Led to Reformation, Science, Witch-Hunts, and the End of Slavery*. Princeton: Princeton University Press.

Stark, Rodney. (2007). *Discovering God: The Origins of the Great Religions and the Evolution of Belief*. New York: Harperone.

Stark, Rodney, and William Sims Bainbridge. (1987). *A Theory of Religion*. New York: Peter Lang Press.

Stark, Rodney, and Roger Finke. (2000). *Acts of Faith: Explaining the Human Side of Religion*. Berkeley: University of California Press.

Stoll, David. (1999). *Rigoberta Menchu and the Story of All Poor Guatemalans*. Boulder: Westview Press.

Stout, Jeffrey. (2008). The Folly of Secularism. *Journal of the American Academy of Religion*, 76 (3): 533–44.

Strenski, Ivan. (2004). The Proper Object of the Study of Religion: Why It Is Better to Know Some of the Questions Than All of the Answers. In Slavica Jakelic and Lori Pearson (eds.), *The Future of the Study of Religion: Proceedings of Congress 2000* (xxx). Leiden: E. J. Brill.

Strenski, Ivan. (2006). *Thinking About Religion: An Historical Introduction to Theories of Religion*. Oxford: Blackwell Publisher.

Taves, Ann. (2011). 'Religion' in the Humanities and the Humanities in the University. *Journal of the American Academy of Religion*, 79 (2): 287–314.

Taylor, Mark. C. (1994). Unsettling Issues. *Journal of the American Academy of Religion* 42 (4): 949–63.

Taylor, Mark C. (1998). Introduction. In Mark C. Taylor (ed.), *Critical Terms for Religious Studies* (1–19). Chicago: University of Chicago Press.

Taylor, Mark C. (1999). *About Religion: Economics of Faith in Virtual Culture*. Chicago: University of Chicago Press.

Taylor, Victor E. (2008). Disfiguring Postmodern Theology. *Bulleting of the Council for the Societies for the Study of Religion*, 37 (2): 41–45.

Thiemann, Ronald F. (1990). The Future of an Illusion: An Inquiry into the Contrast Between Theological and Religious Studies. *Theological Education*, 26 (2): 66–85.

Tomasello, Michael. (1999). *The Cultural Origin of Cognition*. Cambridge: Harvard University Press.

Tomasello, Michael. (2014). *A Natural History of Human Thinking*. Cambridge: Harvard University Press.

Toulmin, Stephen. (1972). *Human Understanding: The Collective Us and Evolution of Concepts*. Princeton: Princeton University Press.

Townes, Emilie M. (2009). Walking on the Rim Bones of Nothingness: Scholarship and Activism. *Journal of the American Academy of Religion*, 77 (1): 1–15.

Tracy, David. (1995). Modernity, Antimodernity, and Postmodernity in the American Setting. In William M. Shea and Peter A. Huff (eds.), *Knowledge and Belief in America: Enlightenment Traditions and Modern Religious Thought* (328–34). Princeton: Princeton University Press.

Trigg, Roger. (2003). Do Science and Religion Need Each Other? http://www.st-edmunds. cam.ac/CIS/trigg/pdf/trigg_lecture_hires.pdf

Tweed, Thomas A. (2016). *Valuing* in the Study of Religion: Improving Difficult Dialogues Within and Beyond the AAR's Big Tent. *Journal of the American Academy of Religion*, 84 (2): 287–322.

Veblen, Thorstein. (1908). *The Higher Learning in America: A Memorandum on the Conduct of the Universities by Business Men*. New York: B. W. Huebsch.

Walls, Andrew F. (1990). Religious Studies in the Universities: Scotland. In Ursula King (ed.), *Turning Points in Religious Studies* (32–45). Edinburgh: T & T Clark.

Wang, Jessica. (1999). *American Science in the Age of Anxiety: Scientists, Anticommunism, and the Cold War*. Chapel Hill: The University of North Carolina Press.

Ward, Keith. (1990). The Study of Truth and Dialogue in Religion. In Ursula King (ed.), *Turning Points in Religious Studies* (32–45). Edinburgh: T & T Clark.

Warne, Randi R. (2002). An Institutional History of the CSSR. CSSR Presidential Address. Unpublished, 26 pp.

Warne, Randi R. (2004). New Approaches to the Study of Religion in North America. In Peter Antes, Armin Geertz and Randi Warne (eds.), *New Approaches to the Study of Religion, Vol. 1: Regional, Critical, and Historical* (13–41). Berlin: Walter de Gruyter.

Wasserstrom, Steven M. (1999). *Religion After Religion: Gershom Scholem, Mircea Eliade, and Henry Corbin at Eranos*. Princeton: Princeton University Press.

Weber, Max. (1946 [1919]). Science as a Vocation. In H. H. Gerth and C. Wright Mills (eds.), *From Max Weber: Essays in Sociology* (129–56). New York: Oxford University Press.

Weinberg, Steven. (2015). *To Explain the World: The Discovery of Modern Science*. New York: Harper.

Welch, Claude. (1971a). Identity Crisis in the Study of Religion? A First Report from the ACLS Study. *Journal of the American Academy of Religion*, 39: 3–18.

Welch, Claude. (1971b). *Graduate Education in Religion: A Critical Appraisal*. Missoula: University of Montana Press.

Werblowsky, R. J. Zwi. (1958). The nth International Congress for the History of Religions, Tokyo. *Numen*, 5 (3): 233–37.

Werblowsky, R. J. Zwi. (1960). Marburg and After. *Numen*, 7 (2): 215–20.

Whitfield, Stephen J. (1991): *The Culture of the Cold War*. Baltimore: The Johns Hopkins Press.

Whitehouse, Harvey. (2000). *Arguments and Icons: Divergent Modes of Religiosity*. Oxford: Oxford University Press.

Wiebe, Donald. (1970). Can Theology Withstand the Impact of Science? M.A. Thesis, University of Guelph, ON, Canada.

Wiebe, Donald. (1973). Comprehensively Critical Rationalism and Commitment. *Philosophical Studies*, 21: 186–201.

Wiebe, Donald. (1974). Science, Religion, and Rationality: Questions of Method in Science and Theology. Ph.D. Thesis, Lancaster University, Lancaster, UK.

Wiebe, Donald. (1975). Explanation and the Scientific Study of Religion. *Religion*, 5: 33–52.

Wiebe, Donald. (1977). Is Religious Belief Problematic? *Christian Scholar's Review*, 7: 22–35.

Wiebe, Donald. (1978). Is a Science of Religion Possible? *Studies in Religion/Sciences de Religieuses*, 7: 5–17.

Wiebe, Donald. (1981). *Religion and Truth: Towards an Alternative Paradigm for the Study of Religion*. The Hague: Mouton Publishers.

Wiebe, Donald. (1983). Theory in the Study of Religion. *Religion*, 13: 283–309.

Wiebe, Donald. (1984). The Failure of Nerve in the Academic Study of Religion. *Studies in Religion/Sciences Religieuses*, 13 (4): 401–22.

Wiebe, Donald. (1988). The Study of Religion: On the New Encyclopedia of Religion. *Annals of Scholarship*, 5: 260–68.

Wiebe, Donald. (1991). *The Irony of Theology and the Nature of Religious Thought*. Montreal and Kingston: McGill-Queen's University Press.

Wiebe, Donald. (1994). Transcending Religious Language: Towards the Recovery of an Academic Agenda. In Ugo Bianchi (ed.), *The Notion of 'Religion' in Comparative Research* (905–12). Rome: L'Erma Di Bretschneider.

Wiebe, Donald. (1997a). A Religious Agenda Continued: A Review of the Presidential Addresses to the AAR. *Method and Theory in the Study of Religion*, 9: 353–75.

Wiebe, Donald. (1997b). Dissolving Rationality: The Anti-Science Phenomenon and Its Implications for the Study of Religions. In J. S. Jensen and L. H. Martin (eds.), *Rationality in the Study of Religion* (167–83). Aarhus: University of Aarhus Press.

Wiebe, Donald. (1998). *The Politics of Religious Studies: The Continuing Conflict with Theology in the Academy*. New York: Palgrave Press.

Wiebe, Donald. (1999a). Responses to Miller and Sutcliffe. *Bulletin of the Council of Societies for the Study of Religion*, 27: 115–18.

Wiebe, Donald. (1999b). Appropriating Religion: Understanding Religion as an Object of Science. In Tore Ahlbäck (ed.), *Approching Religion: Part 1* (253–72). Stockholm: Almquist and Wiksell International.

Wiebe, Donald. (2000). Modernism. In W. Braun and R. McCutcheon (eds.). *Guide to the Study of Religion* (351–64). London: Cassell.

Wiebe, Donald. (2001). On Religious Studies and the Rhetoric of *Religious Reading*. *Method and Theory in the Study of Religion*, 13: 334–51.

Wiebe, Donald. (2002a). Introduction: The Study of Religion. In J. Gordon Melton and Markus Baumann (eds.), *Religions of the World: A Comprehensive Encyclopedia of Beliefs and Practices* (xix–xxv). Santa Barbara: ABC/CLIO.

Wiebe, Donald. (2002b). 'Understanding' in Religious Studies: A Gnostic Aberration in the Modern Study of Religion. *Fu-Jen Religious Studies*, 6: 15–56.

Wiebe, Donald. (2002c). Modern Western Science and the Study of Religion: A Response to Richard King's. *Orientalism and Religion: Postcolonial Theory, India, and the Mystic East*, 14: 265–78.

Wiebe. (2004). Ideology and the Subersion of Rational Inquiry. In Christoph Kleine, Monika Schrimph, and Katja Triplett (eds.), *New Paths in the Study of Religion: Festschrift in Honour of Michael Pye* (81–95). Munich: Biblion Verlag.

Wiebe, Donald. (2005). Beyond Thick Descriptions and Interpretive Sciences: Explaining Religious Meaning. In Renè Gothóni (ed.), *How to do Comparative Religion: Three Ways, Many Goal* (65–82). Berlin: Walter DeGruyter.

Wiebe, Donald. (2006a). The Learned Practice of Religion: A Review of the History of Religious Studies in Canada and Its Portent for the Future. *Studies in Religion/Sciences Religieuses*, 35 (3–4): 475–501.

Wiebe, Donald. (2006b). The Eternal Return All Over Again, The Religious Conversation Endures: A Critical Assessment of Recent Presidential Addresses to the AAR. *Journal of the American Academy of Religion*, 44 (3): 674–96.

Wiebe, Donald. (2008). Secular Theology is Still Theology, Not the Academic Study of Religion. *Bulletin of the Council of Societies for the Study of Religion*, 37 (3): 77–81.

Wiebe, Donald. (2009). Religious Biases in Funding Religious Studies Research. *Religio: Revue Pro Religionistiku*, 17 (2): 125–139.

Wiebe, Donald. (2011). The Congress Director's General Report on the XXth IAHR World Congress. In Donald Wiebe (ed.), *Religion: A Human Phenomenon: Proceedings of the XXth World Congress of the International Association for the History of Religions*. Toronto: IASR Publication.

Wiebe, Donald. (2015). Documenting the Delusion: A Case Study. *Method and Theory in the Study of Religion*, 27: 279–91.

Wiebe, Donald. (2016). Questioning the Quality of the Quality Assurance Process in Ontario's Universities. *Academic Matters (Journal of the Ontario Confederation of University Faculty Associations)*, 19–22.

Wiebe, Donald, and Luther H. Martin. (2016). A Rationale for a Change of Name for the International Association for the History of Religions. In Luther H. Martin and Donald Wiebe (eds.), *Conversations and Controversies in the Scientific Study of Religion: Collaborative and Co-authored Essays by Luther H. Martin and Donald Wiebe* (9–13). Leiden: Brill.

Williams, Cyril. (1990). Religious Studies in the Universities: Wales. In Ursula King (ed.), *Turning Points in Religious Studies* (46–56). Edinburgh: T & T Clark.

Wilson, John. (1987). Modernity and Religion: A Problem of Perspective. In William Nicholls (ed.), *Modernity and Religion, Supplements to Studies in Religion/Sciences Religieuses*, 19 (9–18). Waterloo: Wilfrid Laurier University Press.

Wolin, Richard. (2004). *The Seduction of Unreason: The Intellectual Romance with Fascism, From Nietzsche to Postmodernism*. Princeton: Princeton University Press.

Wolpert, Lewis. (1993). *The Unnatural Nature of Science: Why Science Cannot Make Common Sense*. Cambridge: Harvard University Press.

Worsley, Peter. (1997). *Knowledges: Culture, Counterculture, Subculture*. New York: The New Press.

Wuthnow, Robert. (2004). Is There a Place for 'Scientific' Studies of Religion? *Religious Studies News*, 19 (4): 13 and 32.

Zammito, John H. (2004). *A Nice Derangement of Epistemes: Post-Positivism in the Study of Science from Quine to Latour*. Chicago: University of Chicago Press.

Zoloth, Laurie. (2016). Interpreting Your Life: An Ethics for the Coming Storm. *Journal of the American Academy of Religion*, 84 (1): 3–24.

Index

Lightning Source UK Ltd
Milton Keynes UK
UKHW020659210521
384111UK00003B/86